THE
EVERYTHING
HEALTHY MEAL PREP
COOKBOOK

Dear Reader,

I know, meal prepping a week's worth of food seems like a lot of work, and you'll probably get stuck eating bland and boring food, right? Wrong! This book will prove that meal prepping is a fun and worthwhile skill to learn, enabling you to enjoy healthy and tasty food.

I started meal prepping religiously in 2013, soon after I embarked on my fitness journey. I started doing it for several reasons. First, I was too busy to cook healthy and tasty meals each day. Second, I realized that my physical changes weren't measuring up to the work I was putting into exercising (that's because you can rarely out-work and out-train a bad diet!). I was also constantly tired, not sleeping well, and having fluctuations in my mood.

I quickly realized that planning and cooking all my meals for the week ahead of time was the only option. With this in mind, I started sharing my weekly meal preps on *Instagram*. I loved sharing some tips and healthy recipes along with my weekly preps with others. Now after more than four years, I'm able to distill all that I've learned into this cookbook—an opportunity that I'm forever grateful for.

Meal prepping and eating well has changed my life for the better. I now have more energy than I've ever had and I sleep well nearly every night. My fitness level keeps improving and, most important, I feel amazing!

My goal is to help, inspire, and share healthy, simple, and delicious meal prepping recipes with others. #HappyPrepping

Tina

Welcome to the EVERYTHING® Series!

These handy, accessible books give you all you need to tackle a difficult project, gain a new hobby, comprehend a fascinating topic, prepare for an exam, or even brush up on something you learned back in school but have since forgotten.

You can choose to read an Everything® book from cover to cover or just pick out the information you want from our four useful boxes: e-questions, e-facts, e-alerts, and e-ssentials.

We give you everything you need to know on the subject, but throw in a lot of fun stuff along the way too.

We now have more than 400 Everything® books in print, spanning such wide-ranging categories as weddings, pregnancy, cooking, music instruction, foreign language, crafts, pets, New Age, and so much more. When you're done reading them all, you can finally say you know Everything®!

QUESTION

Answers to
common questions

FACT

Important snippets
of information

ALERT

Urgent
warnings

ESSENTIAL

Quick
handy tips

PUBLISHER Karen Cooper

MANAGING EDITOR Lisa Laing

COPY CHIEF Casey Ebert

ASSOCIATE PRODUCTION EDITOR Jo-Anne Duhamel

ACQUISITIONS EDITOR Zander Hatch

DEVELOPMENT EDITOR Brett Palana-Shanahan

EVERYTHING® SERIES COVER DESIGNER Erin Alexander

THE
EVERYTHING®
HEALTHY MEAL PREP COOKBOOK

Tina Chow

Adams Media

New York London Toronto Sydney New Delhi

To my beloved late mother who taught me many kitchen firsts
and instilled the importance of feeding her family with healthy, delicious food.

Adams Media
An Imprint of Simon & Schuster, Inc.
57 Littlefield Street
Avon, Massachusetts 02322

An Everything® Series Book.
Everything® and everything.com® are registered trademarks of Simon & Schuster, Inc.

First Adams Media trade paperback edition JANUARY 2018

ADAMS MEDIA and colophon are trademarks of Simon and Schuster.

For information about special discounts for bulk purchases, please contact Simon & Schuster Special Sales at 1-866-506-1949 or business@simonandschuster.com.

The Simon & Schuster Speakers Bureau can bring authors to your live event. For more information or to book an event contact the Simon & Schuster Speakers Bureau at 1-866-248-3049 or visit our website at www.simonspeakers.com.

Interior design by Colleen Cunningham
Insert photographs by Tina Chow

Manufactured in the United States of America

10 9 8 7 6 5 4 3 2 1

Library of Congress Cataloging-in-Publication Data
Chow, Tina, (chef), author.
The everything healthy meal prep cookbook / Tina Chow.
Avon, Massachusetts: Adams Media, 2018.
Series: Everything.
Includes index.
LCCN 2017037358 (print) | LCCN 2017050454 (ebook) |
ISBN 9781507205976 (pb) | ISBN 9781507205983 (ebook)
LCSH: Quick and easy cooking. | Dinners and dining. |
Health. | LCGFT: Cookbooks.
LCC TX833 (ebook) | LCC TX833 .C44 2018 (print) |
DDC 641.5/12--dc23
LC record available at https://lccn.loc.gov/2017037358

ISBN 978-1-5072-0597-6
ISBN 978-1-5072-0598-3 (ebook)

Contents

Acknowledgments

First and foremost, thank you to my love and life partner, Robert. I appreciate the unconditional love and support you always provide to me through every journey that I decide to take. You inspire and motivate me more than you know. I love you so much!

To my friends, family, and gym community, thank you for always cheering me on! Your kind words of encouragement always make my day!

To my followers on *Instagram*, thank you! Every like, comment, and follow matters! Although you say I inspire you, you are the ones that inspire and motivate me to continue doing what I do every day. Meal prepping and healthy eating is my passion and I love sharing my journey with you.

Introduction

MEAL PREPPING—PREPARING A WEEK'S worth of food in one sitting to save time during the week—is an organizational tool that can simplify your life and get you eating healthier. Whether you're on a weight loss journey, looking to better manage your mealtimes, or simply trying to eat healthier, meal prepping is the technique to achieve those goals. Like the saying goes, what gets scheduled gets done.

If that's the case, why isn't everyone meal prepping? Most people don't meal prep because it takes planning, work, and time. Unfortunately, time is something that seems to be in short supply for all of us. If you had an extra hour in your day, what would you want to do with it? Probably not stand over a stove cooking! Because of this, dining out or buying premade food is the easy solution for busy people. When you can get a whole meal for a fairly affordable price, why would you bother cooking? But do you know what goes into the food others prepare for you? Is it healthy? Chances are it's not, and the long-term effects it can have on your health can be frightening.

So what can you do to turn your health around and ensure that you're getting the proper nutrition? One major step is to cook fresh meals daily, but in today's world finding the time to cook each night is nearly impossible. Therefore, meal prepping is a great option to manage your limited time and ensure you're eating the right types of food. It will also help you save money!

Let's be honest: getting into the habit of meal prepping is not easy. It takes time, work, motivation, and consistency to continue it on an ongoing basis. Luckily, like all new skills, meal prepping gets easier the more you do it. And it's not an all-or-nothing proposition. Start small by prepping just a couple of days or even just one meal, like lunch. That way it's not as daunting a task.

Once you get into the habit, you'll quickly experience the benefits of a healthy eating routine, such as feeling better, sleeping better, and having higher levels of energy. Before you know it, it will become an essential tool for keeping you on track to maintain that healthy lifestyle.

Now that you're embarking on this journey this book will help you along the way and includes many tips on which preprepped foods keep well (and which don't) as well as ways to save time when you are prepping. If you're prepping for a family who all like to eat different things, the chapters will allow you to pick and choose what meals and sides to make for the week so you can mix and match the meal combos for different family members.

To your health! #HappyPrepping

CHAPTER 1

What Is Meal Prepping?

In short, meal prepping is batch cooking a large amount of food in advance. Usually meal prepping involves cooking a week's worth of food on the weekend for the days ahead. Some people batch cook different dishes and pick and choose (buffet style) what to pack throughout their week. Others pre-portion off their meals in advance into breakfast, lunch, and dinner for the week. In this book, you'll learn reasons why you should meal prep, how to get your kitchen ready, and tips on how to save time and make your meal prep sessions efficient.

Reasons to Meal Prep

There are countless reasons to meal prep, from the money you will save not throwing away food or buying food you never use, to the time you'll save in the mornings when you don't have to struggle to come up with ideas for meals. Here are the top five benefits to meal prep:

Saves Time

Time is valuable, and there never seems to be enough of it, hence the saying "time is money." Most people aren't lucky enough to afford a daily meal delivery service of healthy and fresh foods prepared and ready to eat. However, the next best thing is to prepare all your meals for the week in just one day. The average meal prepping session for one person typically takes two to three hours from start to finish for a week's worth of meals. Compare that to slaving away in the kitchen every night for at least an hour after a long day of work and the commute home. You do the math and see if it's worth it! Your evenings will likely become a lot less stressful because you don't have to worry about fighting rush hour traffic to get home to cook dinner. You also don't have to stress over what to make for dinner, whether you have the right ingredients, and what to pack for lunch the following day. So investing two to three hours a week to prep a week's worth of healthy food is totally worth it. Try it and you'll see!

Saves Money

Most people are trying to eat healthier, but it's expensive to eat out often with most restaurants charging an arm and a leg for a "healthy" meal (which may be advertised as healthy but who knows what really is in it). The average North American probably spends around $10 for lunch on any given day. With meal prepping, you can eat a whole day's worth of food for about $10. This may not always be the case, but it's definitely doable if you know the tips to grocery shopping on a budget.

You're in Control

There are so many additives and unhealthy ingredients in restaurant and store-bought processed foods to make it tastier, but are those foods healthy for you? That's questionable. A restaurant is a business after all, and their priority is the bottom line, not your health. So more often than not restaurants opt for the cheapest ingredients to make their food, like unhealthy oils, added salt, MSG, and sauces to enhance the flavors...not to mention the added calories. Reading the calorie and nutrient breakdown of the typical restaurant meal can be shocking! By cooking your own meals, however, you get to control the way it's prepared, the quality of the ingredients, and exactly what goes into the meals that you're feeding yourself and your family. Don't forget that old saying: you are what you eat! So by eating well, you'll feel better, sleep better, and be healthier.

It Keeps You on Track

If you're trying to lose weight or simply eat better, meal prepping ensures that you always have healthy meals at the ready. Having prepared meals reduces the chances that you will backslide on your healthy eating goals when you are crunched for time and there's a lack of healthy food choices or when you have food cravings. Because your entire week's worth of meals is already prepared, you won't have to decide what to eat every day. It's much easier for you to stay on a healthy lifestyle track. If you are trying to lose weight, remember that losing weight is 80 percent diet and 20 percent exercise.

It Helps with Portion Control

When everything is portioned ahead of time and packed in containers, you will be less likely to overeat. You'll just eat what's in your container and that's it. An empty container signifies the end of the meal. This is a great way to gain control over your portions, especially for the emotional eaters out there.

Steps to a Successful Meal Prep Day

If you haven't meal prepped before, the idea of starting meal prepping for your entire week may be daunting. So start small! You can simply begin with prepping two to three days of your breakfast and lunch and see how you feel. Time yourself and see how long these shorter preps take. You'll soon have a better idea how much time you'll need to prep food for more days. If even that is too much, then start by only prepping your breakfast! When you're ready to start a whole week's prep, here are a few tips to keep in mind.

Keep It Simple

If you're just starting out, try only prepping a couple days' worth of food first or even just breakfast for the first week. It can be overwhelming to cook a whole week's worth of food all at once especially when you want a lot of variety. Because of this even experienced meal preppers sometimes choose just three meals to prep for the entire week—one breakfast (seven portions), one lunch (seven portions), and one dinner (seven portions), and maybe some snacks too. When starting out you should stick to cooking simple meals on your prep days, and don't make extravagant meals because these can be very time-consuming.

Choose What You Like to Eat

Just because fitness gurus are eating sweet potatoes, don't feel you must eat them if you dislike them. Choose what you like to eat because that's the only way you'll stick to a healthy diet. Don't boil your broccoli and chicken just because it's "healthy." Chances are, you won't end up eating it and will choose to eat something else. Healthy eating doesn't mean boring and tasteless food. Like spicy food? Then cook spicy food! There are ways to enjoy spicy food and keep it healthy. The only way that your healthy eating lifestyle will be sustainable is if you really enjoy the process and the food.

Plan Ahead

Plan ahead by picking out a couple of recipes that are simple with not too many ingredients. Write down a list of ingredients you'll need to pick up at the grocery store. Plan the amount of servings you'll need and multiply the recipe amounts accordingly. It's not as hard as it sounds, and you will get the hang of it quickly.

Break Down Your Meals

Instead of cooking an entire meal, break it down into parts that you can cook separately. This allows you to mix and match your meals to keep things interesting throughout your week. Pick a couple options of each food group and cook them separately. For example, proteins can include chicken, ground turkey, or eggs. Your vegetable portions could be kale, broccoli, or bok choy; carbohydrates could include rice, quinoa, and potatoes.

This works really well if you're the type of person that gets easily bored with the same meals every day. Lunch Day 1 can be ground turkey, kale, and quinoa. Lunch Day 2 can be eggs with potatoes and bok choy, and Lunch Day 3 can be chicken and broccoli with rice. You get the idea! You can mix and match one carbohydrate, one protein, and one vegetable and make endless amounts of meal combos out of these!

The other trick is to buy ingredients that you can overlap in recipes. For example, zucchini are very cost effective in the summer. Why not stock up on them and spiralize one batch for Mason jar salad and spiralize another batch for "zoodles" with meatballs.

Prep Now, Cook Later

You don't have to cook everything right away. When you have a few spare minutes, you can prewash and cut up all of your vegetables and season or marinate your proteins ahead of time so that when you get home on a weeknight you can just cook and not have to spend time prepping. You won't have to think or stress over it because you already know what you're cooking and you will save a lot of time.

How to Begin

You might get overwhelmed if you're at the very beginning of your meal prep journey. But don't panic, because there are so many tools out there to help guide you. Blogs and websites dedicated to meal prepping are great at demonstrating how easy it can be and are a great way to see how it's done.

The first thing you need to do is decide which day is your prep day. Which day will you be able to commit a window of time to grocery shop, cook, and clean? Once you've decided, then mark that on your calendar. This will ensure that you don't let distractions get in the way. Remember, if it's important to you, you will make time for it. If not, you will make all the excuses in the world to avoid it.

Get Your Kitchen Ready

Fancy kitchen tools are nice to have, but you really don't need anything beyond the basics when you're just starting out. As time goes on and you start getting more comfortable, then you can slowly invest in more kitchen utensils and equipment. By then you'll also know if you'll actually have a use for that fancy tool or not.

With that said, having a well-equipped kitchen is important. Here is a list of basic kitchen tools and utensils you should have:

- Full set mixing bowls (usually come in a set of four)
- 1 set measuring cups
- 1 set measuring spoons
- 2–3 tongs
- 2 frying pans or skillets (one small and one large), with covers
- 4 baking pans (two large, two medium)
- 1 can opener
- 1 good quality sharp chef's knife (one will do but two would be ideal!)
- 2 chopping boards (one for meat, one for vegetables)
- 1 meat thermometer (a basic one is fine)
- 1 spiralizer (a great time-saver)
- 1 whisk
- 1 steamer basket
- 2 pots (one large, one medium)
- Parchment paper (buy the value size)
- 1 slow cooker (a lifesaver!)
- 1 silicon brush for basting
- 1 pair kitchen scissors
- 1 potato peeler
- 2 spatulas (one wooden, one plastic)
- 1 slotted spoon
- 1 soup ladle
- 1 grater
- 1 zester
- 1 pair oven mitts
- 1 food processor (size will depend on your household size)
- 1 blender

- 1 mandoline
- 1 muffin pan
- 1 colander

If you are a more experienced cook or want to experiment with new recipes and cooking methods, you should also consider having these tools:

- Rice cooker
- Pressure cooker
- Grinder
- Hand mixer
- Food scale
- Lemon juicer
- Egg slicer

Picking Food Storage Containers

So you've just spent half a day meal prepping and two days later your food is starting to spoil! Choosing the wrong container to store your prepped food in is a frustrating and costly mistake. Therefore, making sure you have the right type of containers is so important! Here are some of the features to look for when you're shopping for food containers.

- **Leakproof:** Whether you choose plastic or glass, the first thing to look for is a container with an airtight seal. This will prevent the sauces and food from leaking out, especially when you have to commute with your food.
- **Durability:** Cheap, thin plastic containers may be fine sitting in your refrigerator, but when you have to commute with one, it may not hold up. If you're going with plastic, make sure you invest in stronger and thicker plastic containers; they will last longer and be a better long-term investment.
- **Compartments:** Containers with multiple compartments have become very popular with meal preppers, but beware because the quality can differ from brand to brand. If you're going this route, pick one that is strong and thick and seals tightly when closed. Pick a minimum of two compartments because you can separate the sauced foods from dry ones. This allows you to keep your food for longer.

- **Glass versus plastic:** Glass containers are easier to clean (especially with tomato sauce and oil) as compared to plastic ones. Tomato sauce recipes usually stain plastic containers permanently in a short amount of time. So make sure you pick the right ones to store depending on the type of food you will likely be meal prepping. If you are picking plastic, be sure to pick containers that are both microwave- and dishwasher-safe.
- **Mason jars:** They are affordable and seal very tightly, so they're great for packing salads. They clean well and are easy to take on the go. They also reheat well. One of the downsides is the lids. You will likely have to replace them after a while due to rusting, but this can be mitigated by properly cleaning then drying the lids. Another downside to Mason jars is that they are made of glass and therefore prone to breakage.
- **Plastic food containers:** Pick ones that are BPA-free. Make sure the lids seal well so that they're leakproof. Plastic containers are a great option for when you have to take your food on the go. They're lightweight and usually quite durable.
- **Different sizes:** You'll need different sizes to pack different meals and snacks and sauces. Invest in a variety of them. Don't forget about the bigger ones for when you bulk prep and need to store all that food in the refrigerator.

Grocery Shopping Tips

Knowing exactly how many of what items to buy will make your grocery trips more efficient and will ensure no food goes to waste. You should also try to limit your grocery trips to once a week, usually the day of prep or the day before prep to make sure you are prepping with fresh ingredients. Here are some tips to keep in mind to make the most out of your grocery trips!

Make a List

After reviewing your chosen recipes for prepping, write down exactly what you need of each type of ingredient. You can use apps like Wunderlist or Evernote or even write down your grocery list on a piece of paper. Sticking to this list while shopping is important.

Choose a Time

Go Friday nights or early mornings on the weekends to avoid crowds. This will allow you to shop quicker and also get in and out of the market faster. Don't forget that if you go early, you often get the better picks of fresh produce.

Shop Seasonally

For fresh fruits and vegetables, make an effort to buy the ones that are in season. These will likely taste the best and be the most nutritious. If you're not sure what's in season, do a quick *Google* search. If you don't have time to search, then the food labels at the supermarket usually will tell you. Foods that are in season are typically a lot cheaper than ones that are not.

Shop Locally

Buying produce locally is sometimes a lot cheaper than buying at the supermarket, and you're helping local farmers. Don't forget that buying local means produce gets from the farm to your kitchen in a short span of time, which means you're getting produce at its ripest so it's more nutrient-dense and tastier. Some options for shopping locally would be to visit a farmers' market in your neighborhood, or even visiting a local farm seasonally to harvest your own fruits and vegetables. This can be a lot of fun too since you can make it a family day trip! If you don't have a farm or farmers' market near you, then purchase produce grown as close as possible to you. For example, if you live in Toronto, Ontario, purchase peaches grown in Ontario (when they're in season). Some cities also have farm share or community supported agriculture (CSA) programs that you can sign up for.

Don't Overshop

Before you go shopping, double-check what you already have. You may already have some of the items on your shopping list. Also only buy the quantities of items called for in the recipes you're making. If you buy too much, it will likely spoil before you can make use of it. There is so much food wasted in the standard North American household because of this.

Try Frozen Foods

Some produce and fruits are cheaper when you buy them frozen at bulk food stores. In fact, frozen produce is usually picked at its peak, so it's more nutrient-dense than its fresh counterpart at grocery stores. Most fresh produce is picked before it fully ripens, to account for travel time and shelf life. So don't be hesitant about buying frozen vegetables.

Buy Meat in Bulk

It's usually more cost-effective to buy your meat in large quantities rather than small packages. You may not need to use it all, but you can always portion it out and freeze unused portions for the following week. Partner up with friends and family to source bulk meat—you will save a lot of money.

Storing Your Raw Ingredients

Sometimes if a certain type of protein is on sale, you may want to stock up because it usually does freeze well. Fresh produce, however, usually does not store well for that long. Here are some tips to store some of your raw ingredients to make them last longer.

- **Chicken/beef/pork:** It would be best if you pre-portion them out before freezing them. Use a freezer-safe zip-top bag and portion out your week's worth of protein and then store it.
- **Fish:** Try purchasing fish that comes in individually wrapped fillets. They will last for months in the freezer and are easier to manage since you can either thaw them the night before by putting them in the refrigerator or thaw them by soaking them in warm water right before cooking.

Storing Your Produce

- **Fresh herbs:** Herbs like cilantro and parsley that you can buy with the roots intact will store for weeks if they are kept properly. Fill a jar or large glass with water, place the herbs in it, wrap with a plastic bag, and store it in the refrigerator. You can also buy handy herb storage containers that work in a similar fashion. This keeps the herbs fresh for weeks.

- **Leafy greens:** Leafy greens like spinach, lettuce, and kale can spoil quickly if there is too much moisture present. Simply wrap them in a paper towel, put them in a bag, and tightly seal them. This will keep them fresh much longer than usual—you will be surprised.
- **Fruits:** Pears and apples are staples, and they store well for weeks if kept in the fruit compartment of your refrigerator. Berries, on the other hand, can only be kept for a few days. Blueberries usually store better than other berries like strawberries, raspberries, and blackberries.

Storing Your Cooked Meals

Some foods store well in the refrigerator and still taste pretty good after five days, but some will go bad after just a day or two. Knowing what foods stay fresh is important. But don't worry, you'll soon learn along the way.

Here is a list of things that typically store well in the refrigerator for at least five days:

- Ground meat (turkey, beef, chicken, and pork): Once seasoned and cooked, it will store very well in the refrigerator and will maintain taste and flavor.
- Soups and stews: Slow cooker recipes and one-pot stews usually store really well.
- Egg cups: They store very well for five days and taste amazing.
- Meatloaf
- Cooked quinoa and rice dishes
- Steamed vegetables
- Baked sweet potatoes
- Roasted root vegetables
- Mason jar salads
- Overnight oats
- Fresh vegetables (bell peppers, zucchini, carrots, broccoli, cauliflower, kale)

Things to avoid storing more than a day or two:

- **Any cooked fish dishes:** They do not taste the same after two days. If you want to have fish for the week, I would recommend preparing it each night as a dinner meal. Thaw the fish the night before in the refrigerator and cook it fresh daily. Fish doesn't take long to cook, so it's a quick and easy option to complement other prepped foods.
- **Seafood (except for shrimp):** Scallops and calamari do not keep well. Don't cook them as your weekly prepped meals.
- **Fresh tomato dishes:** Tomato salads do not keep well unless they're placed at the bottom of a Mason jar salad (see recipes in Chapter 8).
- **Fresh herbs:** If your meal prep includes fresh herbs, preserve them by wrapping them in a paper towel and packing them separately. This keeps the moisture out and helps keep the herbs fresh for longer.
- **Boiled eggs:** You can boil eggs ahead of time, but just don't peel them before storing. Keep boiled eggs in their shells, as they will last longer. It's best to boil them the night before.
- **Chicken breasts:** They won't be good after two or more days. It's best to keep them marinated or seasoned, but uncooked. Cooked fresh each day, or at least two or three days at a time, is best.
- **Steaks:** Not good to meal prep with. They do not last more than a day or so. They do not taste the same. Avoid meal prepping these and just enjoy them as weekend meals.
- **Cucumber:** Prepped cucumber with seeds will get slimy and watery after a couple of days. If you want to keep them longer, make sure the seeds are removed.

Common Mistakes of Meal Prepping

Meal prepping is easy to do and will save you countless hours of time during the week, but there are some common mistakes that people make when meal prepping that you should be sure to avoid:

1. **Prepping the same food every week:** Healthy doesn't mean boring! Eating the same things over and over again can be very boring. Even if you like chicken a lot, you can cook it in different ways every week.

2. **Skipping on flavors:** Many people think eating healthy means not adding any spice or flavors to your cooking. If you try that, healthy eating will not last very long because you'll soon realize that life is short and you need some flavors in your life. Don't be afraid to add new spices or herbs that you've never used before. Experiment with your food and maybe you'll actually love sumac after all (that's a Middle Eastern spice).

3. **Packaged dressing/sauces:** You'll notice that this entire book has minimal amounts of prepackaged dressing or sauces. Why? Because often-times, packaged sauces and dressings have an insane amount of calories in them plus a lot of preservatives and ingredients that may not be the best for you.

4. **Not pre-portioning out meals:** Some people cook their food in batches, but don't pre-portion their meals out. This will cause two things: they can overeat and they will not have enough food to last through the week. (Not to mention, most people meal prep to lose weight or live a healthier lifestyle so overeating will not help if this is your goal.)

5. **Shopping too many days ahead:** As mentioned earlier, you should grocery shop the day before or the day of your meal prep to ensure you're using fresh ingredients to prep. If you buy your produce too far in advance and don't store it properly, it may be spoiled by the time you go to prep.

6. **Trying long, complicated recipes:** The key is to keep your preps simple (for example, keep your ingredient list short, to less than five itmes, and the whole prep and cooking process shouldn't take you more than five hours to complete). Don't try to make an extravagant, beautiful meal for a prep, as it will take forever and you'll be so tired, you won't want to continue making more meal options.

7. **Not prepping snacks:** Prep your snacks as well as your meals, because if you're portion controlling your meals, you may not last from lunch to dinner without a snack in between. Forgetting your meals may cause you to grab last-minute snacks or even overeat during dinner. So keep snacks simple, and have an apple, a protein bar, or even two boiled eggs and some carrots.

8. **Being too ambitious with options:** Having different meal options is important, but remember that the more variety you want, the more time you'll need to invest. You don't want to spend your entire day in your kitchen on a Sunday when it's beautiful out. It's about being able to enjoy your weekend as well as cooking healthy food so you can be ready for the

week. You have to find the balance between having options and the time you want to put in. Having three different meals and then repeating the three meals for the entire week may be good enough for some, but others may need five meal options. Find your balance!

9. **Skipping the pre-planning:** If you just walk into a grocery store and start picking up whatever you see, hoping to make something good out of what you find, your chances of having a successful meal prep day will be slim! Like anything, you have to start by meal prepping with a plan (picking recipes, listing out ingredients and how many you'll need of each, checking what you already have versus what you'll have to purchase, and planning your day and time of grocery shopping and cooking). A simple rule to follow is this: what gets planned gets done. Don't skip this important step!

10. **Prepping too much food:** Before you decide the number of meal portions you'll make; you should review your social calendar. Maybe you have three pre-planned dinners out with friends, so therefore you don't need seven meals, you'll only need four for the entire week. If you don't review and plan ahead, it will lead to a lot of wasted food, or not enough prepped meals for the week.

Time-Saving Tips

When you first start out, it may take you longer to get organized, prep the food, cook, and clean. But as you continue, it will get easier and you'll also get more efficient at prepping. Here are a few tips that may help save you time and effort in your meal prep.

- **Use a slow cooker:** Slow cooker recipes are lifesavers, and they usually require only a minimal effort. Just put everything in one pot, hit cook, and go to bed. You'll wake up the next day with a beautiful meal already cooked.
- **Batch-cook your meals:** Cook all of your ground turkey, then cook all of your chicken, and then your vegetables—you get the idea. By doing so, you can mix and match your options to create different meals each day.
- **Pick recipes with different cooking methods:** Choose recipes that require baking, using a slow cooker, and the stovetop so you can multitask.

Doing so will allow you to stir-fry something on the stovetop while something is baking in the oven. You'll save a lot of time this way.

- **Keep things simple:** Steaming your vegetables instead of sautéing them with other ingredients not only saves time but is more nutritious too. It also keeps the calories down.
- **Make one-pot meals:** One-skillet meals like stir-fries or even one-pot stews are great time-savers.
- **Get organized:** Plan ahead so you can move easily from one task to another.
- **Prep before the prep:** If you know you'll be short on time on prep day, then split up the prep work the night before. For example, you can wash and cut the vegetables, cut and season or marinate your meat, and make dressings and sauces so they'll last for a couple of weeks.
- **Buy precut produce and meat:** If you're really crunched for time, you can buy your produce and meat precut. This may be more expensive, but it'll still be cheaper than eating out.
- **Engage a helper:** Make it fun and invite a friend to do it together. You can divide up tasks and tackle the whole prep together.
- **Use kitchen tools:** A spiralizer, mandoline, and grater are great for preparing raw ingredients. These tools can save a lot of time especially when you're new to cooking.
- **Buy pre-mixed dried spices:** If you're too busy to measure out all of the different spices in a recipe, this will save time. Spice mixes are especially good on eggs and proteins.
- **Keep your snacks simple:** Not all snacks need to be homemade to be good. Precut vegetables or fruits with cottage cheese are not only easy to prep, but they are also healthier than reaching for that bag of chips. Tossing some nuts into a small container takes no time.
- **Use a grill:** The grill can cook food quickly and in large amounts. It also imparts that smoky, grilled taste. Grilling also minimizes the amount of oil you use. This again keeps calories in check.
- **Clean as you go:** Don't pile the mess up for the end of your prep. Always clean everything as you go. A clean working space makes your process more enjoyable.
- **Freeze pre-portioned smoothie ingredients in zip-top bags:** This is great if you're having smoothies for breakfast or need a quick lunch or snack on the go.

- **Find recipes with overlapping ingredients:** This way you can prep all of the vegetables for multiple recipes at the same time.
- **Keep your refrigerator and freezer organized and clean:** Don't forget to keep the place that will store your weekly food organized. There's nothing worse than opening up a refrigerator or freezer and not being able to find what you're looking for.
- **Clean your food containers daily:** If you don't do this, containers will pile up in your kitchen sink, and before you know it there's a big mess waiting for you to start your weekend.
- **Portion everything ahead of time:** Pre-portion your breakfasts, lunches, and dinners. This helps with portion control and also makes sure that no food goes to waste. You can purchase inexpensive food scales to help you with proper food portioning.
- **Make sure to cool the food completely before refrigeration:** Hot food can create condensation in a closed container. That will create extra moisture and spoil your food faster.
- **Try one new recipe at a time:** Don't try three different new recipes in one day. This will be overwhelming especially if all three don't turn out very well. Sometimes recipes take time to perfect, so don't risk your entire week's food all at once.
- **Spice up your food:** Don't be afraid to try spices you've never had before.

CHAPTER 2

Eggs

Perfect Boiled Eggs

With these steps you should be able to boil eggs exactly the way you want. Boiled eggs can be kept in the refrigerator with shells on up to 5 days and up to 3 days with shells removed.

INGREDIENTS | SERVES 2

4 large eggs

Wonderfully Versatile Eggs

Eggs can be added to any salads for extra protein and are also a great, quick pre-workout snack. Eggs are affordable and considered a complete protein food source because they contain nine essential amino acids. One egg alone contains 6 grams of protein and is also a good source of vitamin D, vitamin B_{12}, and phosphorus.

1. Fill a medium pot ¾ full with water and bring to a boil over high heat.

2. Use a large slotted spoon to place eggs slowly into the boiling water. Eggs should be completely submerged under water.

3. For soft-boiled eggs with runny yolk: boil on high 7 minutes.

4. For soft but not runny yolk: boil on high 9 minutes.

5. For hard-boiled eggs: boil on high 11 minutes.

6. Once desired time is up, remove pot from heat and drain water. Run eggs under cold water 30 seconds. Crack the eggs and let cracked-shell eggs sit another 5 minutes to cool before peeling.

7. Enjoy right away or store in a food container for future use.

PER SERVING Calories: 143 | Fat: 8.7 g | Protein: 12.6 g | Sodium: 142 mg | Fiber: 0.0 g | Carbohydrates: 0.7 g | Sugar: 0.4 g

Coconut Milk Scrambled Eggs with Chives

Scrambled eggs are a great, quick meal prep when you don't feel like spending hours prepping in the kitchen. When stored properly this dish will keep well in the refrigerator approximately 2–3 days.

INGREDIENTS | SERVES 2

2 large eggs

1 cup egg whites

¼ cup coconut milk

⅛ teaspoon salt

1 teaspoon cooking oil

2 tablespoons chopped fresh chives

⅛ teaspoon freshly ground black pepper

Savory Scrambled Eggs

Scrambled eggs are one of the most versatile meals you can make because you can pretty much add any of your favorite ingredients to them. Chives add a good punch of flavor without taking away from the eggs. Scrambled eggs go well on top of toast or can be served with any of your favorite sides.

1. In a large bowl whisk eggs, egg whites, coconut milk, and salt until well mixed.

2. Heat a medium pan over medium heat and add oil.

3. Once oil is hot, pour egg mixture into pan and cook 30 seconds.

4. Add chives and pepper.

5. With a spatula, stir and turn the eggs to ensure ingredients are thoroughly mixed. Cook 2 minutes if you like eggs that are a bit runny. If you prefer well-done eggs, then cook 3 minutes total or until you no longer see any liquid.

6. Remove from pan and serve.

PER SERVING Calories: 147 | Fat: 12.2 g | Protein: 7.0 g | Sodium: 219 mg | Fiber: 0.1 g | Carbohydrates: 1.4 g | Sugar: 0.2 g

Egg Whites and Chicken Muffins

If you are not a big fan of asparagus, you can use broccoli in this recipe instead. Egg muffins keep in the refrigerator at least 5 days and will hold their taste very well.

INGREDIENTS | SERVES 24

1 tablespoon extra-virgin olive oil, divided

2 cloves garlic, peeled and minced

½ cup frozen green peas

1 cup diced asparagus shoots

2 cups chopped baby spinach

¼ teaspoon salt, divided

¼ teaspoon freshly ground black pepper, divided

1 cup extra-lean ground chicken

¼ teaspoon ground cumin

¼ teaspoon paprika, divided

2 cups egg whites

Egg Muffins

To keep this low in fat and reduce oil use, try using silicon muffin cups. They're easier to clean, and for the most part the eggs can be taken out of the cups with ease. Another option is to apply some cooking oil into the muffin cups before pouring the egg mix into them.

1. Preheat oven to 350°F.

2. Heat a large pan over medium heat and add ½ tablespoon oil. Once oil is hot, add garlic, peas, and asparagus. Stir until asparagus is soft, 3 minutes.

3. Add spinach, ⅛ teaspoon salt, and ⅛ teaspoon pepper and stir until spinach is wilted, 1 minute. Pour into a large bowl and set aside to cool.

4. In the same pan add the remaining ½ tablespoon oil and chicken. Stir with a spatula and use the flat edge to separate into small pieces. Stir 6–8 minutes or until thoroughly cooked.

5. Add remaining salt and pepper, cumin, and ⅛ tablespoon paprika. Pour into a separate bowl and set aside to cool.

6. Once meat and vegetables are cool, line the muffin cups with silicon liners or oil the liners if you're using another type.

7. Fill each muffin cup with ½ tablespoon chicken and 1 tablespoon vegetables, then pour egg whites on top and sprinkle with remaining paprika. Bake 25 minutes.

8. Let cool, then remove from liners, store in food containers, and refrigerate up to 5 days.

PER SERVING (1 muffin) Calories: 30 | Fat: 1.1 g | Protein: 4.4 g | Sodium: 79 mg | Fiber: 0.3 g | Carbohydrates: 0.9 g | Sugar: 0.4 g

Bacon Broccoli Frittata

Frittatas will only keep in the refrigerator 2 days. They will last 2–3 months in the freezer, but allow time to thaw before reheating in the microwave or oven. Reheating in the microwave could make this a bit soggy.

INGREDIENTS | SERVES 6

7 slices low-sodium bacon or turkey bacon

7 large eggs

¼ teaspoon salt

¼ cup coconut cream

1 cup grated sweet carrots

¼ teaspoon freshly ground black pepper

1 teaspoon dried oregano

¼ teaspoon paprika

1 tablespoon coconut oil

¾ cup diced yellow onion

2 cloves garlic, peeled and minced

1 cup diced broccoli florets

Broccoli

Broccoli is a good source of dietary fiber, not to mention the numerous vitamins and minerals found in these mini trees. But did you know that they're part of the cabbage family? Stay healthy by making broccoli a regular staple in your diet.

1. Preheat oven to 350°F.

2. In a medium pan over medium heat fry bacon until crisp. Set aside on a plate to cool. Once bacon is cool to touch, break or cut into ¼" pieces.

3. In a large mixing bowl whisk eggs, salt, and coconut cream until well mixed.

4. Add carrots, pepper, oregano, and paprika and stir until well mixed. Set aside.

5. Heat a large oven-safe skillet over medium heat and add coconut oil.

6. Once oil is hot, add onion, garlic, and broccoli. Stir until vegetables are soft, then add bacon and egg mixture.

7. Use the spatula to fold egg mixture into vegetables to evenly distribute. Keep cooking until firm. With the spatula, pat the eggs evenly across the pan.

8. Transfer pan directly into oven and bake 15 minutes. Serve immediately or let cool and separate into 6 pieces and store separately.

PER SERVING Calories: 208 | Fat: 14.0 g | Protein: 12.1 g | Sodium: 294 mg | Fiber: 1.6 g | Carbohydrates: 6.4 g | Sugar: 2.2 g

Spicy Spinach and Tomato Frittata

If you do not have an oven-safe pan, you can always cook the frittata on a regular pan first, then transfer it to a baking pan or dish that is oven-safe. This frittata will reheat nicely up to 3 days, or you can also enjoy it cold. If you do not like spicy food, then omit the red pepper flakes from this recipe.

INGREDIENTS | SERVES 2

6 large eggs

⅛ teaspoon sea salt

¼ teaspoon freshly ground black pepper

¼ teaspoon red pepper flakes

1 tablespoon coconut oil

½ medium onion, peeled and diced

2 cloves garlic, peeled and minced

1 cup diced and seeded tomatoes

1 (9-ounce) bag baby spinach

5 tomato slices

1. Set oven to broil or preheat it to 475°F.

2. In a large mixing bowl add eggs, salt, pepper, and red pepper flakes and whisk or stir with a fork until combined. Set aside.

3. Heat a large oven-safe pan over medium heat, add oil, and swirl around until the oil covers entire pan.

4. Once the pan is hot, add onions and stir 1 minute. Add garlic and diced tomatoes and stir until soft, 2–3 minutes.

5. Add spinach and stir 30 seconds or until it is wilted.

6. Add whisked egg mixture into the pan and use a spatula to fold eggs into vegetables. Cook until eggs are firm but still a bit runny, 2–3 minutes.

7. With the spatula, pat the eggs evenly across the pan. Lay tomato slices evenly on top of eggs.

8. Place in oven and bake 4 minutes or until eggs are golden brown. Portion out the dish as needed in meal prep containers and then refrigerate up to 3 days.

PER SERVING Calories: 341 | Fat: 19.9 g | Protein: 24.2 g | Sodium: 466 mg | Fiber: 5.0 g | Carbohydrates: 14.6 g | Sugar: 5.9 g

Spinach and Sweet Potato Quiche

Quiche actually originated from Germany; the word quiche *is taken from the German word for cake. The flexible thing about quiches is that they can be served hot or cold. Quiche will only keep 2 days in the refrigerator.*

INGREDIENTS | SERVES 6

1½ tablespoons coconut oil, divided

2 cloves garlic, peeled and minced

1 cup diced Spanish onions

½ pound ground turkey

1 (10-ounce) package frozen spinach leaves, parboiled

¼ teaspoon sea salt

¼ teaspoon freshly ground black pepper

2 large sweet potatoes, peeled and thinly sliced

4 large eggs

¾ cup almond milk (or coconut milk)

¼ cup Cheddar cheese

1. Preheat oven to 395°F.

2. Grease a 9½" ceramic oven-safe dish with ½ tablespoon coconut oil. Set aside.

3. Heat a large pan over medium heat and add 1 tablespoon coconut oil, garlic, and onions. Stir until golden brown, 2–3 minutes.

4. Add ground turkey and stir until thoroughly cooked, 5–7 minutes. Make sure to break up big turkey pieces into smaller ones.

5. Reduce heat to low and add spinach. Stir until spinach is thoroughly cooked, 10–12 minutes. Add salt and pepper. Set aside.

6. In bottom of prepared dish, overlap sweet potato slices to create a crust for the quiche; make sure you do not leave any open gaps. Pour cooked spinach over sweet potatoes.

7. In a separate mixing bowl whisk eggs and almond milk until well blended. Pour egg mixture into the ceramic dish over spinach.

8. Sprinkle and cover the top layer evenly with cheese. Cover with foil and bake 30 minutes.

9. Serve immediately or let cool and cut into 6 slices and store in containers.

PER SERVING Calories: 208 | Fat: 10.3 g | Protein: 13.4 g | Sodium: 283 mg | Fiber: 3.6 g | Carbohydrates: 15.2 g | Sugar: 4.2 g

Spinach and Sweet Potato Egg Cups

This recipe has a good mix of carbohydrates and protein. If you do not like coconut milk, it can be replaced with regular 2% milk. These cups can be kept up to 5 days in the refrigerator.

INGREDIENTS | SERVES 10

1 cup diced sweet potatoes
½ tablespoon coconut oil
½ cup finely diced onions
2 cloves garlic, peeled and minced
1 cup diced red bell peppers
¼ teaspoon salt
¼ teaspoon freshly ground black pepper
¼ teaspoon paprika
2 cups baby spinach, chopped
16 large eggs
¼ cup coconut milk

Are Sweet Potatoes Healthier?

Sweet potatoes are often advocated for use in a healthy diet. But do sweet potatoes have fewer carbohydrates than regular potatoes? They do not; they have the same amount of carbs per serving. However, sweet potatoes have more fiber and are therefore lower on the glycemic index than regular white potatoes.

1. Preheat oven to 350°F. Line a 12-cup muffin pan with silicon liners.

2. Fill a small pot halfway with water and bring to a boil over high heat. Put diced sweet potatoes into boiling water and parboil 3 minutes. Remove from stove, strain, and set aside.

3. Heat a large pan over medium-low heat and add ½ tablespoon oil. Once oil is hot, add onions and garlic. Stir until golden brown, 2–3 minutes.

4. Add blanched sweet potatoes, bell peppers, salt, black pepper, and paprika and stir 3 minutes.

5. Add spinach and stir until it's wilted, 1 minute. Pour into a large bowl and set aside to cool.

6. In a separate large mixing bowl whisk eggs and coconut milk to combine.

7. Add 2 tablespoons vegetable mixture to 10 of the muffin cups and pour egg mixture on top to fill the liners. Fill the remaining cups ⅔ full of water.

8. Bake 30–35 minutes or until eggs are cooked. Let cool, then remove from liners and store in containers.

PER SERVING (1 cup) Calories: 165 | Fat: 9.4 g | Protein: 11.0 g | Sodium: 185 mg | Fiber: 1.3 g | Carbohydrates: 7.0 g | Sugar: 2.6 g

Broccoli and Mushroom Frittata

Frittatas are rich in healthy fats and protein. The combinations of different types of vegetables and proteins that go into a frittata are almost limitless. This frittata will reheat nicely up to 3 days, or you can enjoy it cold.

INGREDIENTS | SERVES 6

2 cups chopped broccoli florets

2 teaspoons coconut oil, divided

1 clove garlic, peeled and minced

8 ounces cremini mushrooms, cleaned and sliced

½ teaspoon sea salt

¼ teaspoon freshly ground black pepper

10 large eggs

1 cup coconut cream

2 tablespoons chopped fresh dill

½ cup grated Cheddar cheese

Coconut Cream

If you cannot find coconut cream, you can replace it with coconut milk or half-and-half. For those following a paleo or Whole30 diet, stick to coconut milk or cream and simply omit the cheese from this recipe. Coconut milk from a sealed container rather than a can is often preferable.

1. Preheat oven to 375°F.

2. Fill a medium pot halfway with water and and bring it to a boil over high heat. Add broccoli and parboil 2 minutes. Remove from stove, drain, and set aside.

3. Heat a large skillet over medium heat and add 1 teaspoon coconut oil.

4. Once oil is hot, add garlic and mushrooms and stir until mushrooms are golden brown, 5 minutes.

5. Add broccoli, salt, and pepper to the skillet and continue to stir 2 minutes. Remove and set aside.

6. Grease a 9" oven-safe pan or pie plate with remaining 1 teaspoon coconut oil. Pour in the vegetables and spread evenly across the bottom of the pie plate.

7. In a large bowl whisk together eggs and coconut cream, add dill to mixture, and whisk to combine. Pour egg mixture over vegetables and sprinkle cheese evenly over the top.

8. Bake 35 minutes or until firm. Let cool and divide into 6 servings and store in the refrigerator.

PER SERVING Calories: 321 | Fat: 24.5 g | Protein: 16.0 g | Sodium: 348 mg | Fiber: 1.9 g | Carbohydrates: 7.3 g | Sugar: 1.5 g

Cheesy Ground Beef Egg Muffins

Egg muffins are easy to make, good for long-term storage, and super nutritious. You can customize them however you like by adding ingredients that you'd prefer and take away ingredients that you don't like. For example, beef can be replaced by ground chicken in this recipe. These can be stored up to 5 days in the refrigerator.

INGREDIENTS | SERVES 12

2 teaspoons coconut oil, divided
8 ounces extra-lean ground beef
2 cups finely chopped broccoli florets
¼ cup drained and finely chopped sun-dried tomatoes
1 cup grated Cheddar cheese
1 teaspoon dried oregano
1 teaspoon dried basil
½ teaspoon garlic powder
½ teaspoon onion powder
¼ teaspoon sea salt
8 large eggs
1 tablespoon finely chopped fresh chives

Ground Beef

If ground beef isn't your thing, try replacing it with Italian sausage or even ground turkey or pork. Just make sure your sausage choice remains low in fat and sodium. Choose extra-lean ground pork if you are making it with pork.

1. Preheat oven to 375°F.

2. Grease a 12-cup muffin pan with 1 teaspoon oil (or use silicon muffin liners to avoid oil).

3. Heat a large pan over medium heat and add remaining oil and ground beef. Stir with spatula until thoroughly cooked, 5–7 minutes. Set aside to cool.

4. In a large mixing bowl combine broccoli, cooked beef, tomatoes, cheese, oregano, basil, garlic powder, onion powder, and salt; mix well.

5. In separate large bowl whisk eggs. Pour broccoli mixture into eggs and mix well.

6. Divide mixture evenly into muffin cups and top with chives.

7. Bake 30 minutes or until a wooden toothpick inserted in the center comes out clean.

8. Remove from oven, let cool, and remove from pan. Store in food containers and refrigerate up to 5 days.

PER SERVING Calories: 120 | Fat: 6.9 g | Protein: 11.1 g | Sodium: 173 mg | Fiber: 0.5 g | Carbohydrates: 1.6 g | Sugar: 0.4 g

Deviled Eggs

Deviled eggs are one of the most appetizing yet easy recipes to make. Serve these as appetizers for your next dinner party. These will keep up to 3 days in the refrigerator.

INGREDIENTS | SERVES 5

10 large hard-boiled eggs
1½ tablespoons mayonnaise
1½ tablespoons Dijon mustard
1 teaspoon ground cayenne pepper
1 teaspoon paprika, divided
1 tablespoon coconut aminos
1 tablespoon chopped fresh chives or green onions

1. Cut hard-boiled eggs in half lengthwise, remove the yolks, and place yolks in a large bowl.

2. With a fork, mash the yolks. Add mayonnaise, mustard, cayenne, ½ teaspoon paprika, and coconut aminos and mix until smooth.

3. Scoop mixture back into hollow egg whites, garnish with chives or green onions, and finish off with a sprinkle of paprika on top.

PER SERVING Calories: 179 | Fat: 11.7 g | Protein: 12.7 g | Sodium: 238 mg | Fiber: 0.3 g | Carbohydrates: 1.9 g | Sugar: 0.5 g

Easy Egg Salad

This dish is great for breakfast or even as a light snack served with toast or another carbohydrate. If you are sticking to a gluten-free diet, try serving this dish on a slice of steamed sweet potato. This salad will last up to 5 days stored in food containers.

INGREDIENTS | SERVES 5

10 large hard-boiled eggs, chopped
½ cup mayonnaise
1 tablespoon Dijon mustard
¼ cup chopped green onions
¼ teaspoon paprika
¼ teaspoon ground cayenne pepper
1 cup diced pears
½ cup diced celery
½ cup diced red bell peppers

Add ingredients to a large bowl and mix until well combined. Serve immediately or store in food containers and refrigerate up to 5 days.

PER SERVING Calories: 328 | Fat: 24.6 g | Protein: 13.3 g | Sodium: 176 mg | Fiber: 1.7 g | Carbohydrates: 7.9 g | Sugar: 4.4 g

Sweet Potato Hash Egg Cups

Layers of potatoes, greens, eggs with cheese—who can say no? This dish can be served hot or cold. If you want to reheat, don't do so for more than 60 seconds. Egg cups usually will keep up to 5 days in the refrigerator.

INGREDIENTS | SERVES 12

1 teaspoon cooking oil
1 cup grated raw sweet potatoes
¼ cup grated Cheddar cheese (optional)
½ tablespoon garlic powder
¼ teaspoon freshly ground black pepper
¼ teaspoon sea salt
1 small zucchini, thinly sliced
12 large eggs

Zucchini

Zucchini is a great source of vitamins C and B₆, and it also contains a small amount of protein. These summer squash are low in calories and carbohydrates yet high in nutrients. They can be added to almost any recipe and are a great complement to most dishes. Try baking or grilling them!

1. Preheat oven to 375°F.

2. Grease a 12-cup muffin pan with oil or line cups with silicon or paper liners.

3. In a large mixing bowl add sweet potato, cheese, garlic powder, pepper, and salt and mix well.

4. Add 1" (about 1 tablespoon) sweet potato mixture to the bottom of each cup.

5. Add 3 pieces sliced zucchini on top, overlapping one another. Crack 1 egg on top of each cup.

6. Bake 15 minutes or until eggs are at desired consistency.

7. Let cool before removing from pan to store.

PER SERVING Calories: 103 | Fat: 5.4 g | Protein: 7.3 g | Sodium: 145 mg | Fiber: 0.7 g | Carbohydrates: 4.8 g | Sugar: 1.2 g

Omelette with a Kick

Omelettes are great examples of how leftovers can be used. Leftover meat and vegetables can easily be transformed into a delicious omelette. While the ingredients can be prepped ahead, the omelette should be cooked the night before for best results and maximum freshness.

INGREDIENTS | SERVES 1

1 tablespoon coconut oil, divided

½ medium tomato, chopped

½ medium yellow onion, chopped

½ cup Mexican Ground Turkey (see Chapter 5)

½ medium jalapeño pepper, seeded (if desired) and sliced thinly

1 handful baby spinach

⅛ teaspoon sea salt

⅛ teaspoon freshly ground black pepper

⅛ teaspoon red pepper flakes

3 large eggs

¼ medium avocado, pitted and flesh removed

Jalapeños

If you want to lower the spice level of this omelette, remove the jalapeño seeds before slicing. You can also omit the jalapeño altogether since the red pepper flakes will give you enough of a kick if you're not a big spice person.

1. Heat a large skillet over medium heat and add ½ tablespoon oil.

2. Once oil is hot, add tomatoes and onions. Stir 3 minutes or until onions are golden brown.

3. Add turkey meat, jalapeño, spinach, salt, pepper, and red pepper flakes. Stir until spinach is wilted, 1 minute. Pour into a bowl and set aside.

4. Crack eggs into a large mixing bowl and whisk until well mixed.

5. In the same skillet over medium heat add remaining oil and once oil is hot pour in egg mixture. Let eggs cook 1 minute.

6. Pour cooked meat and vegetables over one side of eggs. Fold egg in half to cover the filling.

7. Turn heat to low and cook another 3–4 minutes.

8. Serve with a quarter of an avocado.

PER SERVING Calories: 590 | Fat: 33.8 g | Protein: 50.5 g | Sodium: 694 mg | Fiber: 5.9 g | Carbohydrates: 17.7 g | Sugar: 6.9 g

French Omelette

French omelettes are traditionally cooked in a lot of butter and cheese. This French-inspired dish is waistline-friendly yet keeps all the richness of the original. These omelettes are best made the same day or the night before. You can prep the ingredients ahead of time for a week's worth to save time.

INGREDIENTS | SERVES 1

3 large eggs
1 teaspoon coconut oil
1 tablespoon minced fresh rosemary
1 tablespoon minced fresh thyme
⅛ teaspoon sea salt
⅛ teaspoon freshly ground black pepper
¼ cup thinly sliced ham

Fresh Herbs

Fresh herbs are best to bring out the aroma of the dish. But you can certainly opt for dried herbs as well if you don't have fresh ones readily available. However, fresh herbs add that extra element to recipes and are usually inexpensive to buy. Also consider fresh herb storage containers to keep them fresh for longer.

1. Whisk eggs in a large bowl and set aside.

2. Bring a medium skillet to heat over medium heat and add oil. Once the oil is hot, add eggs and sprinkle herbs, salt, and pepper over top.

3. Cook eggs 1 minute, then add ham to the center of eggs.

4. With a spatula, fold two sides of eggs into the center to cover ham.

5. Once cooked to desired firmness, remove and serve. Store in food container for next day use.

PER SERVING Calories: 310 | Fat: 19.1 g | Protein: 27.8 g | Sodium: 967 mg | Fiber: 0.7 g | Carbohydrates: 2.2 g | Sugar: 0.6 g

Gluten-Free Zucchini Fritters

This is a great way to get rid of the abundance of zucchini you may have left over from your garden harvest. These fritters are low in carbohydrates and should be served with some boiled eggs for an extra dose of protein. The fritters are easy to make and keep well 3–4 days in the refrigerator.

INGREDIENTS | SERVES 4

2 large zucchini, grated

¼ teaspoon sea salt, divided

2 large eggs, beaten

¼ cup coconut flour

2 green onion stalks, finely chopped

¼ cup chopped fresh flat Italian parsley

¼ cup grated Parmesan cheese (optional)

¼ teaspoon freshly ground black pepper

2 tablespoons coconut oil (for frying)

Coconut Flour

If you do not have coconut flour, you can replace it with almond flour or any gluten-free flour mix. If you are also dairy-free, the cheese in this recipe is optional and can be removed.

1. Place grated zucchini in large bowl, sprinkle with half of the salt, and mix well.

2. Place zucchini on a large dishcloth or use paper towels and squeeze out as much liquid as possible. Place zucchini back into a bowl.

3. Add eggs, flour, onions, parsley, cheese, remaining salt, and pepper to zucchini bowl and mix well.

4. Heat a large frying pan over medium heat and add oil.

5. Once oil is hot, add mixture in ⅓ cup dollops, making sure fritters are separated. Fry 2–3 minutes on each side or until golden brown.

6. Remove from oil and place on top of paper towels to soak up excess oil. Serve as a side with your favorite protein or on their own as a snack. Store in food container and refrigerate up to 4 days.

PER SERVING Calories: 195 | Fat: 10.8 g | Protein: 9.0 g | Sodium: 338 mg | Fiber: 6.8 g | Carbohydrates: 14.6 g | Sugar: 5.2 g

Sausage and Potato Pancakes

This flourless savory pancake is high in protein and can be served as a complete breakfast. If you don't eat pork, you can replace the sausages with other meat-based ones like chicken or beef, or you can also use a ground meat of your choice (about 1 cup of it). These pancakes keep up to 3 days in the refrigerator.

INGREDIENTS | SERVES 5

2 large Italian mild sausages, chopped into small pieces

1 tablespoon coconut oil, divided

½ medium onion, peeled and diced

½ cup diced red bell peppers

1 teaspoon garlic powder

¼ teaspoon sea salt

¼ teaspoon freshly ground black pepper

1 teaspoon chili powder

1 teaspoon dried basil

8 large eggs

⅓ cup coconut milk

1 cup grated raw yellow potatoes

½ cup chopped fresh parsley

1. Preheat oven to 350°F.

2. Heat a medium skillet over medium heat and thoroughly cook sausages, 5–7 minutes depending on size. Pour into a bowl and set aside.

3. In the same skillet add ½ tablespoon oil, onions, bell peppers, garlic powder, salt, black pepper, chili powder, and basil and stir 3–4 minutes. Add cooked sausages back to skillet, remove from heat, and set aside.

4. In a large mixing bowl whisk eggs with coconut milk.

5. Add grated potato, cooked sausage mixture, and parsley and mix well.

6. Pour mixture into a 10" oven-safe pan greased with remainder of coconut oil.

7. Bake 25 minutes or until eggs reach desired firmness.

8. Set aside to cool, cut into 5 servings, and store.

PER SERVING Calories: 304 | Fat: 19.6 g | Protein: 16.9 g | Sodium: 559 mg | Fiber: 2.1 g | Carbohydrates: 12.3 g | Sugar: 2.2 g

Sweet Potato Egg Bowls

*These are not only showpieces, they are also super delicious and nutritious.
These bowls are gluten-free and Whole30 approved. Serve with ground turkey
bits on top for an extra boost of protein. These will keep up to 3 days.*

INGREDIENTS | SERVES 10

5 medium sweet potatoes

10 large eggs

⅛ teaspoon freshly ground black pepper

⅛ cup chopped fresh chives (optional)

Sweet Potatoes

There are many varieties of sweet potatoes, and depending on the variety one may take longer to bake than the other. Pick the rounder potatoes as opposed to the long skinny ones for this recipe because they'll make better bowls. Also, don't let the potato flesh go to waste. Make a quick sweet potato mash by adding coconut oil, salt, and pepper to the potato flesh.

1. Preheat oven to 375°F.

2. Poke potatoes with a fork and microwave each 8–10 minutes rotating halfway through; or, if you'd prefer baking, bake in oven 45 minutes.

3. Insert a toothpick to the center to ensure potatoes are thoroughly cooked.

4. Remove from oven and set aside 15 minutes or until potatoes are cool enough to touch.

5. Cut potatoes in half lengthwise, scoop out half of the insides, and place in a bowl.

6. Place potatoes on baking sheet, then slowly crack an egg into each potato half and sprinkle with pepper.

7. Bake 20 minutes or until eggs reach desired firmness.

8. Garnish with chopped chives. Store them in food containers, but be careful not to stack them on top of each other.

PER SERVING Calories: 127 | Fat: 4.4 g | Protein: 7.3 g | Sodium: 106 mg | Fiber: 2.0 g | Carbohydrates: 13.5 g | Sugar: 2.9 g

Avocado Egg Bowls

This dish is already high in healthy fats, but for extra added protein, sprinkle bacon bits or cooked ground turkey meat on top. To ensure the egg fits into the hole, crack the egg in a small bowl, then use a spoon to transfer the egg over. Avocado bowls won't keep more than 2 days in the refrigerator.

INGREDIENTS | SERVES 2

1 large avocado
2 large eggs
⅛ teaspoon sea salt
⅛ teaspoon freshly ground black pepper
1 tablespoon chopped green onions
⅛ teaspoon paprika

1. Preheat oven to 400°F.

2. Cut avocado in half, remove seed, then use a spoon to scoop out half of the center to make a bigger hole to fit the egg.

3. Crack egg into hole. Sprinkle salt and black pepper over egg. Bake 20 minutes or until egg reaches desired firmness.

4. Remove from oven and top with green onions and paprika.

PER SERVING Calories: 185 | Fat: 13.7 g | Protein: 7.7 g | Sodium: 193 mg | Fiber: 4.8 g | Carbohydrates: 6.6 g | Sugar: 0.5 g

Avocado Egg Salad

You really can't go wrong with an egg salad for breakfast or even lunch. This dish is Whole30 and paleo approved. Serve this salad over toast or sweet potato slices. Making this salad the night before is recommended as this will not keep fresh for the entire week.

INGREDIENTS | SERVES 2

4 large hard-boiled eggs, chopped
1 large avocado
1 medium lime
¼ cup seeded and diced tomatoes
1 tablespoon chopped fresh parsley
⅛ teaspoon sea salt
⅛ teaspoon freshly ground black pepper
⅛ teaspoon ground cumin
⅛ teaspoon garlic powder
⅛ teaspoon paprika

1. Add eggs to a large bowl.

2. Cut avocado in half, remove seed, and scoop out all the flesh; place in a separate bowl. Squeeze lime juice over avocado, then use a fork to mash.

3. Add avocado, tomatoes, parsley, salt, pepper, cumin, and garlic powder to egg bowl and mix well.

4. Top with paprika and serve. Store in food containers and refrigerate up to 2 days.

PER SERVING Calories: 265 | Fat: 18.1 g | Protein: 14.3 g | Sodium: 266 mg | Fiber: 5.1 g | Carbohydrates: 9.2 g | Sugar: 1.5 g

Mason Jar Eggs

This egg jar recipe stays fresh, usually lasting 5 days, and is so convenient for travel. You'll need 8-ounce glass jars to make this recipe.

INGREDIENTS | SERVES 10

2 tablespoons coconut oil, divided

1 small onion, peeled and finely chopped

¾ cup finely diced red bell peppers

1 cup frozen green peas

1 cup Mexican Ground Turkey (see Chapter 5)

1 cup grated raw sweet potatoes (1 small sweet potato)

⅛ teaspoon salt

¼ teaspoon freshly ground black pepper

½ teaspoon dried parsley

½ teaspoon dried oregano

½ teaspoon garlic powder

¼ teaspoon paprika

12 large eggs

¼ cup coconut milk

Mason Jars

Baking with glassware can be tricky. Mason jars should be baked in a bath of water. They should never be dry-baked. Place the jars in at least ½" hot water. You'll need a deeper baking pan for this (something like a 9" × 13" baking pan or dish).

1. Preheat oven to 375°F.

2. Heat a large skillet over medium heat and add ½ tablespoon oil. Once oil is hot, add onions, red peppers, and peas and cook until soft, 3–4 minutes. Add turkey meat.

3. Add sweet potatoes, salt, black pepper, parsley, oregano, garlic powder, and paprika and stir another 2 minutes. Remove from heat and set aside.

4. Lightly grease inside of jars with the remaining coconut oil.

5. Fill baking dish with ½" hot water and place the jars inside the pan.

6. Evenly divide turkey/potato mixture into the jars.

7. In a large bowl whisk eggs and coconut milk together.

8. Pour egg mixture into the jars, leaving 1" at the top empty (for eggs to rise and room to close the jar).

9. Cover entire pan with foil and bake 25–30 minutes or until egg reaches desired firmness.

10. Remove from oven and let cool completely before placing lids on them. Refrigerate and store up to 5 days.

PER SERVING Calories: 178 | Fat: 9.6 g | Protein: 14.6 g | Sodium: 178 mg | Fiber: 1.6 g | Carbohydrates: 6.9 g | Sugar: 2.2 g

Microwaved Jar Eggs

If you're crunched for time, this is a great prep using Mason jars. This is similar to the Mason Jar Eggs recipe in this chapter, but will take less than half the time. If you want to use lower-fat ingredients, choose turkey bacon instead of regular bacon. These are best made the morning you want to eat them. You can prep the ingredients ahead of time and it will take you less than 5 minutes to put it together in the morning.

INGREDIENTS | SERVES 1

2 large eggs
⅛ teaspoon salt
⅛ teaspoon freshly ground black pepper
⅓ cup chopped spinach
½ tablespoon grated Cheddar cheese
1 strip bacon, cooked and crumbled
¼ teaspoon finely chopped fresh chives

Microwaving Eggs

It is normal for the egg mixture to rise quite a bit while cooking in the microwave, but it will settle back down after it's finished. Don't panic when you see this happening. Make sure you're checking often to ensure it doesn't overflow.

1. In a small bowl whisk eggs with salt and pepper. Add spinach and mix well.

2. Pour mixture into an 8-ounce Mason jar.

3. Microwave on high 2 minutes.

4. Remove from microwave and top with cheese, crumbled bacon, and chives. Serve immediately or cover with lid and serve within 2–3 hours.

PER SERVING Calories: 212 | Fat: 13.6 g | Protein: 17.6 g | Sodium: 598 mg | Fiber: 0.3 g | Carbohydrates: 1.5 g | Sugar: 0.4 g

CHAPTER 3

Overnight Oats

Berry Delicious Oats

These Mason jar overnight oats can be prepped in about 10 minutes. You'll need 16-ounce Mason jars for this recipe. Multiply this recipe by five and make enough for the entire week since this can be refrigerated up to 5 days.

INGREDIENTS | SERVES 1

½ cup rolled oats

½ cup almond milk

1 tablespoon peanut butter

1 teaspoon chia seeds

⅛ teaspoon ground cinnamon

¼ cup diced apples

¼ cup chopped blueberries

Mason Jars

Mason jars are a great investment for your kitchen and very affordable as well. The jars will keep food fresh when completely sealed and last for at least 5 days.

1. In a 16-ounce jar add ingredients in the following order: oats, almond milk, peanut butter, chia seeds, cinnamon, apples, and blueberries.

2. Close jar and refrigerate at least 8 hours.

3. Before serving, remove lid and microwave 2 minutes on high.

PER SERVING Calories: 328 | Fat: 13.4 g | Protein: 10.4 g | Sodium: 80 mg | Fiber: 8.4 g | Carbohydrates: 45.8 g | Sugar: 12.4 g

Protein Chocolate Oats

This is like the previous delicious overnight oats recipe but with an extra punch of protein and chocolate! If you do not have fresh berries, frozen ones also work well. This recipe will store well in the refrigerator up to 5 days.

INGREDIENTS | SERVES 1

½ cup almond milk

¾ cup water

1 scoop chocolate whey protein powder

½ cup rolled oats

1 cup mixed fresh berries

1. In a shaker or sealed cup, add milk, water, and protein powder and mix.

2. In a 16-ounce jar add ingredients in this order: oats, milk/protein powder mix, and berries.

3. Close jar and refrigerate at least 8 hours. Can be refrigerated up to 5 days.

4. Can be served cold, or if you like your oats hot, then remove lid and microwave 2 minutes on high before serving.

PER SERVING Calories: 350 | Fat: 4.9 g | Protein: 23.6 g | Sodium: 194 mg | Fiber: 9.0 g | Carbohydrates: 55.7 g | Sugar: 14.3 g

Chia Oats Pudding

Love chia seed pudding? Then you'll love this! You can also choose to add your favorite fruit as toppings. Multiply this recipe by five and be prepared for the week ahead.

INGREDIENTS | SERVES 1

½ cup plain Greek yogurt
½ cup almond milk
¼ cup rolled oats
½ teaspoon maple syrup
1 teaspoon chia seeds
½ cup chopped strawberries
1 teaspoon raw sliced almonds

1. In a 16-ounce Mason jar add ingredients in the following order: yogurt, milk, oats, maple syrup, and chia seeds.

2. Close jar and give it a good shake until ingredients are properly mixed.

3. Add strawberries and almonds on top and then refrigerate. Serve cold.

PER SERVING Calories: 251 | Fat: 7.1 g | Protein: 15.9 g | Sodium: 116 mg | Fiber: 5.0 g | Carbohydrates: 32.4 g | Sugar: 14.7 g

Zucchini Banana Oats

Zucchini in oatmeal might sound strange at first, but once you try this, you might be hooked! This will store up to 5 days in the refrigerator.

INGREDIENTS | SERVES 1

½ medium banana, peeled and mashed
½ cup rolled oats
¾ cup coconut milk
½ cup grated zucchini
½ teaspoon chia seeds
⅛ teaspoon ground cinnamon
⅛ teaspoon unsweetened coconut flakes

1. In a medium bowl add all ingredients except coconut flakes and mix well.

2. Pour mixture into a 16-ounce Mason jar and top with coconut flakes.

3. Refrigerate overnight.

4. Serve cold or microwave on high 1–2 minutes without the lid for hot oats.

PER SERVING Calories: 553 | Fat: 37.9 g | Protein: 10.1 g | Sodium: 26 mg | Fiber: 6.9 g | Carbohydrates: 48.0 g | Sugar: 9.7 g

Oatmeal Breakfast Muffins

These are great on the go. Serve them for breakfast or an afternoon snack. Your kids will love them too. These will store well in tightly sealed food containers up to 5 days in the refrigerator. Make sure you completely cool them before storing.

INGREDIENTS | SERVES 6

3 large ripe bananas

2½ cups rolled oats

2 large eggs, whisked

1 cup coconut milk

⅛ teaspoon vanilla extract

1 cup frozen mixed berries

1 teaspoon coconut oil (for greasing pan)

Silicon Liners

You can use muffin pan liners to reduce the amount of oil used in this recipe. If you want to help reduce waste, invest in silicon liners. Their naturally nonstick surface is perfect for this kind of recipe, and they can handle high-heat cooking. Most important, they are super easy to clean up since they're dishwasher-safe!

1. Preheat oven to 350°F.

2. In a large bowl mash bananas with a fork.

3. Add oats, eggs, milk, vanilla, and berries and mix until well blended.

4. Grease a 12-cup muffin pan with oil and evenly divide oat mixture into cups.

5. Bake 25 minutes or until cooked thoroughly (poke with a toothpick to test; it should come out clean if cooked properly). Let cool then store them in food containers and refrigerate up to 5 days.

PER SERVING Calories: 362 | Fat: 14.9 g | Protein: 9.6 g | Sodium: 35 mg | Fiber: 7.4 g | Carbohydrates: 50.7 g | Sugar: 13.0 g

Simple Strawberry Overnight Oats

Five-ingredient recipes are hard to come by. Get your breakfast jars ready in less than 10 minutes, and you can use your favorite milk in this recipe. These oats can be refrigerated up to 5 days.

INGREDIENTS | SERVES 1

½ cup rolled oats
½ cup 2% milk
1 teaspoon chia seeds
⅛ teaspoon vanilla extract
½ cup chopped fresh strawberries

Vanilla Extract

Did you know that vanilla helps to reduce inflammation? It also has tons of antioxidants that protect your body from toxins and free-radical damage. Make sure that you pick up pure vanilla extract when shopping for this ingredient.

1. In a 16-ounce Mason jar add ingredients in the following order: oats, milk, chia seeds, vanilla, and then strawberries.

2. Close jar and refrigerate at least overnight.

3. Serve cold, or if you like your oats hot, then remove lid and microwave 2 minutes on high before serving.

PER SERVING Calories: 254 | Fat: 6.5 g | Protein: 10.2 g | Sodium: 57 mg | Fiber: 6.8 g | Carbohydrates: 40.7 g | Sugar: 11.3 g

Sweet Potato Oats

Sweet potatoes are such a wonderfully versatile ingredient that they can be added to almost any recipe. If you have not tasted sweet potatoes mixed in oats, it will amaze you! This dish can be refrigerated up to 5 days and still taste fresh.

INGREDIENTS | SERVES 1

½ cup rolled oats
¾ cup coconut milk
1 teaspoon chia seeds
⅛ teaspoon vanilla extract
½ cup shredded raw sweet potatoes
1 tablespoon raisins

Sweet Potatoes

Sweet potatoes are high in vitamins A, B_5, and B_6, and they contain lots of fiber. Although they are sweet, they do not spike blood sugar levels because of their fiber content, which gives them a low glycemic index number.

1. In a large bowl add all ingredients and mix well.

2. Pour mixture into a 16-ounce Mason jar and refrigerate overnight.

3. This recipe is meant to be served warm. Options for warming are in a water bath on a stove over medium heat for 5 minutes, or you can remove lid and microwave entire jar 1–2 minutes on high.

PER SERVING Calories: 582 | Fat: 38.0 g | Protein: 10.3 g | Sodium: 57 mg | Fiber: 7.4 g | Carbohydrates: 53.5 g | Sugar: 9.2 g

Tropical Oats

Bored of the regular berries and banana oats? This recipe adds a new tropical twist to your regular oats. When chopping the fruits, chop them into finer pieces so it will be easier for you to mix it up. These jars should last up to 5 days in the refrigerator.

INGREDIENTS | SERVES 1

½ cup rolled oats
½ cup coconut milk
1 teaspoon chia seeds
⅛ teaspoon vanilla extract
½ cup finely chopped fresh pineapple
½ cup finely chopped fresh mangoes
¼ teaspoon unsweetened coconut flakes

Pineapples

A pineapple will not ripen any further once it has been picked. When choosing a pineapple, it should smell sweet and be firm and gold-colored with healthy, green leaves.

1. In a 16-ounce Mason jar add ingredients in the following order: oats, milk, chia seeds, vanilla, pineapple, mangoes, and coconut flakes.

2. Close lid and refrigerate overnight.

3. Serve this dish warm or cold. Options for warming are in a water bath on a stove over medium heat for 5 minutes, or you can remove lid and microwave entire jar 1–2 minutes on high.

PER SERVING Calories: 481 | Fat: 27.2 g | Protein: 9.0 g | Sodium: 14 mg | Fiber: 7.7 g | Carbohydrates: 54.9 g | Sugar: 20.5 g

Pumpkin Spice Oats

This is the perfect breakfast for the fall when pumpkins are in season. The cinnamon in this recipe is an excellent source of antioxidants, contains anti-inflammatory properties, and has been shown to reduce the risk of heart disease. This will last up to 5 days stored in the refrigerator.

INGREDIENTS | SERVES 1

½ cup rolled oats
½ cup almond milk
1 teaspoon chia seeds
⅛ teaspoon vanilla extract
½ cup pumpkin purée
½ teaspoon ground cinnamon
⅛ teaspoon ground cloves

1. In a 16-ounce Mason jar add ingredients in the following order: oats, milk, chia seeds, vanilla, pumpkin purée, cinnamon, and cloves.

2. Close lid and refrigerate overnight.

3. Serve this dish warm or cold. Options for warming are in a water bath on a stove over medium heat for 5 minutes, or you can remove lid and microwave entire jar 1–2 minutes on high.

PER SERVING Calories: 220 | Fat: 5.6 g | Protein: 7.1 g | Sodium: 82 mg | Fiber: 8.4 g | Carbohydrates: 38.2 g | Sugar: 6.6 g

Banana Vanilla Protein Oats

The coconut flakes in this recipe are a good source of medium-chain triglycerides, a great fuel for keeping active, and also an antioxidant. Coconut flakes are, however, high in saturated fat, so if you are trying to lose weight, you can omit them or halve the amount in this recipe. This will last up to 5 days stored in the refrigerator.

INGREDIENTS | SERVES 1

½ cup rolled oats
¾ cup water
1 scoop vanilla whey protein powder
½ medium banana, peeled and sliced into rounds
1 teaspoon unsweetened coconut flakes

1. In a medium bowl add oats, water, and protein powder and mix well. Transfer mixture into a 16-ounce Mason jar, then add banana rounds and coconut flakes on top.

2. Close lid and refrigerate overnight.

3. Serve this dish warm or cold. Options for warming are in a water bath on a stove over medium heat for 5 minutes, or you can remove lid and microwave entire jar 1–2 minutes on high.

PER SERVING Calories: 317 | Fat: 4.5 g | Protein: 22.6 g | Sodium: 114 mg | Fiber: 5.8 g | Carbohydrates: 49.4 g | Sugar: 8.7 g

Chocolate Coconut Oats

This is a sweet and delicious way to consume your oats and still feel satisfied. You can also satisfy your chocolate cravings without feeling guilty! You can also add nuts for extra crunch. The coconut milk can be substituted with any other kind of nut milk. This will last up to 5 days stored in the refrigerator.

INGREDIENTS | SERVES 1

½ cup rolled oats
⅔ cup coconut milk
2 tablespoons cocoa powder
1 teaspoon honey
1 teaspoon chia seeds
1 teaspoon unsweetened coconut flakes

1. In a medium bowl add oats, milk, cocoa powder, honey, and chia seeds and mix well.

2. Transfer mixture into a 16-ounce Mason jar, then add coconut flakes on top.

3. Close lid and refrigerate overnight.

4. Serve this dish warm or cold. Options for warming are in a water bath on a stove over medium heat for 5 minutes, or you can remove lid and microwave entire jar 1–2 minutes on high.

Cocoa Powder

Cocoa powder, like all chocolate products, contains a mild dose of caffeine. One tablespoon of cocoa powder contains 12 milligrams of caffeine compared to 95 milligrams in a typical cup of coffee. Use caution when consuming cocoa close to bedtime.

PER SERVING Calories: 518 | Fat: 36.8 g | Protein: 10.9 g | Sodium: 21 mg | Fiber: 9.4 g | Carbohydrates: 45.0 g | Sugar: 7.0 g

Chocolate Peanut Butter Oats

Make sure you buy an all-natural peanut butter because there are many brands with unnecessary and unhealthy added ingredients. It's very easy to overindulge in peanut butter, since it is high in calories and fat, so enjoy in moderation. This will last up to 5 days stored in the refrigerator.

INGREDIENTS | SERVES 1

½ cup rolled oats
¾ cup almond milk
1 scoop chocolate whey protein powder
1 tablespoon natural peanut butter
1 teaspoon chia seeds

1. In a medium bowl add oats, milk, protein powder, peanut butter, and chia seeds and mix well.

2. Transfer mixture into a 16-ounce Mason jar, close lid, and refrigerate overnight.

3. Serve this dish warm or cold. Options for warming are in a water bath on a stove over medium heat for 5 minutes, or you can remove lid and microwave entire jar 1–2 minutes on high.

PER SERVING Calories: 410 | Fat: 13.8 g | Protein: 26.7 g | Sodium: 295 mg | Fiber: 5.9 g | Carbohydrates: 46.4 g | Sugar: 8.3 g

Mango Coconut Oats

Mangoes are usually high on many people's favorite fruits list. But if you are weight conscious, enjoy this fruit in moderation because it is quite high in sugar. For example, 1 cup of mango contains approximately 24 grams of sugar. That's about two-thirds the amount of sugar in a can of soda. This will last up to 5 days stored in the refrigerator.

INGREDIENTS | SERVES 1

½ cup rolled oats
¾ cup coconut milk
1 teaspoon chia seeds
½ cup chopped mangoes
1 tablespoon coconut cream
1 teaspoon unsweetened coconut flakes

1. In a 16-ounce Mason jar add ingredients in the following order: oats, milk, chia seeds, mangoes, coconut cream, and coconut flakes.

2. Close lid and refrigerate overnight.

3. Serve this dish warm or cold. Options for warming are in a water bath on a stove over medium heat for 5 minutes, or you can remove the lid and microwave entire jar 1–2 minutes on high.

PER SERVING Calories: 608 | Fat: 44.3 g | Protein: 10.3 g | Sodium: 22 mg | Fiber: 7.0 g | Carbohydrates: 47.0 g | Sugar: 12.4 g

Peachy Oats

Try this recipe in the summertime when peaches are fresh. The flaxseed in this recipe is super high in fiber and an excellent source of omega-3 fats, vitamin B$_1$, and magnesium. Multiply this recipe by five for a full week's worth of breakfast meals.

INGREDIENTS | SERVES 1

½ cup rolled oats
½ cup almond milk
2 teaspoons ground flaxseed
½ teaspoon pure maple syrup
½ cup diced peaches
¼ teaspoon ground cinnamon

1. In a 16-ounce Mason jar add ingredients in the following order: oats, milk, flaxseed, maple syrup, peaches, and cinnamon.

2. Close lid and refrigerate overnight.

3. Serve this dish warm or cold. Options for warming are in a water bath on a stove over medium heat for 5 minutes, or you can remove lid and microwave entire jar 1–2 minutes on high.

PER SERVING Calories: 243 | Fat: 6.2 g | Protein: 7.1 g | Sodium: 81 mg | Fiber: 6.8 g | Carbohydrates: 42.4 g | Sugar: 13.0 g

Mocha in a Jar

Love the taste of coffee flavor in everything? Try it in oats! If you are vegan, replace the yogurt with an extra ¼ cup almond milk. This will last up to 5 days stored in the refrigerator.

INGREDIENTS | SERVES 1

½ cup rolled oats
½ cup unsweetened almond milk
1 teaspoon chia seeds
1 teaspoon cocoa powder
½ teaspoon espresso powder
¼ cup plain Greek yogurt
1 tablespoon pitted and chopped dates
1 tablespoon raisins
1 tablespoon chopped raw almonds

1. In a 16-ounce Mason jar add ingredients in the following order: oats, milk, chia seeds, cocoa, espresso powder, yogurt, dates, raisins, and almonds.

2. Close lid and refrigerate overnight.

3. Serve this dish warm or cold. Options for warming are in a water bath on a stove over medium heat for 5 minutes, or you can remove lid and microwave entire jar 1–2 minutes on high.

PER SERVING Calories: 331 | Fat: 11.2 g | Protein: 14.6 g | Sodium: 98 mg | Fiber: 7.9 g | Carbohydrates: 47.9 g | Sugar: 14.9 g

Taco Tuesday Overnight Oats

Sweet oats not your cup of tea? Try savory overnight oats for a change. It might sound weird if you've never tried it before, but savory oats are like Chinese rice porridge. They're traditionally eaten in the mornings in Asian culture. This meal should last up to 5 days in the refrigerator.

INGREDIENTS | SERVES 1

½ cup rolled oats

1 cup unsweetened almond milk

1 teaspoon coconut oil

1 clove garlic, peeled and minced

¼ cup diced onions

¼ cup diced red bell peppers

⅛ teaspoon sea salt

⅛ teaspoon freshly ground black pepper

¼ teaspoon paprika

⅛ teaspoon ground cayenne pepper

¼ cup Mexican Ground Turkey (see Chapter 5)

½ tablespoon chopped fresh cilantro

Cilantro

Did you know that cilantro is also known as coriander? Most often *coriander* is the name used for the seeds, and *cilantro* for the leaves. This herb is native to the Mediterranean region and packs a punch in terms of healthy plant compounds that have been shown to play a role in disease prevention. When shopping for cilantro, look for vibrant green leaves with firm stems that are free from any spoilage or yellow discoloration.

1. In a 16-ounce Mason jar add oats and milk and set aside.

2. Heat a medium pan over medium heat and add oil. Once oil is hot, add garlic, onions, and bell peppers and sauté 2–3 minutes. Add salt, black pepper, paprika, and cayenne.

3. Add Mexican Ground Turkey to pan and stir another minute.

4. Remove from stove and pour over oats in jar. Set aside to let completely cool.

5. Once cooled, garnish with cilantro, close lid, and refrigerate overnight.

6. This dish should be served warm. Options for warming are either in a water bath on a stove over medium heat for 5 minutes, or you can remove lid and microwave entire jar 1–2 minutes on high. Mix well and then enjoy.

PER SERVING Calories: 326 | Fat: 11.5 g | Protein: 21.6 g | Sodium: 512 mg | Fiber: 6.2 g | Carbohydrates: 35.5 g | Sugar: 4.5 g

Vegetarian Overnight Oats

If eating meat first thing in the morning is not your thing, try this vegetarian option. If you're looking for more protein, try adding a poached or boiled egg on top of this. Protein is an important macronutrient, but it does not always have to come from meat. This will last up to 5 days stored in the refrigerator.

INGREDIENTS | SERVES 1

½ cup rolled oats
1 cup unsweetened almond milk
1 teaspoon coconut oil
1 clove garlic, peeled and minced
½ cup julienned onions
½ cup julienned red bell peppers
⅛ teaspoon sea salt
⅛ teaspoon freshly ground black pepper
½ teaspoon dried oregano
¼ teaspoon paprika
2 cups baby spinach
½ tablespoon chopped fresh parsley

1. In a 16-ounce Mason jar add oats and milk and set aside.

2. Heat a medium pan over medium heat and add oil. Once oil is hot, add garlic, onions, and bell peppers and sauté 2–3 minutes.

3. Add salt, black pepper, oregano, and paprika and stir another minute.

4. Add spinach and stir until spinach is wilted, 1–2 minutes.

5. Remove from stove and pour pan contents over oats in jar. Set aside to let completely cool.

6. Once cooled, garnish with parsley, close lid, and refrigerate overnight.

7. This dish should be served warm. Options for warming are either in a water bath on a stove over medium heat for 5 minutes, or you can remove the lid and microwave entire jar 1–2 minutes on high. Mix well and then enjoy.

PER SERVING Calories: 274 | Fat: 10.1 g | Protein: 9.2 g | Sodium: 445 mg | Fiber: 7.9 g | Carbohydrates: 39.3 g | Sugar: 5.8 g

Bacon Cheddar Savory Oats

If you're a bacon lover, you'll love this one. The cheese and bacon leave you feeling satisfied all morning. You can replace the sweet potatoes with grated pumpkin or butternut squash. This will last up to 5 days stored in the refrigerator.

INGREDIENTS | SERVES 1

½ cup rolled oats

1 cup unsweetened almond milk

1 strip bacon

1 teaspoon coconut oil

1 clove garlic, peeled and minced

½ cup diced onions

½ cup grated raw sweet potatoes

⅛ teaspoon sea salt

⅛ teaspoon freshly ground black pepper

¼ teaspoon paprika

1 tablespoon shredded Cheddar cheese

Bacon

There's a way to cook bacon that you probably weren't aware of. Because of the fat content, bacon is likely to splatter the hot fat out while it cooks. You can avoid this by simply adding a little water to cover the bottom of the pan. The result is crispy and browned bacon that is chewy—and a lot less messy to cook.

1. In a 16-ounce Mason jar add oats and milk and set aside.

2. Heat a medium pan over medium heat, add bacon, and cook until light brown on both sides, 2–3 minutes per side. Remove from pan and set on top of a plate with paper towels to soak up the extra fat. Once bacon is cool, chop into bits.

3. Clean pan with paper towels, then add oil. Once oil is hot, add garlic, onions, and sweet potatoes and sauté 2–3 minutes. Add salt, pepper, and paprika and stir another minute. Set side.

4. Pour vegetable mix over oats in jar, add bacon, and top with cheese. Set aside to let completely cool.

5. Once cooled, close lid and refrigerate overnight.

6. This dish should be served warm. Options for warming are either in a water bath on a stove over medium heat for 5 minutes, or you can remove lid and microwave entire jar 1–2 minutes on high. Mix well and then enjoy.

PER SERVING Calories: 393 | Fat: 15.8 g | Protein: 13.8 g | Sodium: 671 mg | Fiber: 7.7 g | Carbohydrates: 49.6 g | Sugar: 7.3 g

Mushroom Kale Oats

This recipe is just as creamy and filling as mushroom risotto but much friendlier to your waistline. If you're looking to add more protein to this recipe, add a poached or boiled egg. This will last up to 5 days stored in the refrigerator.

INGREDIENTS | SERVES 1

½ cup rolled oats
¼ cup coconut milk
¼ cup chicken broth
1 teaspoon coconut oil
1 clove garlic, peeled and minced
½ cup diced onions
½ cup sliced cremini or white mushrooms
⅛ teaspoon sea salt
⅛ teaspoon freshly ground black pepper
1 cup chopped kale
1 teaspoon chopped fresh cilantro

1. In a 16-ounce Mason jar add oats, milk, and broth and set aside.

2. Heat a medium pan over medium heat and add oil. Once oil is hot, add garlic, onions, and mushrooms and sauté 2–3 minutes. Add salt and pepper and stir another minute.

3. Add kale and stir until wilted, 2–3 minutes.

4. Pour vegetable mix over oats in jar and top with cilantro. Set aside to let completely cool.

5. Once cooled, close lid and refrigerate overnight.

6. This dish should be served warm. Options for warming are either in a water bath on a stove over medium heat for 5 minutes, or you can remove lid and microwave entire jar 1–2 minutes on high. Mix well and then enjoy.

PER SERVING Calories: 352 | Fat: 18.7 g | Protein: 9.2 g | Sodium: 482 mg | Fiber: 6.3 g | Carbohydrates: 40.5 g | Sugar: 5.7 g

Rosemary, Pumpkin, and Leek Oats

This dish is super herby and perfect for a rainy morning. It's warm and fills you up. For extra protein, add a boiled egg. This will last up to 5 days stored in the refrigerator.

INGREDIENTS | SERVES 1

½ cup rolled oats

¼ cup coconut milk

½ cup chicken broth

½ cup pumpkin purée

1 teaspoon coconut oil

¼ cup chopped leeks

½ teaspoon minced fresh rosemary

⅛ teaspoon sea salt

⅛ teaspoon freshly ground black pepper

Rosemary

Rosemary is quite an impressive herb. It is rich in iron, calcium, and vitamin B_6. Rosemary was traditionally used to help alleviate muscle pain, improve memory, and boost the immune system. It's great as a dried herb to garnish your meals, or even as a tea to warm you up.

1. In a 16-ounce Mason jar add oats, milk, broth, and pumpkin and set aside.

2. Heat a medium pan over medium heat and add oil. Once oil is hot, add leeks and sauté until soft, 2–3 minutes. Add rosemary, salt, and pepper and stir another minute.

3. Pour leek mixture over oats in jar. Set aside to let completely cool.

4. Once cooled close lid and refrigerate overnight.

5. This dish should be served warm. Options for warming are either in a water bath on a stove over medium heat for 5 minutes, or you can remove lid and microwave entire jar 1–2 minutes on high. Mix well and then enjoy.

PER SERVING Calories: 339 | Fat: 18.9 g | Protein: 8.3 g | Sodium: 708 mg | Fiber: 7.0 g | Carbohydrates: 37.0 g | Sugar: 4.4 g

CHAPTER 4

Smoothies

Banana Strawberry Protein Smoothie

This is a smoothie staple. Prep your ingredients ahead by peeling your bananas and portioning your berries, and freezing them in zip-top bags. You should not store a blended smoothie for more than 24 hours.

INGREDIENTS | SERVES 1

½ medium banana, peeled and sliced

1 cup frozen strawberries

1 cup ice cubes

1 cup water

1 scoop vanilla whey protein powder

1. In a blender add banana, strawberries, ice cubes, water, and protein powder and blend until smooth.

2. Serve immediately or store in the refrigerator in a sealed container or Mason jar up to 24 hours.

PER SERVING Calories: 208 | Fat: 0.4 g | Protein: 18.1 g | Sodium: 118 mg | Fiber: 4.7 g | Carbohydrates: 35.5 g | Sugar: 14.4 g

Blender

One of the best investments you can add to your kitchen arsenal is a good quality blender. It will last a lifetime and the money is definitely worth it, especially when you meal prep or cook on a regular basis.

Pear Spinach Smoothie

The pear adds a natural hint of delicious sweetness to this smoothie. When choosing your whey protein, always choose isolate over whey blend. Isolate is a purer form of whey, which means it has a higher concentration of protein per gram. You should not store a blended smoothie for more than 24 hours.

INGREDIENTS | SERVES 1

½ medium banana, peeled and chopped

1 cup chopped pears

3 cups baby spinach

1 scoop vanilla whey protein powder (optional)

1 cup water

1 cup ice cubes

1 teaspoon chia seeds

1. In a blender add banana, pear, spinach, protein powder, water, and ice cubes and blend until smooth.

2. Top with chia seeds.

3. Serve immediately or store in the refrigerator in a sealed container or Mason jar up to 24 hours.

PER SERVING Calories: 283 | Fat: 1.9 g | Protein: 21.2 g | Sodium: 188 mg | Fiber: 9.6 g | Carbohydrates: 51.1 g | Sugar: 23.6 g

Kale and Avocado Smoothie

This is a green super smoothie, packed with vitamin K and healthy fats. The kale in this recipe is also loaded with minerals like magnesium, copper, potassium, and manganese. You should not store a blended smoothie for more than 24 hours.

INGREDIENTS | SERVES 1

2 cups chopped kale (frozen or fresh)
½ medium banana, peeled and sliced
½ medium avocado, pitted and flesh removed
1 cup coconut water
1 scoop vanilla whey protein powder (optional)
1 cup ice cubes
1 teaspoon chia seeds

1. In a blender add kale, banana, avocado, coconut water, protein powder, and ice cubes and blend until smooth.

2. Top with chia seeds.

3. Serve immediately or store in the refrigerator in a sealed container or Mason jar up to 24 hours.

PER SERVING Calories: 344 | Fat: 10.9 g | Protein: 21.3 g | Sodium: 187 mg | Fiber: 8.4 g | Carbohydrates: 42.4 g | Sugar: 18.1 g

Blueberry Avocado Smoothie

This might not look like the most appetizing drink, but you will quickly move past that as soon as you take the first sip. You should not store a blended smoothie for more than 24 hours.

INGREDIENTS | SERVES 1

1 cup frozen blueberries
½ medium avocado, pitted and flesh removed
1 cup coconut milk
1 scoop vanilla whey protein powder (optional)
1 cup ice cubes
1 teaspoon chia seeds

1. In a blender add blueberries, avocado, coconut milk, protein powder, and ice cubes and blend until smooth.

2. Top with chia seeds.

3. Serve immediately or store in the refrigerator in a sealed container or Mason jar up to 24 hours.

PER SERVING Calories: 757 | Fat: 56.5 g | Protein: 24.0 g | Sodium: 142 mg | Fiber: 9.9 g | Carbohydrates: 40.9 g | Sugar: 13.6 g

Banana Peanut Butter Smoothie

Are you a peanut butter lover? You'll love how satisfying this smoothie is!
You should not store a blended smoothie for more than 24 hours.

INGREDIENTS | SERVES 1

½ medium banana, peeled and sliced

½ cup coconut milk

½ cup water

1 scoop chocolate whey protein powder (optional)

1 cup ice cubes

1 tablespoon peanut butter

1 teaspoon milled flaxseed

1. In a blender add banana, milk, water, protein powder, ice cubes, peanut butter, and flaxseed and blend until smooth.

2. Serve immediately or store in the refrigerator in a sealed container or Mason jar up to 24 hours.

PER SERVING Calories: 485 | Fat: 31.6 g | Protein: 23.8 g | Sodium: 193 mg | Fiber: 3.0 g | Carbohydrates: 29.3 g | Sugar: 9.3 g

Strawberry Watermelon Blast

Watermelon is another fruit that you can't get enough of in the summer. If you're not a big fan, you can omit the mint in this recipe. You should not store a blended smoothie for more than 24 hours.

INGREDIENTS | SERVES 1

½ cup chopped seeded watermelon

½ cup frozen whole strawberries

½ cup coconut milk

½ cup water

1 scoop vanilla or strawberry whey protein powder (optional)

1 cup ice cubes

1 tablespoon minced fresh mint

1. In a blender add watermelon, strawberries, milk, water, protein powder, and ice cubes and blend until smooth.

2. Top with mint.

3. Serve immediately or store in the refrigerator in a sealed container or Mason jar up to 24 hours.

PER SERVING Calories: 375 | Fat: 23.0 g | Protein: 20.0 g | Sodium: 126 mg | Fiber: 2.0 g | Carbohydrates: 24.4 g | Sugar: 8.5 g

Piña Colada Smoothie

You can enjoy this smoothie without alal the guilt and calories of a traditional piña colada. You should not store a blended smoothie for more than 24 hours.

INGREDIENTS | SERVES 1

1 cup frozen pineapple chunks
½ cup coconut cream
½ cup water
1 scoop vanilla whey protein powder (optional)
1 cup ice cubes

1. In a blender add pineapple, coconut cream, water, protein powder, and ice cubes and blend until smooth.

2. Serve immediately or store in the refrigerator in a sealed container or Mason jar up to 24 hours.

PER SERVING Calories: 593 | Fat: 39.3 g | Protein: 22.6 g | Sodium: 111 mg | Fiber: 5.3 g | Carbohydrates: 40.4 g | Sugar: 4.3 g

Coconut Cream

You can use 1 cup of coconut milk instead of the cream and water. Also look for coconut cream in a paper carton if your market carries it; it's better than the canned version due to it being 100% pure cream with no other added ingredients.

Mango Coconut Dream

Mangoes and coconuts are delicious together! However, mangoes are high in sugar and the coconut cream is high in fat, so if you are weight conscious, reduce the portion to ½ cup mangoes and replace the coconut cream with coconut milk. You can also freeze this recipe overnight to make a frozen treat. You should not store a blended smoothie for more than 24 hours.

INGREDIENTS | SERVES 1

1 cup chopped mangoes (frozen or fresh)
½ cup coconut cream
½ cup water
1 scoop vanilla whey protein powder (optional)
1 cup ice cubes

1. In a blender add mangoes, coconut cream, water, protein powder, and ice cubes and blend until smooth.

2. Serve immediately or store in the refrigerator in a sealed container or Mason jar up to 24 hours.

PER SERVING Calories: 620 | Fat: 39.3 g | Protein: 21.2 g | Sodium: 115 mg | Fiber: 5.3 g | Carbohydrates: 48.4 g | Sugar: 28.3 g

Chocolate Espresso Shake

A fan of the chocolate-coffee flavor combination? Then this shake is perfect for you. You should not store a blended smoothie for more than 24 hours.

INGREDIENTS | SERVES 1

½ cup chilled coffee

1 tablespoon cocoa powder

½ cup coconut milk

1 scoop chocolate whey protein powder (optional)

1 cup ice cubes

⅛ teaspoon ground cinnamon

1. In a blender add coffee, cocoa, milk, protein powder, and ice cubes and blend until smooth.

2. Top with cinnamon.

3. Serve immediately or store in the refrigerator in a sealed container or Mason jar up to 24 hours.

PER SERVING Calories: 339 | Fat: 23.6 g | Protein: 20.4 g | Sodium: 124 mg | Fiber: 2.2 g | Carbohydrates: 15.0 g | Sugar: 0.4 g

Whey Protein

If you are vegan, then replace the whey protein with plant-based chocolate protein. If you choose to omit protein powder, then add 1 teaspoon of sweetener (honey or maple syrup). It will be bitter if you do not.

Very Berry Goji

Goji berries have been used in Chinese medicine and cooking for thousands of years. They contain over twenty vitamins and minerals and have been shown to support vision, help with the immune system, and improve memory. You should not store a blended smoothie for more than 24 hours.

INGREDIENTS | SERVES 1

1 cup frozen mixed berries

½ medium banana, peeled and sliced

3 tablespoons goji berries

½ cup coconut milk

½ cup water

1 scoop vanilla whey protein powder (optional)

1 cup ice cubes

1. In a blender add mixed berries, banana, goji berries, milk, water, protein powder, and ice cubes and blend until smooth.

2. Serve immediately or store in the refrigerator in a sealed container or Mason jar up to 24 hours.

PER SERVING Calories: 516 | Fat: 23.2 g | Protein: 23.8 g | Sodium: 181 mg | Fiber: 16.0 g | Carbohydrates: 59.5 g | Sugar: 19.3 g

Buttercup Cinnamon Smoothie

If you love squash and cinnamon, you'll love this smoothie. If you do not have frozen squash, you can also use any type of squash purée to make this smoothie. You should not store a blended smoothie for more than 24 hours.

INGREDIENTS | SERVES 1

1 cup frozen cooked buttercup squash chunks

1 tablespoon milled flaxseed

1 cup unsweetened almond milk

1 scoop vanilla whey protein powder (optional)

1 cup ice cubes

⅛ teaspoon ground cinnamon

1. In a blender add squash, flaxseed, milk, protein powder, and ice cubes and blend until smooth.

2. Top with cinnamon.

3. Serve immediately or store in the refrigerator in a sealed container or Mason jar up to 24 hours.

PER SERVING Calories: 234 | Fat: 5.6 g | Protein: 20.6 g | Sodium: 274 mg | Fiber: 4.9 g | Carbohydrates: 27.1 g | Sugar: 3.5 g

Coconut Lover

If you love the taste of coconut in all its various forms, then this smoothie is for you. You should not store a blended smoothie for more than 24 hours.

INGREDIENTS | SERVES 1

½ cup coconut meat

½ cup coconut water

½ cup coconut cream

1 scoop vanilla whey protein powder (optional)

1 cup ice cubes

1. In a blender add coconut meat, water, cream, protein powder, and ice cubes and blend until smooth.

2. Serve immediately or store in the refrigerator in a sealed container or Mason jar up to 24 hours.

PER SERVING Calories: 663 | Fat: 51.9 g | Protein: 22.8 g | Sodium: 150 mg | Fiber: 6.2 g | Carbohydrates: 27.7 g | Sugar: 7.6 g

Coconut Meat

There are many ways you can get coconut meat. You can find it frozen, canned, or in fresh young coconuts. If you choose the prepackaged variety, make sure to pick one without added sugar or additives.

Can't Beet This!

Beets: you either love them or hate them. If you love them, then you'll love this smoothie. You should not store a blended smoothie for more than 24 hours.

INGREDIENTS | SERVES 1

1 cup chopped oven-roasted beets

1 cup coconut milk

1 scoop vanilla whey protein powder (optional)

1 cup ice cubes

2 tablespoons pomegranate seeds

½ teaspoon chia seeds

1. In a blender add beets, milk, protein powder, and ice cubes and blend until smooth.

2. Top with pomegranate and chia seeds.

3. Serve immediately or store in the refrigerator in a sealed container or Mason jar up to 24 hours.

PER SERVING Calories: 645 | Fat: 47.5 g | Protein: 24.3 g | Sodium: 288 mg | Fiber: 4.8 g | Carbohydrates: 32.7 g | Sugar: 12.6 g

Beets

Beets are one of the healthiest root vegetables to incorporate in your diet. They are a good source of fiber, folate, potassium, iron, and vitamin C. They can also help to purify blood, improve circulation, and increase stamina.

Pear Ginger Smoothie

If your stomach is out of sorts, this should help your recovery. Ginger has long been used to relieve digestive issues like nausea and upset stomach. You should not store a blended smoothie for more than 24 hours.

INGREDIENTS | SERVES 1

1 cup chopped pears

1 tablespoon peeled and grated fresh ginger

1 cup unsweetened almond milk

1 scoop vanilla whey protein powder (optional)

1 cup ice cubes

1. In a blender add pear, ginger, milk, protein powder, and ice cubes and blend until smooth.

2. Serve immediately or store in the refrigerator in a sealed container or Mason jar up to 24 hours.

PER SERVING Calories: 229 | Fat: 3.1 g | Protein: 18.6 g | Sodium: 268 mg | Fiber: 5.1 g | Carbohydrates: 34.0 g | Sugar: 16.1 g

Cauliflower Almond Smoothie

If you have a hard time eating your daily servings of vegetables, adding them to a smoothie is an easy way to eat them. They are more tolerable because cold temperatures reduce our sensitivity to flavors. You should not store a blended smoothie for more than 24 hours.

INGREDIENTS | SERVES 1

1 cup frozen cauliflower florets

1 cup unsweetened almond milk

1 scoop vanilla whey protein powder (optional)

1 tablespoon almond butter

1 cup ice cubes

1/8 teaspoon ground cinnamon

1. In a blender add cauliflower, milk, protein powder, butter, and ice cubes and blend until smooth.

2. Top with cinnamon.

3. Serve immediately or store in the refrigerator in a sealed container or Mason jar up to 24 hours.

PER SERVING Calories: 263 | Fat: 11.0 g | Protein: 23.9 g | Sodium: 299 mg | Fiber: 4.9 g | Carbohydrates: 17.9 g | Sugar: 4.0 g

Tropical Paradise

This smoothie will remind you of a tropical vacation. You can simply add a handful of spinach or kale to turn this into a green smoothie. You should not store a blended smoothie for more than 24 hours.

INGREDIENTS | SERVES 1

1 cup chopped papaya

½ medium banana, peeled and sliced

½ cup chopped pineapples

1 scoop vanilla whey protein powder (optional)

1 tablespoon goji berries

1 cup ice cubes

1 teaspoon chia seeds

1. In a blender add papaya, banana, pineapple, protein powder, goji berries, ice cubes, and chia seeds and blend until smooth.

2. Serve immediately or store in the refrigerator in a sealed container or Mason jar up to 24 hours.

PER SERVING Calories: 298 | Fat: 1.7 g | Protein: 20.2 g | Sodium: 136 mg | Fiber: 9.3 g | Carbohydrates: 55.8 g | Sugar: 28.0 g

Sweet Pea Smoothie

Peas make a wonderful addition to smoothies because they are naturally sweet and creamy when blended. They are also a great source of protein. You should not store a blended smoothie for more than 24 hours.

INGREDIENTS | SERVES 1

½ cup cooked frozen peas

½ cup chopped pears

2 cups baby spinach

1 cup almond milk

1 scoop vanilla whey protein powder (optional)

1 cup ice cubes

1. In a blender add peas, pears, spinach, milk, protein powder, and ice cubes and blend until smooth.

2. Serve immediately or store in the refrigerator in a sealed container or Mason jar up to 24 hours.

PER SERVING Calories: 284 | Fat: 3.2 g | Protein: 24.0 g | Sodium: 371 mg | Fiber: 8.2 g | Carbohydrates: 42.3 g | Sugar: 19.2 g

Super Green Shake

Looking to get your raw greens into your diet? This shake will be easier than eating endless servings of salads. You should not store a blended smoothie for more than 24 hours.

INGREDIENTS | SERVES 1

½ cup chopped frozen zucchini

2 cups baby spinach

2 cups chopped kale

½ medium avocado, pitted and peeled

1 cup unsweetened almond milk

1 scoop vanilla whey protein powder (optional)

⅔ cup ice cubes

1 teaspoon chia seeds

1. In a blender add zucchini, spinach, kale, avocado, milk, protein powder, and ice cubes and blend until smooth.

2. Top with chia seeds.

3. Serve immediately or store in the refrigerator in a sealed container or Mason jar up to 24 hours.

PER SERVING Calories: 301 | Fat: 13.5 g | Protein: 23.6 g | Sodium: 335 mg | Fiber: 8.9 g | Carbohydrates: 22.6 g | Sugar: 3.1 g

Frozen Options

Purchasing prepackaged frozen fruits and vegetables is a great option, and sometimes an even better option than buying fresh. Why? Because they're usually picked at their peak and instantly frozen, whereas fresh fruits are prematurely picked and left to ripen as they transport and sit on grocery store shelves.

Apple Arugula Blend

Arugula is usually found on pizza or salads, but this is an easy way to drink your daily dose of vegetables. You should not store a blended smoothie for more than 24 hours.

INGREDIENTS | SERVES 1

1 cup chopped green apples

2 cups baby arugula

1 cup water

1 scoop vanilla whey protein powder (optional)

1 teaspoon lime juice

1 cup ice cubes

1 teaspoon chia seeds

1. In a blender add apples, arugula, water, protein powder, lime juice, ice cubes, and chia seeds and blend until smooth.

2. Serve immediately or store in the refrigerator in a sealed container or Mason jar up to 24 hours.

PER SERVING Calories: 194 | Fat: 1.4 g | Protein: 19.0 g | Sodium: 127 mg | Fiber: 4.9 g | Carbohydrates: 26.6 g | Sugar: 11.7 g

Matcha Green Tea

Matcha is a trend that's popping up in the health and wellness industry. This green tea is a great way to make use of your matcha powder. You should not store a blended smoothie for more than 24 hours.

INGREDIENTS | SERVES 1

½ cup plain yogurt

½ cup coconut milk

½ cup water

2 teaspoons matcha powder

1 scoop vanilla whey protein powder (optional)

1 cup ice cubes

1. In a blender add yogurt, milk, water, matcha, protein powder, and ice cubes and blend until smooth.

2. Serve immediately or store in the refrigerator up to 24 hours.

PER SERVING Calories: 423 | Fat: 25.5 g | Protein: 30.5 g | Sodium: 161 mg | Fiber: 0.0 g | Carbohydrates: 17.7 g | Sugar: 4.9 g

Matcha Powder

Matcha green tea is an antioxidant, has anti-aging properties, and aids with lowering bad cholesterol and weight loss. It also is high in fiber and a great substitute for coffee.

CHAPTER 5

Poultry

Simple Oven-Baked Chicken Breasts

It doesn't get easier than this: six simple ingredients and an oven.
Cooked chicken breasts will store well 2–3 days.

INGREDIENTS | SERVES 5

5 medium (5–6-ounce) skinless, boneless chicken breasts

1 tablespoon dried oregano

½ teaspoon sea salt

½ teaspoon freshly ground black pepper

½ tablespoon olive oil

½ tablespoon lemon juice

Chicken Breasts

Overcooking chicken breasts causes them to dry out. If you cook on lower heat for less amount of time, it should prevent the chicken from drying out. You can also marinate this ahead of time and let sit overnight in the refrigerator.

1. Preheat oven to 350°F.

2. In a large mixing bowl add chicken, oregano, salt, pepper, oil, and lemon juice and mix until well combined. Line a baking sheet with tinfoil or parchment paper and place chicken on top.

3. Bake 25–30 minutes, depending on the thickness of the breasts. Make sure they're cooked thoroughly before removing. Ensure doneness by using a thermometer to check that the internal temperature reaches at least 165°F.

4. Let rest 10 minutes before cutting up for storage.

PER SERVING Calories: 197 | Fat: 5.7 g | Protein: 34.6 g | Sodium: 481 mg | Fiber: 0.3 g | Carbohydrates: 0.7 g | Sugar: 0.1 g

Roasted Whole Chicken

Three ingredients and a whole chicken—
this recipe is a perfect dinner for two or meal prep for 2–3 days.

INGREDIENTS | SERVES 3

1 (5–6-pound) whole chicken

1 tablespoon dried oregano

½ teaspoon sea salt

½ teaspoon freshly ground black pepper

1. Preheat oven to 375°F. Line a 17" baking pan with tinfoil or parchment paper. Place chicken on top of foil. Sprinkle with oregano, salt, and pepper to cover the whole chicken. Bake 1 hour and 30 minutes, basting every 25–30 minutes with the fat drippings.

2. Make sure chicken is cooked thoroughly before removing. Ensure doneness by using a thermometer to check that the internal temperature reaches at least 165°F.

3. Let rest 10 minutes before carving. Divide evenly into storage containers.

PER SERVING Calories: 708 | Fat: 13.9 g | Protein: 129.4 g | Sodium: 789 mg | Fiber: 0.5 g | Carbohydrates: 0.9 g | Sugar: 0.0 g

Easy BBQ Chicken Drumsticks

Chicken drumsticks are juicy, tender, and easy to cook. They will keep a bit longer than white meat as well. These will last up to 5 days in the refrigerator.

INGREDIENTS | SERVES 5

10 large chicken drumsticks

½ teaspoon freshly ground black pepper

1 tablespoon barbecue sauce

½ tablespoon coconut aminos (or tamari or soy sauce)

1 teaspoon garlic powder

1 tablespoon chopped fresh parsley

1. Preheat oven to 350°F. Line a 17" baking pan with tinfoil or parchment paper.

2. In a large mixing bowl add chicken, pepper, barbecue sauce, coconut aminos, and garlic powder and mix until well combined.

3. Place chicken on top of foil and bake 12–15 minutes. Turn drumsticks over and bake an additional 12–15 minutes or until chicken is lightly brown.

4. Make sure drumsticks are cooked thoroughly before removing. Ensure doneness by using a thermometer to check that the internal temperature reaches at least 165°F.

5. Let rest 10 minutes before storing in containers.

PER SERVING Calories: 427 | Fat: 22.2 g | Protein: 51.7 g | Sodium: 498 mg | Fiber: 0.2 g | Carbohydrates: 2.3 g | Sugar: 1.2 g

Gluten-Free Chicken Meatballs

These meatballs are great with sides or even served on top of spaghetti or spiralized zucchini with tomato sauce. These store well in the refrigerator and will last up to 5 days.

INGREDIENTS | SERVES 6

2½ pounds ground chicken
1 large egg, whisked
½ teaspoon sea salt
½ teaspoon freshly ground black pepper
4 cloves garlic, peeled and minced
½ medium onion, peeled and minced
¼ cup finely chopped fresh basil
1 tablespoon olive oil

Substitutions

If you have a hard time finding ground chicken, you can substitute ground turkey instead. If you do not have fresh basil, you can also substitute dried basil. It won't be as fresh, but should still be good.

1. Preheat oven to 350°F. Line a 17" baking pan with tinfoil or parchment paper.

2. In a large mixing bowl combine chicken, egg, salt, pepper, garlic, onions, basil, and oil and mix thoroughly.

3. Roll into golf-ball-sized balls. This should yield 35–40 balls.

4. Place balls in pan and bake 25–30 minutes. You may have to do this in batches depending on the size of your pan.

5. Make sure they're cooked thoroughly before removing. Ensure doneness by using a thermometer to check that the internal temperature reaches at least 165°F.

6. Let rest 10 minutes before transferring into storage containers.

PER SERVING Calories: 264 | Fat: 12.4 g | Protein: 37.2 g | Sodium: 508 mg | Fiber: 0.3 g | Carbohydrates: 1.6 g | Sugar: 0.4 g

Coconut Chicken Curry

This curry sauce can also be used to marinate meat or as a drizzle on top of any cooked protein or grilled vegetables. If you pre-portion this meal, make sure you store it in containers with dividers and separately from the rice or sides. This stores well in the refrigerator and will last up to 3 days.

INGREDIENTS | SERVES 5

1 tablespoon coconut oil

1 medium onion, peeled and chopped finely

3 cloves garlic, peeled and minced

2 tablespoons yellow curry powder

½ teaspoon sea salt

½ teaspoon freshly ground black pepper

1 teaspoon red pepper flakes

1 teaspoon grated fresh ginger

2 cups canned crushed tomatoes

1 cup coconut cream

1 tablespoon olive oil

5 (5–6-ounce) chicken breasts

1. Heat a large pan over medium heat and add oil. Once oil is hot, add onion and stir 2–3 minutes or until lightly brown.

2. Add garlic, curry powder, salt, black pepper, red pepper flakes, ginger, and tomatoes. Keep stirring 5 more minutes. Remove and let cool 10 minutes.

3. Transfer mixture into a food processor, add coconut cream, and blend until smooth.

4. Let completely cool, then transfer the curry sauce into a storage container.

5. In a large mixing bowl add olive oil and chicken breasts. Combine until well mixed.

6. Preheat barbecue grill on high.

7. Grill chicken until fully cooked, 10–15 minutes depending on thickness of meat. Make sure it's cooked thoroughly before removing. Ensure doneness by using a thermometer to check that the internal temperature reaches at least 165°F.

8. Pour ½ cup curry sauce over chicken and reheat everything together in the microwave before serving. Store them in food containers and refrigerate.

PER SERVING Calories: 439 | Fat: 25.7 g | Protein: 38.6 g | Sodium: 665 mg | Fiber: 4.7 g | Carbohydrates: 14.3 g | Sugar: 5.2 g

Turkey Burgers

Turkey burgers are a great substitute for beef burgers because they're low in fat and high in protein. These can be stored in the refrigerator 3–4 days before cooking. You can also freeze them. They're best cooked fresh, but you can store cooked patties up to 3 days in the refrigerator.

INGREDIENTS | SERVES 10

2 pounds extra-lean ground turkey

¾ cup finely chopped onions

1½ cups finely chopped Chinese or regular celery

¾ cup finely diced red bell peppers

2 large eggs, whisked

1 tablespoon garlic powder

4 cloves garlic, peeled and minced

1 teaspoon paprika

1 teaspoon dried basil

1 teaspoon dried parsley

1 teaspoon onion powder

1 teaspoon ground cumin

½ teaspoon ground cayenne pepper

½ teaspoon sea salt

½ teaspoon freshly ground black pepper

1 tablespoon olive oil

1. Cut 4" × 4" squares of parchment paper to use as liners to separate patties for storage.

2. In a large mixing bowl add all ingredients and mix until well combined.

3. Make 5–6-ounce patties, place on top of a piece of parchment paper, and stack on top of each other in a container.

4. To cook patties place in a medium pan with 1 teaspoon coconut oil over medium heat. Cook each side a minimum of 4–5 minutes. Cover pan if necessary to prevent oil splashing over stovetop.

5. You can also grill on a barbecue grill. They should take 7–8 minutes on high. Make sure they're cooked thoroughly before removing. Ensure doneness by using a thermometer to check that the internal temperature reaches at least 165°F.

PER SERVING Calories: 146 | Fat: 3.8 g | Protein: 23.4 g | Sodium: 168 mg | Fiber: 1.0 g | Carbohydrates: 4.0 g | Sugar: 1.3 g

Herbed Baked Chicken Breasts

This recipe includes a lot of the herbs you probably have in your kitchen. Chicken breasts are best cooked fresh daily. You can store raw marinated chicken breasts up to 3 days in the refrigerator. If cooked, they will also store up to 3 days in the refrigerator.

INGREDIENTS | SERVES 5

5 (5–6-ounce) chicken breasts
1 teaspoon paprika
1 teaspoon garlic powder
1 tablespoon dried basil
1 tablespoon dried parsley
1 teaspoon onion powder
½ teaspoon ground cayenne pepper
½ teaspoon sea salt
½ teaspoon freshly ground black pepper
1 teaspoon red pepper flakes
1 tablespoon olive oil

1. In a large mixing bowl add all ingredients and mix until well combined. For best results let sit overnight or at least 5–6 hours before cooking.

2. Preheat oven to 350°F. Line a baking sheet with parchment paper.

3. Place chicken on sheet and bake 30–35 minutes, depending on the thickness of the breasts. Make sure they're cooked thoroughly before removing. Ensure doneness by using a thermometer to check that the internal temperature reaches at least 165°F.

4. Cut into chunks or store as whole breasts in storage containers.

PER SERVING Calories: 214 | Fat: 7.1 g | Protein: 35.0 g | Sodium: 483 mg | Fiber: 0.6 g | Carbohydrates: 1.7 g | Sugar: 0.1 g

Asian Chicken Lettuce Wraps

This is a refreshing way of eating chicken that will soon have you hooked. It's light but also filling. You should store the lettuce and chicken separately until right before serving since you will reheat the chicken but not your lettuce. Serve these wraps with sides like steamed rice or baked sweet potatoes.

INGREDIENTS | SERVES 4

2½ cups diced skinless, boneless chicken thighs

½ tablespoon soy sauce or tamari

½ tablespoon oyster sauce

½ teaspoon garlic powder

½ teaspoon freshly ground black pepper

1 tablespoon coconut oil

1 medium onion, peeled and diced

1 cup diced celery

1 cup diced carrots

3 cloves garlic, peeled and minced

½ tablespoon grated fresh ginger

10 iceberg or butter lettuce leaves

2 tablespoons chopped fresh cilantro

½ teaspoon sesame seeds (for garnish)

Hoisin Sauce

You can replace oyster sauce with hoisin sauce. It gives it a sweeter twist. Hoisin sauce is a staple in Chinese cuisine, and it can be easily found in an Asian grocery store. If you cannot find this, replace with 1 tablespoon soy sauce or tamari and ½ tablespoon rice wine vinegar.

1. In a large bowl add chicken, soy sauce, oyster sauce, garlic powder, and pepper; mix to combine and set aside.

2. Heat a large skillet or wok over medium heat and add coconut oil. Once oil is hot, add onions and stir 2–3 minutes or until light brown.

3. Add celery, carrots, garlic, and ginger and stir another 3–4 minutes. Then add chicken and stir until chicken is cooked, 6–8 minutes.

4. Put 2–3 lettuce leaves in each storage container (you'll need 4 containers) and divide chicken mixture evenly into containers. Finish by topping with cilantro and sesame seeds.

5. Once fully cooled, store in refrigerator.

PER SERVING Calories: 194 | Fat: 9.1 g | Protein: 17.7 g | Sodium: 263 mg | Fiber: 2.2 g | Carbohydrates: 8.3 g | Sugar: 3.1 g

Almond-Crusted Chicken Breasts

This recipe is completely gluten-free but still gives you the satisfying crunch of a traditional breaded chicken. These can be stored in the refrigerator up to 3 days.

INGREDIENTS | SERVES 4

1 tablespoon olive oil
1 large egg, whisked
1 tablespoon Dijon mustard
½ teaspoon sea salt
½ teaspoon freshly ground black pepper
1 teaspoon garlic powder
½ teaspoon paprika
1 teaspoon dried parsley
1 cup crushed raw almonds
½ cup milled flaxseed
2 (7–8-ounce) skinless, boneless chicken breasts

Dijon

If you're not a fan of Dijon mustard, you can eliminate it from this recipe, or you can replace it with regular mustard or even honey mustard.

1. Preheat oven to 375°F.

2. In a shallow bowl mix together oil, egg, mustard, salt, and pepper.

3. On a separate large plate mix together garlic powder, paprika, parsley, crushed almonds, and flaxseed.

4. Place chicken breasts one at a time between two pieces of parchment paper and use a meat mallet to pound ½" thick. Cut chicken in half. You should now have 4 pieces.

5. Completely submerge and cover each of the pieces in egg mixture, then coat each with nut mixture. Ensure chicken is completely coated on both sides.

6. Place chicken on baking sheet and bake 20–25 minutes or until the breading is light brown. Make sure they're cooked thoroughly before removing. Ensure doneness by using a thermometer to check that the internal temperature is at least 165°F. Store in food containers and refrigerate up to 5 days.

PER SERVING Calories: 424 | Fat: 27.0 g | Protein: 33.7 g | Sodium: 477 mg | Fiber: 9.0 g | Carbohydrates: 12.2 g | Sugar: 1.5 g

Spicy Chicken Satay

You don't have to go to a Thai restaurant to enjoy a really good satay—make it for your next meal prep! This can be served as an appetizer or a main dish to go with your sides in your meal preps for the week. This will last up to 3 days in the refrigerator.

INGREDIENTS | SERVES 5

1 cup coconut milk

3 cloves garlic, peeled and minced

1 tablespoon grated fresh ginger

1 tablespoon yellow curry powder

½ teaspoon sea salt

½ teaspoon freshly ground black pepper

1 tablespoon red pepper flakes

4 (7–8-ounce) skinless, boneless chicken breasts

1. In a large bowl add coconut milk, garlic, ginger, curry powder, salt, black pepper, and red pepper flakes and mix until well combined.

2. Cut each chicken breast lengthwise into 3 or 4 strips. Put chicken strips into prepared mixture and marinate overnight or at least 4–5 hours.

3. Soak wooden skewer sticks in water at least 1 hour before use. Skewer chicken strips onto the wooden sticks.

4. You can grill or bake these. To grill, preheat grill on high heat. Grill at least 8–10 minutes or until cooked evenly on all sides.

5. To bake, preheat oven to 350°F. Bake 25–30 minutes, turning halfway through to ensure it's cooked on both sides. Make sure they're cooked thoroughly before removing. Ensure doneness by using a thermometer to check that the internal temperature reaches at least 165°F before removing.

PER SERVING Calories: 292 | Fat: 13.9 g | Protein: 38.1 g | Sodium: 320 mg | Fiber: 0.8 g | Carbohydrates: 2.9 g | Sugar: 0.1 g

Mexican Ground Turkey

This ground turkey will go well on salads or served as a main dish to many of your sides. Leftovers can even be used for omelettes. This meat can be stored up to 5 days in the refrigerator.

INGREDIENTS | SERVES 5

½ tablespoon coconut oil

2 pounds extra-lean ground turkey

½ tablespoon garlic powder

½ tablespoon chili powder

1 tablespoon ground cumin

1 tablespoon paprika

1 teaspoon ground cayenne pepper

½ teaspoon sea salt

½ teaspoon freshly ground black pepper

½ tablespoon red pepper flakes

½ tablespoon dried parsley

1. Heat a large skillet or pan over medium heat and add oil. Once oil is hot, add ground turkey and stir 5–6 minutes or until meat only has a bit of pink left. Use the flat side of a wooden spatula to break larger chunks into smaller ones while it's cooking. Drain meat and return pan to stove.

2. Turn heat to low, then add garlic powder, chili powder, cumin, paprika, cayenne, salt, black pepper, red pepper flakes, and parsley and stir 4–5 minutes to ensure it is thoroughly cooked.

3. Set aside to cool and store in food containers.

PER SERVING Calories: 229 | Fat: 4.7 g | Protein: 43.5 g | Sodium: 350 mg | Fiber: 1.1 g | Carbohydrates: 2.7 g | Sugar: 0.3 g

Chinese Five-Spice Chicken Thighs

Chinese five-spice powder is a mixture of star anise, cloves, cinnamon, fennel seeds, and Szechuan pepper. It is very aromatic and great on all proteins. Store these in food containers and they last up to 3 days in the refrigerator.

INGREDIENTS | SERVES 5

10 bone-in, skin-on chicken thighs

1 teaspoon olive oil

½ tablespoon five-spice powder

1 teaspoon garlic powder

½ teaspoon ground ginger

1 tablespoon soy sauce or tamari

½ teaspoon freshly ground black pepper

1. In a large mixing bowl add chicken, oil, five-spice powder, garlic powder, ginger, soy sauce, and pepper. Mix until well combined. Let marinate in the refrigerator at least 3–4 hours or overnight for best results.

2. When ready to cook preheat oven to 375°F.

3. Bake 40–45 minutes or until chicken is lightly brown.

4. Turn oven to broil and broil 5 minutes.

5. Make sure chicken is cooked thoroughly before removing. Ensure doneness by using a thermometer to check that the internal temperature reaches at least 165°F.

6. Set aside to cool, then store in containers.

PER SERVING Calories: 867 | Fat: 58.5 g | Protein: 64.3 g | Sodium: 505 mg | Fiber: 0.3 g | Carbohydrates: 2.4 g | Sugar: 0.3 g

Turmeric Ground Turkey

This turkey is good in salads or even on top of egg jars. Turmeric is a very powerful spice. It is an antioxidant and fights inflammation and can help prevent cancer. It also may help delay aging and age-related chronic diseases. This meat can be stored up to 5 days in the refrigerator.

INGREDIENTS | SERVES 5

½ tablespoon coconut oil

2 pounds extra-lean ground turkey

½ tablespoon garlic powder

½ tablespoon ground ginger

1 tablespoon ground turmeric

½ teaspoon sea salt

½ teaspoon freshly ground black pepper

½ tablespoon red pepper flakes

1. Heat a large skillet or pan over medium heat and add oil. Once oil is hot, add ground turkey and stir 5–6 minutes or until meat only has a bit of pink left. Use the flat side of a wooden spatula to break larger chunks into smaller ones while it's cooking. Drain meat and return pan to stove.

2. Turn heat to low, then add garlic powder, ginger, turmeric, salt, black pepper, and red pepper flakes and stir 4–5 minutes to ensure it is thoroughly cooked.

3. Set aside to cool and store in food containers.

PER SERVING Calories: 225 | Fat: 4.2 g | Protein: 43.1 g | Sodium: 280 mg | Fiber: 0.7 g | Carbohydrates: 2.5 g | Sugar: 0.1 g

Spicy Turkey Meatloaf

Ground turkey is one of the leanest proteins you can find. High in protein and low in fat, it's an amazing choice when you're weight conscious. This recipe stores really well and will last up to 5 days in the refrigerator.

INGREDIENTS | SERVES 6

4 cups extra-lean ground turkey

1 large egg, whisked

¾ cup finely diced onions

3 cloves garlic, peeled and minced

1 tablespoon soy sauce or tamari

½ tablespoon balsamic vinegar

1 teaspoon garlic powder

¼ teaspoon sea salt

½ teaspoon freshly ground black pepper

½ cup chopped green chilies

1 cup diced bell peppers

1 teaspoon coconut oil (for greasing pan)

1. Preheat oven to 375°F.

2. In a large mixing bowl add turkey, egg, onion, garlic, soy sauce, vinegar, garlic powder, salt, pepper, chilies, and bell peppers. Mix until well combined. Grease a 9" loaf pan with coconut oil or line with parchment paper, then pour in meat mixture.

3. Bake 50–55 minutes or until cooked thoroughly. Use a thermometer to check that the internal temperature reaches at least 165°F. Set aside to cool, then slice and store in containers.

PER SERVING Calories: 214 | Fat: 3.9 g | Protein: 37.8 g | Sodium: 316 mg | Fiber: 1.2 g | Carbohydrates: 6.0 g | Sugar: 2.8 g

Rosemary Lemon Chicken

*If you don't have fresh rosemary you can substitute with dried rosemary.
Chicken breasts are always best cooked the night before, but if you had to
cook them all at once, they will last up to 3 days in the refrigerator.*

INGREDIENTS | SERVES 5

5 (5–6-ounce) skinless, boneless chicken breasts

1 teaspoon olive oil

1 tablespoon minced fresh rosemary

1 teaspoon garlic powder

Juice and zest from 1 medium lemon

½ teaspoon sea salt

½ teaspoon freshly ground black pepper

1. In a large mixing bowl add chicken, oil, rosemary, garlic powder, lemon juice, lemon zest, salt, and pepper. Mix until well combined. Let marinate in the refrigerator at least 3–4 hours or overnight for best results.

2. When ready to bake preheat oven to 350°F.

3. Bake 30–35 minutes or until thoroughly cooked.

4. Make sure chicken is cooked thoroughly before removing. Ensure doneness by using a thermometer to check that the internal temperature reaches at least 165°F.

5. Set aside to cool, then store in containers.

PER SERVING Calories: 195 | Fat: 5.3 g | Protein: 34.7 g | Sodium: 481 mg | Fiber: 0.3 g | Carbohydrates: 1.3 g | Sugar: 0.2 g

Turmeric Chicken Stir-Fry

Stir-fries are so easy to make, and they keep well up to a week in the refrigerator. You can substitute boneless, skinless chicken thighs for the breasts if you prefer.

INGREDIENTS | SERVES 5

1 teaspoon coconut oil

1 medium onion, peeled and diced

3 cloves garlic, peeled and minced

½ tablespoon minced fresh ginger

2 cups diced jicama

1 cup diced celery

1 cup diced red bell peppers

3 (5–6-ounce) skinless, boneless chicken breasts, cubed

½ teaspoon sea salt

½ teaspoon freshly ground black pepper

1 teaspoon garlic powder

½ tablespoon ground turmeric

¼ cup chopped fresh cilantro

1. Heat a large skillet or pan over medium heat and add oil. Once oil is hot, add onion and stir 2–3 minutes or until lightly brown.

2. Add garlic, ginger, jicama, celery, and red peppers and stir 3–5 minutes.

3. Add chicken, salt, pepper, garlic powder, and turmeric and stir 5 minutes or until chicken is thoroughly cooked.

4. Turn off heat and add cilantro.

5. Set aside to cool, then store in containers.

PER SERVING Calories: 165 | Fat: 3.6 g | Protein: 22.1 g | Sodium: 384 mg | Fiber: 4.2 g | Carbohydrates: 10.8 g | Sugar: 3.4 g

Appetizer Friendly

This can be served as an appetizer if you're hosting a party. Place smaller portions inside lettuce leaves and serve as lettuce wraps.

Diced Chicken Stir-Fry

This dish is very refreshing and crispy. You can usually find jicama at international supermarkets although it is becoming more widely available at mainstream grocery chains. If you cannot find it, you can substitute zucchini or more celery. This stores well in the refrigerator and will last up to 3 days.

INGREDIENTS | SERVES 5

1 teaspoon coconut oil

1 medium onion, peeled and diced

3 cloves garlic, peeled and minced

2 cups diced jicama

2 cups diced celery

1 cup diced carrots

3 (5–6-ounce) skinless, boneless chicken breasts, cubed

½ teaspoon sea salt

½ teaspoon freshly ground black pepper

¼ cup chopped green onions

1. Heat a large skillet or pan over medium heat and add oil. Once oil is hot, add onion and stir 2–3 minutes or until lightly brown.

2. Add garlic, jicama, celery, and carrots and stir 3–5 minutes.

3. Add chicken, salt, and pepper and stir 5 minutes or until chicken is thoroughly cooked.

4. Turn off heat and add green onions.

5. Set aside to cool, then store in containers.

PER SERVING Calories: 166 | Fat: 3.6 g | Protein: 22.1 g | Sodium: 417 mg | Fiber: 4.5 g | Carbohydrates: 11.2 g | Sugar: 3.7 g

Thai Green Curry

This dish is extra rich so enjoy it in moderation. Make sure you read the ingredients on the curry paste and avoid any that have added sugar or additives. No salt is needed since the paste itself is quite salty. Store the curry separately from your rice. This will store well in the refrigerator up to 3 days. Serve this dish with white or brown rice.

INGREDIENTS | SERVES 6

3 tablespoons green curry paste

1 tablespoon water

3 cups cubed skinless, boneless chicken thighs

1 teaspoon coconut oil

1 medium onion, peeled and chopped

4 cloves garlic, peeled and minced

2 cups chopped Chinese eggplant

2 cups chopped red bell peppers

1 cup canned sliced water chestnuts

2 cups canned bamboo shoots, cut into strips

2 cups canned baby corn, cut into 1" pieces

2½ cups coconut milk

½ cup chopped fresh cilantro

½ cup fresh Thai basil leaves

1. Preheat oven to 375°F.

2. In a small bowl add curry paste and water; use a fork to mix well to loosen up paste. Set aside.

3. In a large mixing bowl add chicken and mix in paste. Mix until well combined.

4. Transfer chicken to a 17" baking pan and bake 30 minutes. Remove from oven and set aside.

5. Heat a large wok over medium heat and add oil. Once oil is hot, add onion and stir 2–3 minutes or until lightly brown. Add garlic and stir 1 minute.

6. Add eggplant and stir another 3 minutes. Add red peppers, water chestnuts, bamboo shoots, and corn and stir another 2–3 minutes.

7. Add chicken to wok and stir another minute.

8. Add coconut milk and lower heat to a simmer. Let simmer 3–4 minutes.

9. Top with cilantro and basil.

10. Set aside to cool, then store in containers.

PER SERVING Calories: 596 | Fat: 42.0 g | Protein: 30.0 g | Sodium: 479 mg | Fiber: 5.2 g | Carbohydrates: 18.3 g | Sugar: 6.8 g

Slow Cooker Chicken Taco Meat

You can serve this meat on corn tortillas, or for a lower-calorie option serve it on lettuce wraps. If tacos are too much hassle, then serve this on a salad or with your favorite sides. This recipe stores well in the refrigerator and will last up to 3 days.

INGREDIENTS | SERVES 6

3 (5–6-ounce) skinless, boneless chicken breasts

8 (3–4-ounce) skinless, boneless chicken thighs

3 cups diced tomatoes

1 medium onion, peeled and diced

4 cloves garlic, peeled and minced

2 small jalapeño peppers, seeded and chopped

1 tablespoon ground cumin

1 teaspoon chili powder

1 teaspoon paprika

½ teaspoon sea salt

1 teaspoon freshly ground black pepper

1 teaspoon ground coriander

½ cup chopped fresh cilantro

1. Place all ingredients except cilantro in a slow cooker and cook on high 5 hours.

2. Remove chicken to a large plate and shred with two forks.

3. Place shredded chicken back into the slow cooker, mix well, and cook on high 1 more hour.

4. Top with cilantro and serve.

PER SERVING Calories: 262 | Fat: 6.6 g | Protein: 41.1 g | Sodium: 431 mg | Fiber: 2.1 g | Carbohydrates: 7.2 g | Sugar: 3.4 g

Tangy Orange Chicken

Love Chinese takeout? This will allow you to enjoy it without feeling too guilty. Serve this on white rice with steamed vegetables or serve on cauliflower "fried rice" to lower the calories and carbohydrates. This stores well in the refrigerator and will last up to 3 days.

INGREDIENTS | SERVES 5

2 tablespoons soy sauce or tamari

2 tablespoons orange juice

1 teaspoon orange zest

4 cloves garlic, peeled and minced

2 tablespoons tomato paste

1 tablespoon rice vinegar

2 tablespoons honey

½ teaspoon freshly ground black pepper

4 (5–6-ounce) skinless, boneless chicken breasts, cubed

1 teaspoon roasted sesame seeds (for garnish)

¼ cup chopped green onions (for garnish)

1. Add soy sauce, orange juice, orange zest, garlic, tomato paste, vinegar, honey, and pepper to a large bowl and whisk until well combined.

2. Add chicken and stir to coat.

3. Place chicken in a slow cooker and cook on low 5 hours.

4. Transfer the sauce only into a small saucepan and simmer 15 minutes to thicken.

5. Divide chicken into storage containers, top with sauce, and then top with sesame seeds and green onions.

PER SERVING Calories: 193 | Fat: 3.8 g | Protein: 28.9 g | Sodium: 638 mg | Fiber: 0.7 g | Carbohydrates: 10.6 g | Sugar: 8.3 g

Spicy Basil Chicken Stir-Fry

If you can't find Thai basil, you can substitute regular basil. If you're sick of eating chicken, you can substitute beef or pork as well. This stores well in the refrigerator and will last up to 3 days. This dish is best served with steamed rice.

INGREDIENTS | SERVES 5

4 (5–6-ounce) skinless, boneless chicken breasts, sliced

1 tablespoon oyster sauce

1 tablespoon soy sauce or tamari

1 tablespoon coconut oil

4 cloves garlic, peeled and minced

2 green Thai chilies, seeded and chopped

1 teaspoon red pepper flakes

3 cups fresh Thai basil leaves

1. In a large bowl add chicken, oyster sauce, and soy sauce and let marinate 30 minutes.

2. Heat a large wok over medium heat and add oil. Once oil is hot, add garlic and chilies and stir 30 seconds.

3. Add chicken and red pepper flakes and stir 5–6 minutes or until chicken is thoroughly cooked.

4. Reduce heat to low, add basil, and stir until wilted, 1 minute.

5. Divide chicken into storage containers.

PER SERVING Calories: 225 | Fat: 6.9 g | Protein: 32.8 g | Sodium: 524 mg | Fiber: 7.8 g | Carbohydrates: 11.3 g | Sugar: 0.6 g

Mom's Lemongrass Chicken

You can find lemongrass stalks in an Asian supermarket. You can grind these ahead of time and just freeze them in a bag for later. They last for long periods of time in the freezer. This dish is best served with steamed rice. This stores well in the refrigerator and will last up to 5 days.

INGREDIENTS | SERVES 5

¼ cup diced fresh lemongrass
3 cloves garlic, peeled
1 tablespoon oyster sauce
½ tablespoon water
½ tablespoon honey
1 tablespoon soy sauce or tamari
10 (3–4-ounce) skinless, boneless chicken thighs

1. In a food processor add lemongrass and garlic and process until finely ground. Pour mixture into a medium bowl.

2. Add oyster sauce, water, honey, and soy sauce to the bowl. Whisk until marinade is well combined. Set aside.

3. In a large mixing bowl add chicken and ⅔ of the marinade. Mix until well combined. Marinate overnight for best results or at least 3–4 hours.

4. Preheat oven to 375°F. Line a 17" baking pan with parchment paper and place chicken on top of the parchment.

5. Bake 30–35 minutes, depending on thickness of the thighs. Every 10 minutes turn chicken and brush on remaining marinade.

6. Make sure chicken is cooked thoroughly before removing. Ensure doneness by using a thermometer to check that the internal temperature reaches at least 165°F.

7. Divide chicken into storage containers.

PER SERVING Calories: 289 | Fat: 8.0 g | Protein: 45.1 g | Sodium: 489 mg | Fiber: 0.1 g | Carbohydrates: 3.7 g | Sugar: 1.7 g

Jerk Chicken

Want to add extra zing to your lunch? You'll love this served with baked plantains and coleslaw! If you want to make this even spicier try adding some cayenne pepper and red chili flakes on top of the jerk seasoning. This dish stores well in the refrigerator and will last up to 5 days.

INGREDIENTS | SERVES 5

10 large skin-on chicken drumsticks
1 tablespoon Jamaican jerk seasoning
½ tablespoon water
3 cloves garlic, peeled and minced
½ tablespoon soy sauce or tamari
½ teaspoon freshly ground black pepper
1 teaspoon red pepper flakes (optional)
1 teaspoon garlic powder

Jerk Seasoning

Make sure you read the labels when purchasing jerk seasoning to ensure there are no additives outside of herbs and spices. If you prefer a less spicy dish, remove red pepper flakes; use half the jerk seasoning and replace the other half with soy sauce.

1. Cut 2 or 3 short shallow slits into each drumstick to allow marinade to absorb better.

2. In a small bowl add jerk seasoning, water, garlic, soy sauce, black pepper, red pepper flakes, and garlic powder and mix until well combined. Set aside.

3. In a large mixing bowl add chicken and marinade. Mix until well combined. Marinate overnight for best results or at least 3–4 hours.

4. Preheat oven to 375°F. Line a 17" baking pan with parchment paper and place chicken on top of parchment.

5. Bake 30–35 minutes or until thoroughly cooked. Turn each drumstick over at least once halfway through cooking.

6. Turn the oven to broil and broil an additional 2–3 minutes. Keep an eye on chicken to make sure it doesn't burn.

7. Make sure chicken is cooked thoroughly before removing. Ensure doneness by using a thermometer to check that the internal temperature reaches at least 165°F.

8. Divide chicken into storage containers.

PER SERVING Calories: 432 | Fat: 22.2 g | Protein: 51.9 g | Sodium: 685 mg | Fiber: 0.2 g | Carbohydrates: 3.7 g | Sugar: 0.0 g

Moroccan Chicken

If you cannot find harissa in your local grocery store, you can make your own. Simply combine equal servings of paprika, cumin, coriander, ginger, turmeric, cinnamon, and black pepper in a small bowl. Store this chicken dish in food containers and refrigerate up to 3 days.

INGREDIENTS | SERVES 5

10 skin-on, bone-in chicken thighs
1 tablespoon harissa spice blend
½ teaspoon freshly ground black pepper
1 teaspoon red pepper flakes (optional)
1 teaspoon garlic powder

1. Cut 2 or 3 short shallow slits into each thigh to allow the seasoning to absorb better.

2. In a large mixing bowl add chicken, harissa, black pepper, red pepper flakes, and garlic powder. Mix until well combined. Let sit overnight for best results or at least 3–4 hours.

3. Preheat oven to 375°F. Line a 17" baking pan with parchment paper and place chicken on top of parchment.

4. Bake 30–35 minutes or until thoroughly cooked.

5. Turn the oven to broil and broil an additional 2–3 minutes. Keep an eye on chicken to make sure it doesn't burn.

6. Make sure chicken is cooked thoroughly before removing. Ensure doneness by using a thermometer to check that the internal temperature reaches at least 165°F.

7. Divide chicken into storage containers.

PER SERVING Calories: 862 | Fat: 57.9 g | Protein: 64.2 g | Sodium: 331 mg | Fiber: 0.7 g | Carbohydrates: 2.2 g | Sugar: 0.2 g

Sriracha Chicken

Sriracha is a staple in most Asian households, and now it's so popular that it's finding its way into a lot of other households. Just make sure you don't overuse it because it's quite high in sodium. You'll love this chicken served with baked plantains and coleslaw. This stores well in the refrigerator and will last up to 3 days.

INGREDIENTS | SERVES 5

4 (5–6-ounce) skinless, boneless chicken breasts
1 tablespoon sriracha
1 tablespoon soy sauce or tamari
3 cloves garlic, peeled and minced
1 teaspoon garlic powder
½ teaspoon freshly ground black pepper
1 teaspoon red pepper flakes (optional)
1 teaspoon dried basil
¼ cup chopped fresh basil

1. Cut 2 or 3 short shallow slits into each breast to allow the marinade to absorb better.

2. In a small bowl add sriracha, soy sauce, garlic, garlic powder, black pepper, red pepper flakes, and dried basil and mix until well combined. Set aside.

3. In a large mixing bowl add chicken and marinade. Mix until well combined. Marinate overnight for best results or at least 3–4 hours.

4. Preheat oven to 375°F. Line a baking pan with parchment paper and place chicken on top of parchment.

5. Bake 30–35 minutes or until thoroughly cooked.

6. Make sure chicken is cooked thoroughly before removing. Ensure doneness by using a thermometer to check that the internal temperature reaches at least 165°F.

7. Cut into chunks, sprinkle basil on top, and either serve or divide evenly into storage containers.

PER SERVING Calories: 173 | Fat: 2.3 g | Protein: 31.2 g | Sodium: 285 mg | Fiber: 0.3 g | Carbohydrates: 2.1 g | Sugar: 0.7 g

Red Meat

Spicy Meatballs

These are great with sides or even served on top of spaghetti or spiralized zucchini and tomato sauce. These meatballs store and reheat really well. They can be stored in food containers and last up to 5 days.

INGREDIENTS | SERVES 6

2½ pounds extra-lean ground beef

1 large egg, whisked

½ teaspoon sea salt

½ teaspoon freshly ground black pepper

4 cloves garlic, peeled and minced

½ medium onion, peeled and minced

1 tablespoon dried parsley

½ tablespoon dried rosemary

2 medium jalapeño peppers, seeded and finely diced

1 teaspoon red pepper flakes

1 tablespoon olive oil

1. Preheat oven to 350°F. Line a 17" baking pan with tinfoil or parchment paper.

2. In a large mixing bowl combine beef, egg, salt, black pepper, garlic, onions, parsley, rosemary, jalapeños, red pepper flakes, and oil and mix thoroughly.

3. Roll into golf-ball-sized balls. This should yield 35–40 balls.

4. Place balls on parchment and bake 20–25 minutes or until thoroughly cooked. You may have to do this in batches depending on the size of your pan.

5. Let rest 10 minutes before transferring into storage containers.

PER SERVING Calories: 257 | Fat: 8.3 g | Protein: 42.9 g | Sodium: 294 mg | Fiber: 0.5 g | Carbohydrates: 2.1 g | Sugar: 0.6 g

Five-Spice Slow Cooker Beef Stew

Stews are so satisfying and are great for cold or rainy days. Choose beef with a lower fat content if you're weight conscious, or replace the beef with chicken breast or another lean protein. Store this stew separately in containers. This stores well in the refrigerator and will last up to 5 days.

INGREDIENTS | SERVES 8

½ tablespoon coconut oil

2½ pounds cubed stew beef

1 (26-ounce) can diced tomatoes

2 tablespoons tomato paste

1 tablespoon five-spice powder

4 cloves garlic, peeled and minced

1 teaspoon sea salt

1 teaspoon freshly ground black pepper

1 teaspoon paprika

½ teaspoon ground cayenne pepper

1 teaspoon red pepper flakes

1 teaspoon ground cinnamon

2 cups chopped carrots

2 cups chopped red bell peppers

1 medium onion, peeled and chopped

1 cup beef broth

¼ cup chopped green onions (for garnish)

¼ cup chopped fresh cilantro (for garnish)

1. Heat a large skillet over medium-high heat and add oil. Once oil is hot add beef and stir to brown on all sides, 5–7 minutes. Remove excess oil and set aside.

2. In a slow cooker add meat and remaining ingredients except for green onions and cilantro. Cook on low 7–8 hours.

3. Garnish with green onions and cilantro. Place in food containers and store in the refrigerator up to 5 days.

PER SERVING Calories: 326 | Fat: 13.9 g | Protein: 29.0 g | Sodium: 564 mg | Fiber: 4.2 g | Carbohydrates: 13.7 g | Sugar: 7.5 g

Homemade Beef Burgers

These are easy to make and also keep well in the refrigerator. Store in refrigerator uncooked up to 5 days. You can also freeze them to keep longer.

INGREDIENTS | SERVES 8

2½ pounds extra-lean ground beef

½ medium red onion, peeled and finely chopped

1 large egg, whisked

1 cup finely chopped red bell peppers

1 cup finely chopped celery

4 cloves garlic, peeled and minced

½ tablespoon garlic powder

½ teaspoon freshly ground black pepper

½ teaspoon sea salt

1 tablespoon dried parsley

1 tablespoon olive oil

Meatballs

You can turn these into meatballs, too, if you're looking to prep a week ahead. Meatballs will keep longer than burgers. Once cooked, they can keep up to 5 days in the refrigerator. They're best grilled or pan-fried fresh daily.

1. Cut 8 (4" × 4") pieces parchment paper for lining containers and separating burgers for storage.

2. In a large mixing bowl combine beef, onions, egg, red pepper, celery, garlic, garlic powder, black pepper, salt, parsley, and oil and mix until well combined.

3. Make 5–6-ounce burger patties and place on top of a piece of parchment paper, one on top of another, in a storage container.

4. To grill: grill on high 6–7 minutes or until cooked thoroughly. To pan-fry: pan-fry over medium heat 3–4 minutes per side or until cooked thoroughly.

PER SERVING Calories: 201 | Fat: 6.3 g | Protein: 32.5 g | Sodium: 231 mg | Fiber: 0.9 g | Carbohydrates: 3.3 g | Sugar: 1.3 g

Ground Beef Stuffed Peppers

Bell peppers come in all sizes and shapes, but for this recipe make sure you pick large round ones. They will sit easier as well as have more room for you to stuff. This stores well in the refrigerator and will last up to 5 days.

INGREDIENTS | SERVES 5

10 medium bell peppers (any color)
1 tablespoon coconut oil
1 medium onion, peeled and diced
1 cup diced carrots
4 cloves garlic, peeled and minced
10 kale leaves, stems removed, chopped
2 pounds extra-lean ground beef
½ tablespoon garlic powder
½ teaspoon freshly ground black pepper
½ teaspoon sea salt
¼ cup tomato paste

1. Preheat oven to 350°F.

2. Cut the top of bell peppers off and remove seeds and core.

3. Line a 17" baking pan with parchment paper and place peppers on it. Bake peppers 15 minutes. Remove and set aside.

4. Heat a large wok or skillet over medium heat and add oil. Once oil is hot, add onions and stir 2–3 minutes or until lightly brown.

5. Add carrots and garlic and stir another minute.

6. Add kale and keep stirring until wilted, 1 minute.

7. Add beef and stir 2–3 minutes. Make sure you use a flat wooden spatula to break up the big pieces.

8. Add garlic powder, black pepper, salt, and tomato paste and stir another 2–3 minutes.

9. Remove from stove and stuff meat mixture evenly into pepper cups.

10. Store in food containers.

PER SERVING Calories: 328 | Fat: 8.0 g | Protein: 43.3 g | Sodium: 438 mg | Fiber: 5.9 g | Carbohydrates: 20.2 g | Sugar: 11.8 g

BBQ Beef Kebabs

If you're having these as a dinner, it's better to grill them fresh daily. You can store them in the refrigerator up to 3 days cooked. These are great served with Spicy Chimichurri (see Chapter 10) on the side.

INGREDIENTS | SERVES 5

1 tablespoon olive oil

¼ teaspoon sea salt

½ teaspoon freshly ground black pepper

½ teaspoon garlic powder

3 medium bell peppers, seeded and cut into 1½" pieces

2 medium onions, peeled and cut into 1½" pieces

2 medium zucchini, cut into 1" rounds

2 pounds beef (grilling steak)

1. Soak 15 wooden skewers in water at least 30 minutes before use.

2. In a small bowl whisk together oil, salt, pepper, and garlic powder. Set aside.

3. In a large mixing bowl add peppers, onions, zucchini, and oil mixture. Mix until well combined.

4. Skewer beef and vegetables on their own skewers to enable even cooking. You should be able to make 13–15 skewers.

5. Grill over medium heat 7–8 minutes or until desired doneness of beef.

6. Store in food containers.

PER SERVING Calories: 345 | Fat: 12.5 g | Protein: 42.0 g | Sodium: 204 mg | Fiber: 2.5 g | Carbohydrates: 9.3 g | Sugar: 5.6 g

Healthy Beef and Broccoli Stir-Fry

This is a classic Chinese dish. It's best served with white or brown rice. Always choose a leaner but tender cut of beef for this recipe. This recipe works well with chicken too. This stir-fry stores well in the refrigerator up to 5 days.

INGREDIENTS | SERVES 5

1 tablespoon coconut oil

1 cup sliced carrots

1 tablespoon peeled and minced fresh ginger

4 cups broccoli florets

3 cloves garlic, peeled and minced

1 tablespoon water

2 pounds beef, sliced

¼ teaspoon sea salt

½ teaspoon freshly ground black pepper

½ teaspoon garlic powder

1. Heat a large wok or skillet over medium heat and add oil. Once oil is hot, add carrots and ginger and stir 1–2 minutes or until carrots are soft.

2. Add broccoli and garlic. Stir another minute. Add water and stir for about 30 seconds.

3. Add beef, stir 2 minutes, then add salt, pepper, and garlic powder. Continue stirring another 2 minutes or until beef is cooked to desired doneness.

4. Store in food containers.

PER SERVING Calories: 338 | Fat: 17.0 g | Protein: 38.9 g | Sodium: 282 mg | Fiber: 2.8 g | Carbohydrates: 8.5 g | Sugar: 2.5 g

Taco Tuesday Beef

This beef is great to add to a salad or served with your favorite sides. It's also a great addition to your favorite omelette. This meat can be stored up to 5 days in the refrigerator.

INGREDIENTS | SERVES 5

1 tablespoon coconut oil

2 pounds extra-lean ground beef

½ tablespoon teaspoon garlic powder

¼ teaspoon sea salt

½ teaspoon freshly ground black pepper

2 tablespoons ground cumin

1 tablespoon paprika

½ tablespoon chili powder

1 teaspoon ground cayenne pepper

2 tablespoons tomato paste

1. Heat a large skillet or pan over medium heat and add oil. Once oil is hot, add beef and stir 5–6 minutes or until the meat only has a bit of pink left. Use the flat side of a wooden spatula to break larger chunks into smaller ones while it's cooking. Drain meat.

2. Reduce heat to low, then add garlic powder, salt, black pepper, cumin, paprika, chili powder, cayenne, and tomato paste and stir 2–3 minutes.

3. Set aside to cool and store in food containers.

PER SERVING Calories: 256 | Fat: 8.5 g | Protein: 41.1 g | Sodium: 291 mg | Fiber: 1.5 g | Carbohydrates: 4.5 g | Sugar: 1.1 g

Spaghetti Squash with Ground Beef Sauce

Spaghetti squash is low in calories and high in fiber, and loaded with micronutrients. It is easy to cook and great alone or paired with other proteins in place of the ground beef. This stores well in the refrigerator up to 5 days.

INGREDIENTS | SERVES 6

2 medium spaghetti squash

1 tablespoon coconut oil

1 medium onion, peeled and diced

1 cup diced red bell peppers

4 cloves garlic, peeled and minced

2 pounds extra-lean ground beef

3 cups tomato sauce

¼ cup tomato paste

1 cup water

1 tablespoon dried oregano

1 tablespoon dried parsley

½ teaspoon ground thyme

½ teaspoon dried rosemary

¼ teaspoon ground cinnamon

¼ teaspoon sea salt

½ teaspoon freshly ground black pepper

¼ cup chopped fresh parsley (for garnish)

1. Preheat oven to 375°F. Line a 17" baking pan with parchment paper.

2. Cut spaghetti squash in half lengthwise and remove the seeds.

3. Place squash facedown on prepared pan and bake 30–35 minutes. Set aside and let cool.

4. Heat a large skillet over medium heat and add oil. Once oil is hot, add onions and stir 2–3 minutes or until light brown.

5. Add peppers and garlic and stir another minute.

6. Add beef; stir and break the larger pieces into smaller pieces as it cooks. Stir 2–3 minutes.

7. Add tomato sauce, tomato paste, water, oregano, dried parsley, thyme, rosemary, cinnamon, salt, and pepper. Turn heat to simmer. Let simmer 30 minutes. Set aside.

8. Use a fork to pull spaghetti squash into strands; divide evenly into storage containers.

9. Add meat sauce on top and garnish with fresh parsley.

PER SERVING Calories: 321 | Fat: 7.3 g | Protein: 37.6 g | Sodium: 897 mg | Fiber: 7.2 g | Carbohydrates: 29.8 g | Sugar: 14.1 g

Mini Beef Muffins

These are like beef meatloaves except in a mini version. The muffin shape makes these easy to store as well as portion off. You can pair these with any of your favorite sides. These muffins store well in the refrigerator up to 5 days.

INGREDIENTS | SERVES 6

2 pounds extra-lean ground beef

½ tablespoon olive oil

1 medium onion, peeled and finely chopped

1 cup finely diced red bell peppers

4 cloves garlic, peeled and minced

2 large eggs, whisked

2 tablespoons chopped fresh parsley

¼ teaspoon sea salt

½ teaspoon freshly ground black pepper

1 teaspoon balsamic vinegar

1. Preheat oven to 350°F. Line a 12-cup muffin pan with liners.

2. In large bowl add beef, oil, onions, bell peppers, garlic, eggs, parsley, salt, black pepper, and vinegar and mix until well combined.

3. Divide meat evenly into muffin cups.

4. Bake 25–30 minutes.

5. Remove and let cool before storing in containers.

PER SERVING Calories: 225 | Fat: 6.9 g | Protein: 35.9 g | Sodium: 203 mg | Fiber: 0.9 g | Carbohydrates: 4.2 g | Sugar: 2.0 g

Korean Short Ribs

If you love Korean food, this will be a great prep for you! Serve these ribs with steamed rice and a side of vegetables. These store well in the refrigerator and will last up to 5 days.

INGREDIENTS | SERVES 5

2 tablespoons soy sauce or tamari

½ tablespoon garlic powder

1 teaspoon onion powder

1 teaspoon ground ginger

1 tablespoon honey

¼ teaspoon freshly ground black pepper

1 tablespoon coconut oil

2 tablespoons rice wine vinegar

2 pounds beef short ribs

1. In a small bowl whisk together soy sauce, garlic powder, onion powder, ginger, honey, black pepper, oil, and vinegar.

2. Place ribs in a large mixing bowl and add marinade. Combine until well mixed.

3. For best results let sit in the refrigerator overnight or at least 2 hours.

4. Grill on high 2–3 minutes per side. Serve immediately or store in food containers.

PER SERVING Calories: 360 | Fat: 19.1 g | Protein: 35.4 g | Sodium: 470 mg | Fiber: 0.3 g | Carbohydrates: 5.2 g | Sugar: 3.5 g

Healthy Bibimbap

All of these ingredients can be prepped ahead of time and will take less than 5 minutes to assemble when it's mealtime. Store the ingredients in separate food containers and they will last up to 5 days in the refrigerator.

INGREDIENTS | SERVES 5

4 teaspoons coconut oil, divided

2 pounds extra-lean ground beef

¼ teaspoon sea salt

½ teaspoon freshly ground black pepper

1 tablespoon soy sauce or tamari

10 cups baby spinach

2 cups bean sprouts

5 cups steamed white rice

1½ cups grated carrots

1½ cups julienned cucumbers

1½ cups kimchi

1 tablespoon sesame seeds (for garnish)

¼ cup finely chopped green onions (for garnish)

5 large eggs

1. Heat a large skillet over medium heat and add 1 teaspoon oil. Once oil is hot, add beef and stir 4–5 minutes. Make sure to break up larger chunks of meat into smaller ones while cooking.

2. Add salt, pepper, and soy sauce and stir another minute.

3. Remove from stove, pour into storage container, and set aside.

4. In the same skillet over medium heat add 1 teaspoon oil, then add spinach and stir until wilted. You may need to do this in batches depending on the size of your skillet. Remove and place in another container.

5. In the same skillet over medium heat add 1 teaspoon oil and sprouts. Stir until sprouts are soft. Remove and store in another container.

6. When ready to serve, in a shallow large bowl add 1 cup steamed white rice, ¾ cup meat, and ⅓ cup each carrots, cucumbers, sprouts, and kimchi.

7. Sprinkle on sesame seeds and green onions as garnish.

8. Heat a small skillet over medium heat, fry each egg using remaining oil, and add 1 egg on top of each container to finish off.

PER SERVING Calories: 626 | Fat: 14.3 g | Protein: 55.2 g | Sodium: 944 mg | Fiber: 5.1 g | Carbohydrates: 65.3 g | Sugar: 4.7 g

Slow Cooker Shredded Beef

This beef is great in a salad, served as a main course with your side dishes, or added to a tortilla as a topping for your tacos. Store cooked beef in food containers and refrigerate up to 5 days.

INGREDIENTS | SERVES 8

2 tablespoons chili powder

1 tablespoon garlic powder

1 tablespoon ground cumin

1 teaspoon red pepper flakes

¼ teaspoon sea salt

½ teaspoon freshly ground black pepper

1 (2-pound) beef shoulder roast

2 cups beef broth

5 cloves garlic, peeled

1. In a small bowl mix together chili powder, garlic powder, cumin, red pepper flakes, salt, and black pepper.

2. In a large mixing bowl add beef and seasoning mix and mix until well combined.

3. In a slow cooker add beef, pour broth on top, then add garlic cloves.

4. Cover and cook on high 7 hours.

5. Once cooked, remove meat, use two forks to shred the meat, and put it back into the pot and cook 1 more hour.

6. Remove and store in food containers when completely cooled.

PER SERVING Calories: 158 | Fat: 5.1 g | Protein: 26.0 g | Sodium: 423 mg | Fiber: 1.0 g | Carbohydrates: 2.9 g | Sugar: 0.2 g

Simple Beef Sliders

These are great as appetizers for your next party or can be packed for a hearty lunch. These can be stored in the refrigerator up to 3 days or in the freezer up to a month.

INGREDIENTS | SERVES 5

2 pounds extra-lean ground beef
1 large egg, whisked
1 cup minced onions
½ teaspoon sea salt
½ teaspoon freshly ground black pepper
1 teaspoon ground thyme
1 teaspoon garlic powder
1 tablespoon coconut oil

1. Preheat oven to 350°F. Line a baking sheet with parchment paper.

2. In a large bowl mix beef, egg, onion, salt, pepper, thyme, and garlic powder until well combined. Form 16 sliders (1" thick) and place on a serving plate.

3. Heat a large pan over medium heat and add oil. Once oil is hot, sauté the sliders 2 minutes per side. As the sliders turn brown, transfer them to prepared sheet.

4. Bake 10–12 minutes or until no pink remains in the middle of the patty. Transfer into storage containers to store.

PER SERVING Calories: 261 | Fat: 8.6 g | Protein: 41.6 g | Sodium: 322 mg | Fiber: 0.7 g | Carbohydrates: 3.8 g | Sugar: 1.4 g

Beef Balls with Mint

Mint balls without chocolate might sound weird, but you'll love them. Serve this dish with your favorite greens or other delicious sides. Store in the refrigerator up to 3 days or in the freezer up to a month.

INGREDIENTS | SERVES 5

2 pounds extra-lean ground beef
3 medium shallots, peeled and minced
4 cloves garlic, peeled and minced
¼ cup minced fresh mint
½ teaspoon sea salt
½ teaspoon freshly ground black pepper
½ tablespoon balsamic vinegar
1 tablespoon coconut oil

1. Preheat oven to 350°F. Line a 17" baking pan with parchment paper.

2. In a large bowl mix beef, shallots, garlic, mint, salt, pepper, and vinegar until well combined.

3. Roll meat into 1½"-thick balls and place on a serving plate. Heat a large pan over medium heat and add oil. Once oil is hot, sauté balls 2 minutes per side. Transfer to prepared pan.

4. Bake 10–12 minutes or until no pink remains. Transfer into storage containers.

PER SERVING Calories: 255 | Fat: 7.7 g | Protein: 40.7 g | Sodium: 310 mg | Fiber: 1.0 g | Carbohydrates: 5.4 g | Sugar: 2.2 g

Ginger Beef with Leeks

Stir-fries are great, quick meals to put together, especially when you're crunched for time. Serve this dish with brown or white steamed rice. This dish stores well in the refrigerator and will last up to 5 days.

INGREDIENTS | SERVES 5

2 pounds sliced sirloin

3 cloves garlic, peeled and minced

½ teaspoon sea salt

½ teaspoon freshly ground black pepper

½ tablespoon oyster sauce

1 tablespoon coconut oil

¼ cup julienned fresh ginger

2 cups sliced leeks

Leeks

Leeks are packed with many different vitamins, including vitamins K, A, and C. If you can't find leeks or they're not in season, you can replace them in this recipe with onions.

1. In a medium bowl mix beef, garlic, salt, pepper, and oyster sauce until well combined. Set aside.

2. Heat a large wok or skillet over medium heat and add oil. Once oil is hot, add ginger and stir 1 minute. Add leeks and stir until leeks are soft, 1–2 minutes.

3. Add beef and stir 2–3 minutes or until beef is fully cooked.

4. Transfer into storage containers.

PER SERVING Calories: 418 | Fat: 22.7 g | Protein: 37.6 g | Sodium: 338 mg | Fiber: 0.8 g | Carbohydrates: 6.8 g | Sugar: 1.5 g

Garlic Beef Roast

Beef roasts are great as a main dish, and if you have leftovers you can add them to sandwiches or even soups! If you're tired of beef, try this recipe with pork tenderloin or even pork shoulder meat. This beef will last up to 3 days in the refrigerator.

INGREDIENTS | SERVES 6

1 (3-pound) beef roast
4 cloves garlic, peeled and cut into thin slivers
½ tablespoon minced fresh rosemary
½ teaspoon sea salt
½ teaspoon freshly ground black pepper
1 tablespoon olive oil

1. Preheat oven to 350°F.

2. Allow meat to come to room temperature, 30–60 minutes.

3. Using the tip of your knife, cut slits 1" deep in meat and stuff garlic slivers inside making sure that the garlic is secure.

4. In a small bowl whisk together rosemary, salt, pepper, and oil. Coat roast in oil mixture.

5. Transfer roast to a roasting pan and roast at least 1 hour or to desired doneness.

6. Check temperature using a meat thermometer before removing: 140°F for medium rare, 150°F for medium, or 160°F for well done.

7. Let rest 10 minutes before carving. Place in food containers for storage.

PER SERVING Calories: 361 | Fat: 15.0 g | Protein: 49.3 g | Sodium: 256 mg | Fiber: 0.1 g | Carbohydrates: 0.8 g | Sugar: 0.0 g

Butternut Squash with Spicy Ground Beef

Butternut squash is such a versatile squash, and it'll work with most proteins. This stores well in the refrigerator and will last up to 5 days.

INGREDIENTS | SERVES 5

3 cups peeled and cubed butternut squash

½ tablespoon coconut oil

1 medium onion, peeled and diced

2 pounds extra-lean ground beef

4 cloves garlic, peeled and minced

½ teaspoon salt

½ teaspoon freshly ground black pepper

½ tablespoon red pepper flakes

1 teaspoon paprika

1 teaspoon ground cumin

¼ cup chopped fresh parsley (for garnish)

Butternut Squash

If you don't have time to peel and cut the squash yourself, look for peeled and precut packages in your local grocery store. They're a huge time-saver! Butternut squash is low in carbohydrates and a great source of fiber.

1. Fill a large pot halfway with water and bring to a boil over high heat. Add squash and parboil 2–3 minutes. Remove, strain, and set aside.

2. Heat a large skillet over medium heat and add oil. Once oil is hot, add onions and stir 2–3 minutes or until light brown.

3. Add beef and garlic and stir 3–4 minutes. Add salt, black pepper, red pepper flakes, paprika, and cumin and stir another 2 minutes.

4. Add squash to skillet, stir 1 minute, then cover, lower heat to a simmer, and simmer 4–5 minutes or until squash is soft.

5. Garnish with parsley and place in food containers for storage.

PER SERVING Calories: 273 | Fat: 6.7 g | Protein: 41.3 g | Sodium: 313 mg | Fiber: 2.4 g | Carbohydrates: 13.2 g | Sugar: 2.8 g

Quinoa Beef Stuffed Peppers

Quinoa comes in many varieties and colors, but white, red, and black are the most common. It usually comes with cooking instructions on the package, or if you want to save time and effort, you can also cook it in a rice cooker. This stores well in the refrigerator up to 5 days.

INGREDIENTS | SERVES 5

10 medium red bell peppers

1 tablespoon coconut oil

1 medium onion, peeled and diced

2 pounds extra-lean ground beef

1 cup cooked quinoa

4 cloves garlic, peeled and minced

½ teaspoon salt

½ teaspoon freshly ground black pepper

1 teaspoon garlic powder

¼ cup chopped green onions (for garnish)

1. Preheat oven to 350°F. Line a 17" baking pan with parchment paper.

2. Cut the tops off bell peppers and remove seeds and core. Place peppers on prepared pan and bake 15 minutes. Remove and set aside.

3. Heat a large wok or skillet over medium heat and add oil. Once oil is hot, add onions and stir 2–3 minutes or until lightly brown.

4. Add beef and stir 2–3 minutes. Make sure you use a flat wooden spatula to break up the big pieces into smaller pieces.

5. Add quinoa, garlic, salt, pepper, and garlic powder and stir another 2–3 minutes.

6. Remove from stove and stuff meat mixture evenly into pepper cups. Garnish with green onions.

7. Store in food containers.

PER SERVING Calories: 350 | Fat: 8.6 g | Protein: 44.0 g | Sodium: 364 mg | Fiber: 5.7 g | Carbohydrates: 23.0 g | Sugar: 9.3 g

Spicy Kale Ground Beef

The Thai chilies in this recipe give it a real kick. Serve with steamed brown or white rice. You can replace kale with spinach if you're not a big fan of kale. This recipe stores well and will refrigerate up to 5 days.

INGREDIENTS | SERVES 6

1 tablespoon coconut oil

1 medium onion, peeled and diced

1 cup diced red bell peppers

4 cloves garlic, peeled and minced

2 pounds extra-lean ground beef

½ teaspoon salt

½ teaspoon freshly ground black pepper

2 red Thai chilies, seeded and minced

10 kale leaves, stems removed, chopped

¼ cup chopped fresh cilantro (for garnish)

1. Heat a large skillet over medium heat and add oil. Once oil is hot, add onions and stir 2–3 minutes or until light brown.

2. Add bell peppers and garlic and stir 1–2 minutes. Add beef, salt, black pepper, and chilies and stir 1 minute.

3. Add kale and stir until wilted, 1 minute.

4. Remove, garnish with cilantro, and place in food containers for storage.

PER SERVING Calories: 213 | Fat: 6.5 g | Protein: 34.0 g | Sodium: 296 mg | Fiber: 1.1 g | Carbohydrates: 4.4 g | Sugar: 2.0 g

Curry Cinnamon Ground Beef

Cinnamon is not a common pairing with beef, but it definitely should be because these two pair very well together. Serve this beef over steamed brown or white rice and sides or on top of salads. Store this in a food container and refrigerate up to 5 days.

INGREDIENTS | SERVES 5

1 tablespoon coconut oil

1 medium onion, peeled and minced

4 cloves garlic, peeled and minced

½ tablespoon grated fresh ginger

2 pounds extra-lean ground beef

½ teaspoon salt

½ teaspoon freshly ground black pepper

1½ tablespoons ground cinnamon

1 tablespoon yellow curry powder

¼ cup chopped green onions (for garnish)

1. Heat a large skillet over medium heat and add oil. Once oil is hot, add onions and stir 2–3 minutes or until light brown.

2. Add garlic, ginger, and beef and stir 3–4 minutes. Add salt, pepper, cinnamon, and curry powder and stir 2 minutes or until beef is cooked.

3. Remove and garnish with green onions and place in food containers for storage.

PER SERVING Calories: 259 | Fat: 8.4 g | Protein: 40.7 g | Sodium: 122 mg | Fiber: 2.5 g | Carbohydrates: 5.8 g | Sugar: 1.2 g

Tomato Basil Beef Meatloaf

Meatloaf is a culinary staple that you can pair with so many things.
Meatloaf also stores very well in the refrigerator up to a week.

INGREDIENTS | SERVES 8

2 pounds extra-lean ground beef

½ tablespoon coconut oil

1 tablespoon coconut flour

¼ cup tomato paste

⅓ cup chopped fresh basil

2 large eggs, whisked

½ tablespoon garlic powder

1 medium onion, peeled and minced

½ teaspoon sea salt

½ teaspoon freshly ground black pepper

1 tablespoon minced fresh basil (for garnish)

Topping

Because this is a healthier version of meat-loaf there is no sauce on top. But if you need something extra on top, try whisking together equal amounts of tomato paste and apple cider vinegar and brush it on top before cooking.

1. Preheat oven to 375°F.

2. In a large bowl add beef, oil, flour, tomato paste, chopped basil, eggs, garlic powder, onions, salt, and pepper and mix until well combined.

3. Pour mixture into a 9" loaf pan and bake 40–45 minutes or until meat is thoroughly cooked. To ensure it is cooked through, poke a toothpick through the meat; if it comes out clean, it is cooked.

4. Remove and garnish with minced basil. Let cool 15–20 minutes.

5. Once cool, cut up into portion servings and store in food containers.

PER SERVING Calories: 173 | Fat: 5.3 g | Protein: 27.3 g | Sodium: 277 mg | Fiber: 1.0 g | Carbohydrates: 3.9 g | Sugar: 1.7 g

CHAPTER 7

Pork

Chinese Five-Spice Pork Chops

Pork chops are great to prep, and they cook easily in the oven or on the grill in the summer. They also store well and the meat remains very juicy. Serve these chops over steamed brown or white rice. Store these in a food storage container up to 5 days.

INGREDIENTS | SERVES 5

2 pounds pork chops
1 tablespoon five-spice powder
1 tablespoon soy sauce or tamari
1 teaspoon garlic powder

Five-Spice Powder

The longer the chops season for, the better they will taste. But if you don't have a lot of time, then let sit at least 2 hours. Five-spice powder can be purchased in an Asian market if you can't find it in the spice section of your grocery store. The five spices consist of cinnamon, cloves, fennel, star anise, and Szechuan peppercorns.

1. In a large mixing bowl add pork, five-spice powder, soy sauce, and garlic powder and mix until well combined. Let marinate in the refrigerator at least 2 hours before cooking, or for best results, refrigerate overnight before cooking.

2. Preheat oven to 350°F. Line a 17" baking pan with parchment paper.

3. Transfer pork to prepared pan and bake 30–35 minutes, depending on the thickness of the meat. Make sure they're cooked thoroughly before removing. Ensure doneness by using a thermometer to check that the temperature reaches at least 145°F.

4. Remove and place in food containers for storage.

PER SERVING Calories: 360 | Fat: 20.3 g | Protein: 36.0 g | Sodium: 334 mg | Fiber: 0.3 g | Carbohydrates: 1.7 g | Sugar: 0.6 g

Rosemary Almond-Crusted Pork Tenderloin

Pork tenderloin goes well with roasted root vegetables and is also good on top of a salad. Store this in a food container and refrigerate up to 3 days. You can also pair this with Mango Chutney (see Chapter 10).

INGREDIENTS | SERVES 5

1 (2-pound) pork tenderloin
1 tablespoon coconut oil
1 tablespoon minced fresh rosemary
1 teaspoon paprika
1 teaspoon garlic powder
1 teaspoon onion powder
½ teaspoon salt
½ teaspoon freshly ground black pepper
¾ cup chopped almonds

Tenderloin

This is one of the leanest cuts of pork so be careful about overcooking it. Keep an eye on the pork's temperature because cooking time will vary depending on thickness of the meat.

1. Preheat to 375°F.

2. Bring pork to room temperature by removing it from the refrigerator half an hour before cooking.

3. In a small bowl mix the oil, rosemary, paprika, garlic powder, onion powder, salt, and pepper. Set aside.

4. Use a food processor and pulse almonds until finely chopped. Transfer to a plate.

5. Coat pork with oil mixture then coat with chopped almonds.

6. Transfer pork to a 17" baking pan and bake 35–40 minutes. Check the pork's temperature frequently to ensure it does not overcook. Once it reaches 145°F, remove from oven.

7. Let rest at least 15 minutes before slicing for storage.

PER SERVING Calories: 371 | Fat: 15.0 g | Protein: 50.8 g | Sodium: 336 mg | Fiber: 2.2 g | Carbohydrates: 4.4 g | Sugar: 0.7 g

Slow Cooker Pulled Pork Burrito Bowls

The beauty of this bowl is you can add any of your favorite toppings to make a flavorful, healthy meal. Store this in a food container and refrigerate up to 5 days.

INGREDIENTS | SERVES 4

Pulled Pork:

1 (1½-pound) pork butt or shoulder

3 cloves garlic, peeled and minced

2 tablespoons lime juice

2 tablespoons ground cumin

2 tablespoons paprika

1 tablespoon chili powder

½ teaspoon sea salt

1 teaspoon freshly ground black pepper

1 medium jalapeño pepper, seeded and minced

1 medium onion, peeled and chopped

2 tablespoons tomato paste

1 cup chicken broth

Toppings:

1 cup canned corn

1 cup canned black or red beans

4 cups chopped romaine lettuce

1 cup seeded and diced tomatoes

½ cup diced red onion

½ cup chopped fresh cilantro

4 lime wedges

1. In a slow cooker add pork, garlic, lime juice, cumin, paprika, chili powder, salt, pepper, jalapeño, chopped onion, tomato paste, and broth. Cook on low 6 hours.

2. After 6 hours remove pork and use two forks to shred pork, then place shredded pork back into slow cooker and cook 1 more hour.

3. In each food container, bowl, or Mason jar assemble your burrito bowl by adding ¼ cup corn, ¼ cup beans, 1 cup lettuce, ¼ cup diced tomato, ⅛ cup diced onion, ¾ cup pork, and top off with ⅛ cup cilantro and a lime wedge.

4. For storage, pack pulled pork separately until time of serving.

PER SERVING Calories: 387 | Fat: 10.6 g | Protein: 40.4 g | Sodium: 1,018 mg | Fiber: 10.5 g | Carbohydrates: 31.9 g | Sugar: 7.0 g

Toppings

You can also cut a quarter of an avocado and add it on top right before serving. If you are using a Mason jar, remember to layer the tomatoes at the bottom of the jar and lettuce and cilantro on top.

Pork Sausage Patties

These are great for breakfast with sweet potatoes, a side of greens, and some eggs. They also store well in the refrigerator. Keep in food containers and store up to 5 days.

INGREDIENTS | SERVES 4

2 pounds lean ground pork

½ teaspoon ground sage

1 teaspoon garlic powder

½ teaspoon ground thyme

½ teaspoon onion powder

½ teaspoon salt

½ teaspoon freshly ground black pepper

½ teaspoon paprika

½ medium onion, peeled and minced

3 cloves garlic, peeled and minced

1 tablespoon coconut oil

1. Preheat to 350°F. Line baking sheet with parchment paper.

2. In a large bowl add pork, sage, garlic powder, thyme, onion powder, salt, pepper, paprika, minced onion, minced garlic, and oil and mix until well combined.

3. Form 16 equal mini patties and place on prepared sheet. Bake 15–20 minutes or until temperature reaches 145°F. Check with meat thermometer before removing.

4. Remove, set aside to cool, and then pack in storage containers.

PER SERVING Calories: 313 | Fat: 12.3 g | Protein: 48.3 g | Sodium: 442 mg | Fiber: 0.4 g | Carbohydrates: 2.5 g | Sugar: 0.1 g

Pork and Garlic Scapes Stir-Fry

Garlic scapes are mild and sweet, very similar to chives and scallions but with a hint of garlicky taste. Serve with white or brown rice or with your favorite sides. This dish stores well in the refrigerator in food containers up to 5 days.

INGREDIENTS | SERVES 5

1 tablespoon coconut oil

1 teaspoon grated fresh ginger

2 cloves garlic, peeled and minced

1 (1½-pound) pork center loin, sliced

3 cups garlic scapes, chopped into 1½" sticks

¼ teaspoon sea salt

½ tablespoon soy sauce or tamari

¼ tablespoon freshly ground black pepper

½ tablespoon water

1. Heat a large wok or skillet over medium heat and add oil. Once oil is hot, add ginger and garlic and stir-fry 30 seconds.

2. Add pork and stir 3–4 minutes.

3. Add garlic scapes, salt, soy sauce, pepper, and water and stir another 2–3 minutes.

4. Remove from stove and place in storage containers.

PER SERVING Calories: 232 | Fat: 6.6 g | Protein: 31.0 g | Sodium: 271 mg | Fiber: 1.1 g | Carbohydrates: 8.3 g | Sugar: 2.1 g

Rosemary Garlic Pork Chops

These can be baked in the winter and grilled on your barbecue grill in the summer. Pork chops are best baked or grilled; when cooked they store up to 3 days in the refrigerator.

INGREDIENTS | SERVES 5

3 cloves garlic, peeled and minced

½ tablespoon minced fresh rosemary

½ teaspoon sea salt

1 teaspoon freshly ground black pepper

½ teaspoon garlic powder

¼ cup balsamic vinegar

¼ cup Worcestershire sauce

1 tablespoon olive oil

2 pounds pork chops or 1 (2-pound) center loin, sliced 1" thick

Worcestershire Sauce

If you don't have Worcestershire sauce, you can substitute tamari or coconut aminos. If you don't have any of these, then use more balsamic vinegar. This recipe would be great with chicken breasts as well or other cuts of pork like tenderloin.

1. In a small bowl whisk together garlic, rosemary, salt, pepper, garlic powder, vinegar, Worcestershire sauce, and oil.

2. In a large mixing bowl combine marinade with pork and mix until well combined. Let marinate at least 2 hours or overnight for best results.

3. Preheat oven to 350°F. Line a 17" baking pan with parchment paper.

4. Put pork on top of parchment paper and bake 30–35 minutes or until pork is no longer pink. Ensure doneness by using a thermometer to check that the temperature reaches 145°F before removing.

5. Remove and set aside to cool.

6. Place in storage containers and refrigerate.

PER SERVING Calories: 402 | Fat: 22.8 g | Protein: 35.8 g | Sodium: 449 mg | Fiber: 0.2 g | Carbohydrates: 6.0 g | Sugar: 3.3 g

Lime Cilantro Tenderloin

Love lime? Try zesting one of the limes and add it to the marinade too. This tenderloin is best baked or grilled the same day; when cooked it stores up to 3 days in the refrigerator.

INGREDIENTS | SERVES 5

1 tablespoon olive oil
½ teaspoon sea salt
½ teaspoon freshly ground black pepper
3 medium limes, juiced
½ teaspoon ground cumin
2 cloves garlic, peeled and minced
½ cup chopped fresh cilantro
1 (2-pound) pork tenderloin

1. In a food processor pulse oil, salt, pepper, lime juice, cumin, garlic, and cilantro until smooth.

2. Put tenderloin in a large zip-top bag; pour in marinade and rub into meat to ensure meat is coated all over.

3. Marinate in refrigerator 2–3 hours or for best results overnight.

4. Preheat oven to 350°F. Line a 17" baking pan with parchment paper.

5. Transfer pork to prepared pan and bake 35–40 minutes or until pork is no longer pink. Ensure doneness by using a thermometer to check that the temperature reaches 145°F before removing.

6. Remove and set aside to cool before slicing up to serving sizes.

7. Place in storage containers and refrigerate.

PER SERVING Calories: 289 | Fat: 8.2 g | Protein: 47.7 g | Sodium: 291 mg | Fiber: 0.2 g | Carbohydrates: 2.0 g | Sugar: 0.3 g

Vietnamese Lemongrass Grilled Pork Chops

Lemongrass is so refreshing and fragrant, and it also has lots of health benefits too. This dish stores well in the refrigerator. Keep it in food containers and refrigerate up to 5 days.

INGREDIENTS | SERVES 5

½ cup chopped lemongrass

3 cloves garlic, peeled

1 teaspoon garlic powder

½ teaspoon onion powder

1 tablespoon soy sauce or tamari

½ teaspoon freshly ground black pepper

1 teaspoon honey

1 tablespoon oyster sauce

½ tablespoon water

1 teaspoon Chinese five-spice powder

2 pounds pork chops or 1 (2-pound) pork center loin

Lemongrass

Lemongrass can be purchased fresh in Asian markets. It comes in large stalks that are hard to cut. Cut lemongrass stalks into rounds and then freeze for future uses.

1. In a food processor or spice grinder process lemongrass and garlic until finely ground.

2. Pour lemongrass mixture into a medium bowl and add garlic powder, onion powder, soy sauce, pepper, honey, oyster sauce, water, and five-spice powder. Whisk until well combined. Set aside.

3. Put pork chops in a large zip-top bag, pour the marinade into the bag, and rub marinade into the meat to make sure it's well coated.

4. Marinate in refrigerator 2–3 hours or for best results overnight.

5. Preheat grill on high heat.

6. Grill, basting with reserved marinade, 3–4 minutes per side or until thoroughly cooked (this depends on the thickness). Ensure doneness by using a thermometer to check that the temperature reaches 145°F before removing.

7. Remove and set aside to cool.

8. Place into storage containers and refrigerate.

PER SERVING Calories: 373 | Fat: 20.3 g | Protein: 36.3 g | Sodium: 410 mg | Fiber: 0.3 g | Carbohydrates: 5.1 g | Sugar: 1.4 g

Slow Cooker Balsamic Pulled Pork

Can't think of how to serve this? Change it up and serve this over a burrito bowl with your favorite toppings. You can also use this as a topping on your tacos or burritos. A healthier option is to serve this over a big salad. This dish stores well in the refrigerator up to 5 days.

INGREDIENTS | SERVES 6

½ cup balsamic vinegar

1 tablespoon soy sauce or tamari

½ tablespoon freshly ground black pepper

1 tablespoon maple syrup

1 tablespoon paprika

½ tablespoon red pepper flakes

½ teaspoon sea salt

1 (3-pound) pork center loin

4 cloves garlic, peeled, mashed, and chopped

1 medium onion, peeled and cut into wedges

2 cups chicken broth

1. In a medium bowl whisk together the vinegar, soy sauce, black pepper, maple syrup, paprika, red pepper flakes, and salt. Set aside.

2. In a slow cooker add pork, garlic, onions, and chicken broth. Then pour vinegar mixture all over the pork ensuring it's well covered.

3. Cook on low 7 hours.

4. Remove meat and transfer to a plate. With two forks shred pork and then put it back into the slow cooker and cook 1 more hour on low.

5. Let cool, then store in containers.

PER SERVING Calories: 335 | Fat: 6.6 g | Protein: 51.3 g | Sodium: 748 mg | Fiber: 0.9 g | Carbohydrates: 9.5 g | Sugar: 6.4 g

Crispy Pecan Pork Chops

You can use bread crumbs or panko as a traditional breading, but for a healthier, more nutritious breading use chopped nuts instead. You can replace pecans with almonds, walnuts, or cashews as well. This dish stores well in the refrigerator up to 3 days.

INGREDIENTS | SERVES 6

1 cup pecans

3 tablespoons milled flaxseed

1 teaspoon paprika

¼ teaspoon ground cayenne pepper

½ teaspoon sea salt

2 large eggs, whisked

1 teaspoon soy sauce or tamari

2 pounds pork chops

2 tablespoons coconut oil

1. In a food processor pulse pecans until finely chopped. You can also put pecans in a zip-top bag and use a meat pounder to crush finely. Place pecans on a large plate.

2. In a shallow bowl mix together flaxseed, paprika, cayenne, and salt.

3. In another shallow bowl whisk together eggs and soy sauce.

4. Dip each pork chop into flaxseed mixture, then egg mixture, and coat it with crushed pecans. Place on plate and continue until all chops are coated.

5. Heat a large skillet or frying pan over medium heat and add oil. Once oil is hot, fry chops 8 minutes or until the internal temperature reaches 145°F.

6. Let cool, then store in food containers.

PER SERVING Calories: 480 | Fat: 34.2 g | Protein: 34.0 g | Sodium: 333 mg | Fiber: 2.7 g | Carbohydrates: 3.7 g | Sugar: 0.8 g

Paleo Stuffed Pork Tenderloin

It's so hard to find a stuffed protein recipe without cheese in it. This dish is gluten-free and paleo compliant. It stores well in the refrigerator up to 5 days.

INGREDIENTS | SERVES 5

½ tablespoon coconut oil

1 cup sliced mushrooms

½ cup sliced onions

1 tablespoon minced fresh rosemary, divided

1 teaspoon minced fresh thyme, divided

3 cloves garlic, peeled and chopped

1 teaspoon sea salt, divided

1 teaspoon freshly ground black pepper, divided

2 cups baby spinach

1 (2-pound) pork tenderloin

Adding Cheese

You can add a soft cheese like feta into the stuffing if you do not follow a paleo or dairy-free diet. This can make the pork even more juicy to cut into. But be careful of the added calories and fat in cheese.

1. Preheat oven to 375°F. Line a 16" baking pan with parchment paper.

2. Heat a medium pan over medium heat and add oil. Once oil is hot, add mushrooms, onions, ½ tablespoon rosemary, ½ tablespoon thyme, and garlic and stir 2 minutes. Add ½ teaspoon salt, ½ teaspoon pepper, and spinach and stir until spinach is wilted. Set aside.

3. Butterfly pork by slicing down the center, but don't cut all the way through, and open up like a book.

4. Use a meat tenderizer and pound until ½" thick. Season meat with remaining salt, pepper, rosemary, and thyme.

5. Spread spinach mixture over pork, then roll up and secure with toothpicks or tie with kitchen twine.

6. Place on prepared pan and bake 45 minutes or until temperature of the meat reaches 145°F. Use a meat thermometer to check before removing.

7. Let cool, remove toothpicks or twine, then slice into 1" rounds.

8. Store in food containers.

PER SERVING Calories: 285 | Fat: 6.9 g | Protein: 48.6 g | Sodium: 488 mg | Fiber: 0.8 g | Carbohydrates: 3.0 g | Sugar: 0.8 g

Thanksgiving Pork Tenderloin

This will make your house smell like Thanksgiving, except this meat is much juicier and harder to dry out than the conventional roast turkey. This is best served immediately; however it will still store well in the refrigerator up to 3 days.

INGREDIENTS | SERVES 5

½ tablespoon coconut oil

½ cup sliced onions

1 cup peeled and sliced butternut squash

3 cloves garlic, peeled and chopped

½ cup diced apples (any kind)

2 tablespoons cranberry sauce

½ teaspoon sea salt, divided

½ teaspoon freshly ground black pepper, divided

1 tablespoon minced fresh rosemary, divided

2 cups baby spinach

1 tablespoon olive oil

1 teaspoon ground thyme

1 teaspoon ground sage

1 (2-pound) pork tenderloin

Turkey

If you're looking for something that's lower in fat content, you can use the same recipe to stuff turkey breasts as well. If turkey breasts are hard to find, then use chicken breasts; they work just as well.

1. Preheat oven to 375°F. Line a 16" baking pan with parchment paper.

2. Heat a medium pan over medium heat and add oil. Once oil is hot, add onions and sauté 2 minutes. Add squash, garlic, apples, and cranberry sauce and stir another 3–4 minutes. Add ¼ teaspoon salt, ¼ teaspoon pepper, ½ tablespoon rosemary, and spinach and stir until spinach is wilted. Set aside.

3. In a small bowl whisk oil, remaining rosemary, thyme, sage, and remaining salt and pepper until combined.

4. Butterfly pork by slicing down the center, but don't cut all the way through, and open up like a book.

5. Use a meat tenderizer and pound until ½" thick. Season meat with rosemary-oil mixture, making sure meat is well coated.

6. Spread spinach mix all over pork, then roll meat up and secure with toothpicks or tie with kitchen twine.

7. Place on prepared baking pan and bake 45 minutes or until temperature of the meat reaches 145°F. Use a meat thermometer to check before removing.

8. Let cool, remove toothpicks or twine, then slice into 1" rounds.

9. Store in food containers.

PER SERVING Calories: 335 | Fat: 9.5 g | Protein: 48.5 g | Sodium: 303 mg | Fiber: 1.7 g | Carbohydrates: 10.2 g | Sugar: 5.1 g

CHAPTER 8

Mason Jar Salads

Taco in a Jar

This is one of the most satisfying meals you'll have. You can also shake it up and eat it right out of the jar. This dish keeps well in the refrigerator up to 5 days.

INGREDIENTS | SERVES 1

3 tablespoons plain Greek yogurt

3 tablespoons Pico de Gallo (see Chapter 11)

¼ cup diced tomatoes

⅛ cup diced red onions

¼ cup chopped bell peppers

2 tablespoons canned corn

2 tablespoons red kidney beans or black beans

1 tablespoon sliced black olives

¾ cup Mexican Ground Turkey (see Chapter 5)

⅛ cup chopped fresh cilantro

1 cup mixed field greens

1. In a 32-ounce Mason jar layer ingredients in the following order: yogurt, Pico de Gallo, tomatoes, onions, peppers, corn, beans, olives, turkey, cilantro, and greens.

2. Close lid and refrigerate.

3. When ready to serve, shake it up and enjoy straight out of the jar or pour into a large bowl and enjoy.

PER SERVING Calories: 356 | Fat: 6.8 g | Protein: 52.1 g | Sodium: 580 mg | Fiber: 6.3 g | Carbohydrates: 24.2 g | Sugar: 7.9 g

Layering Your Mason Jar

Mason jar salads can last all week depending on how you layer them. Here are some tips for layering your jars: First pack all of the wet ingredients like dressing, salsa, or chopped tomatoes at the bottom. Next add the harder vegetables like carrots and peppers. Then add the protein like ground meat or chicken. Add the leafy greens or herbs at the top (this will keep them nice and dry). You can also add cheese as a topping to this jar.

Taco in a Jar (Chapter 8)

Easy Gluten-Free Protein Pancakes (Chapter 16)

Shakshuka (Chapter 16)

Ground Beef Stuffed Peppers (Chapter 6)

Quinoa Israeli Salad (Chapter 9)

Perfectly Roasted Japanese Sweet Potatoes
(Chapter 11)

Turkey Burgers (Chapter 5)

Parchment Paper Baked Salmon (Chapter 16)

Fresh Spring Rolls (Chapter 14)

Egg Whites and Chicken Muffins (Chapter 2)

Rob's Roasted Potatoes (Chapter 11)

Slow Cooker Pulled Pork Burrito Bowls (Chapter 7)

Mushroom Kale Oats (Chapter 3)

Mom's Lemongrass Chicken (Chapter 5)

Sausage and Potato Skillet (Chapter 13)

Tropical Oats (Chapter 3)

Spicy Pickled Cabbage Slaw (Chapter 11)

Grilled Steak with Spicy Chimichurri (Chapter 16)

Cajun Sweet Potato Wedges (Chapter 11)

Pear Spinach Smoothie (Chapter 4)

Cinnamon Roasted Butternut Squash (Chapter 11)

Asian Chicken Lettuce Wraps (Chapter 5)

Protein Coconut Chia Seed Pudding (Chapter 15)

Sweet Potato Egg Bowls (Chapter 2)

Chicken with Olive Dressing

If you love olives, this is a good salad to try. This recipe keeps well in the refrigerator up to 3 days.

INGREDIENTS | SERVES 1

1 tablespoon Olive Tapenade Dressing (see Chapter 10)

¼ cup thinly sliced fennel

½ cup chopped baby cucumbers

½ cup cherry tomatoes

1 cup Simple Oven-Baked Chicken Breasts (see Chapter 5)

1 cup baby arugula

1. In a 32-ounce jar layer ingredients in the following order: dressing, fennel, cucumbers, tomatoes, chicken, and arugula.

2. Close lid and refrigerate.

3. When ready to serve, shake it up and enjoy straight out of the jar or pour into a large bowl and enjoy.

PER SERVING Calories: 345 | Fat: 11.9 g | Protein: 47.9 g | Sodium: 848 mg | Fiber: 3.4 g | Carbohydrates: 9.9 g | Sugar: 5.9 g

Sumac Shrimp Zoodles

Who doesn't love shrimp? These little gems are low in fat and high in protein. They are also a great addition to salads. These zoodles keep well in the refrigerator up to 5 days.

INGREDIENTS | SERVES 1

1 tablespoon Sumac Vinaigrette (see Chapter 10)

½ cup spiralized carrots

1 cup spiralized zucchini

½ cup thinly sliced jicama

½ cup chopped red bell peppers

¼ cup chopped parsley

⅔ cup shrimp (5 or 6), boiled

1. In a 32-ounce jar, layer ingredients in the following order: dressing, carrots, zucchini, jicama, peppers, parsley, and shrimp.

2. Close lid and refrigerate.

3. When ready to serve, shake it up and enjoy straight out of the jar or pour into a large bowl and enjoy.

PER SERVING Calories: 154 | Fat: 3.5 g | Protein: 9.4 g | Sodium: 396 mg | Fiber: 8.4 g | Carbohydrates: 21.5 g | Sugar: 10.3 g

Shrimp

If you're in a rush, you can either buy shrimp that have the shells already removed or simply buy precooked ones. This will speed up your prep quite a lot.

Roasted Beets Egg Salad

You can't beat beets when it comes to a great root vegetable with nutrients and tons of fiber. You can also add other proteins like chicken or ground turkey to this jar to give it variety. This salad keeps well in the refrigerator up to 5 days.

INGREDIENTS | SERVES 1

⅛ cup Simple Balsamic Dressing (see Chapter 10)

1 cup Oven-Roasted Beets (see Chapter 11)

½ cup diced celery

¼ cup shredded carrots

¼ cup chopped fresh parsley

2 large hard-boiled eggs, chopped

1. In a 32-ounce jar layer ingredients in the following order: dressing, beets, celery, carrots, parsley, and eggs.

2. Close lid and refrigerate.

3. When ready to serve, shake it up and enjoy straight out of the jar or pour into a large bowl and enjoy.

PER SERVING Calories: 289 | Fat: 12.9 g | Protein: 15.9 g | Sodium: 437 mg | Fiber: 6.0 g | Carbohydrates: 23.2 g | Sugar: 15.6 g

Vegan Quinoa Salad

Need a meatless Monday salad that's filling? Try this one out. This dish keeps well in the refrigerator up to 5 days.

INGREDIENTS | SERVES 1

⅛ cup Simple Balsamic Dressing (see Chapter 10)

½ cup diced red bell peppers

½ cup seeded and diced tomatoes

½ cup seeded and diced cucumbers

⅔ cup Basic Steamed Quinoa (see Chapter 11)

¼ cup chopped parsley

¼ medium avocado, pitted, flesh removed, and sliced (for serving)

1 lemon wedge (for serving)

1. In a 32-ounce jar layer ingredients in the following order: dressing, peppers, tomatoes, cucumbers, quinoa, and parsley.

2. Close lid and refrigerate.

3. When ready to serve, shake it up, add avocado, and squeeze the lemon on top. Enjoy straight out of the jar or pour into a large bowl.

PER SERVING Calories: 285 | Fat: 9.7 g | Protein: 8.4 g | Sodium: 152 mg | Fiber: 8.6 g | Carbohydrates: 41.2 g | Sugar: 9.7 g

Healthy Taco Tuesday Jar

This is a dairy-free option, and the addition of jalapeños gives this dish a little kick. This salad keeps well in the refrigerator up to 5 days. As an option you can add ¼ of an avocado on top at time of serving.

INGREDIENTS | SERVES 1

⅛ cup Lime Vinaigrette (see Chapter 10)

½ cup diced bell peppers

¼ cup shredded purple cabbage

¼ cup seeded and diced tomatoes

¾ cup Mexican Ground Turkey (see Chapter 5)

2 tablespoons canned red kidney beans

2 tablespoons canned corn

3 or 4 sliced jalapeño rounds

½ cup chopped kale

¼ cup chopped fresh cilantro

⅛ cup chopped green onions

1. In a 32-ounce jar layer ingredients in the following order: dressing, peppers, cabbage, tomatoes, turkey, beans, corn, jalapeño, kale, cilantro, and onions.

2. Close lid and refrigerate.

3. When ready to serve, shake it up and enjoy straight out of the jar or pour into a large bowl.

PER SERVING Calories: 349 | Fat: 7.8 g | Protein: 47.9 g | Sodium: 515 mg | Fiber: 6.7 g | Carbohydrates: 23.9 g | Sugar: 8.8 g

Kale

If you want to make your kale softer to eat, chop it up, sprinkle it with a bit of sea salt, and hand massage the leaves for a few minutes before putting them into the salad. You can use this method to prepare kale salad as well.

Paleo Taco Tuesday Jar

This recipe is free of legumes and dairy, so it's great if you're looking for something that's paleo or Whole30 approved. As an option you can add ¼ of an avocado on top at time of serving. This dish keeps well in the refrigerator up to 5 days.

INGREDIENTS | SERVES 1

⅛ cup Lime Vinaigrette (see Chapter 10)
¼ cup seeded and diced tomatoes
¼ cup shredded purple cabbage
½ cup diced bell peppers
¾ cup Taco Tuesday Beef (see Chapter 6)
1 cup baby spinach
¼ cup chopped fresh cilantro
⅛ cup chopped green onions

Dressing

If you're looking to minimize fat and sodium, skip the dressing and just add a wedge of lime or lemon at time of serving. The juice along with the seasoned beef should be enough to make this dish very tasty.

1. In a 32-ounce jar layer ingredients in the following order: dressing, tomatoes, cabbage, peppers, beef, spinach, cilantro, and onions.

2. Close lid and refrigerate.

3. When ready to serve, shake it up and enjoy straight out of the jar or pour into a large bowl.

PER SERVING Calories: 366 | Fat: 11.4 g | Protein: 44.8 g | Sodium: 440 mg | Fiber: 7.4 g | Carbohydrates: 22.7 g | Sugar: 12.7 g

Protein Jar

If you're looking for a jar with a variety of protein sources, then this is worth a try. As an option you can add ¼ of an avocado on top at time of serving. This jar keeps well in the refrigerator up to 5 days.

INGREDIENTS | SERVES 1

⅛ cup Lime Vinaigrette (see Chapter 10)
¼ cup canned pinto beans
½ cup diced bell peppers
¼ cup seeded and diced tomatoes
⅛ cup julienned radish
½ cup Mexican Ground Turkey (see Chapter 5)
1 hard-boiled egg, chopped
½ cup Basic Steamed Quinoa (see Chapter 11)
⅛ cup chopped fresh cilantro

1. In a 32-ounce jar layer ingredients in the following order: dressing, beans, bell peppers, tomatoes, radish, turkey, egg, quinoa, and cilantro.

2. Close lid and refrigerate.

3. When ready to serve, shake it up and enjoy straight out of the jar or pour into a large bowl.

PER SERVING Calories: 479 | Fat: 12.2 g | Protein: 45.1 g | Sodium: 614 mg | Fiber: 10.5 g | Carbohydrates: 45.4 g | Sugar: 11.2 g

Cubed Vegetables Salad

This salad is full of crunch. Add some nuts on top for a bigger crunch. This salad keeps well in the refrigerator up to 5 days.

INGREDIENTS | SERVES 1

⅛ cup Sumac Vinaigrette (see Chapter 10)
½ cup diced celery
½ cup diced carrots
½ cup diced zucchini
¼ cup seeded and diced tomatoes
¾ cup Taco Tuesday Beef (see Chapter 6)
¼ cup chopped fresh parsley

1. In a 32-ounce jar layer ingredients in the following order: dressing, celery, carrots, zucchini, tomatoes, beef, and parsley.

2. Close lid and refrigerate.

3. When ready to serve, shake it up and enjoy straight out of the jar or pour into a large bowl.

PER SERVING Calories: 371 | Fat: 14.3 g | Protein: 43.8 g | Sodium: 581 mg | Fiber: 6.4 g | Carbohydrates: 18.0 g | Sugar: 8.1 g

Simple Mason Jar Salad

*This salad has only six simple ingredients and is easy to make.
It also keeps well in the refrigerator up to 5 days.*

INGREDIENTS | SERVES 1

⅛ cup Simple Balsamic Dressing (see Chapter 10)

½ cup diced bell peppers

¼ cup chopped Spanish onions

½ cup cherry tomatoes

¾ cup Taco Tuesday Beef (see Chapter 6)

2 cups mixed greens

1. In a 32-ounce jar layer ingredients in the following order: dressing, peppers, onions, cherry tomatoes, beef, and mixed greens.

2. Close lid and refrigerate.

3. When ready to serve, shake it up and enjoy straight out of the jar or pour into a large bowl.

PER SERVING Calories: 358 | Fat: 11.4 g | Protein: 44.0 g | Sodium: 412 mg | Fiber: 5.7 g | Carbohydrates: 21.5 g | Sugar: 11.6 g

Apple Walnut Salad

*Need a vegan option for your salads? Here is a nutty one! If you do eat meat and need more protein,
add some baked chicken or boiled eggs. This salad keeps well in the refrigerator up to 5 days.*

INGREDIENTS | SERVES 1

¼ cup Almond Butter Vinaigrette (see Chapter 10)

½ cup diced celery

¼ cup diced bell peppers

¼ cup thinly sliced radishes

¼ medium green apple, sliced

⅓ cup walnuts

2 cups mixed greens

¼ cup chopped fresh cilantro

1. In a 32-ounce jar layer ingredients in the following: dressing, celery, peppers, radish, apples, walnuts, greens, and cilantro.

2. Close lid and refrigerate.

3. When ready to serve, shake it up and enjoy straight out of the jar or pour into a large bowl.

PER SERVING Calories: 727 | Fat: 56.6 g | Protein: 17.6 g | Sodium: 265 mg | Fiber: 11.7 g | Carbohydrates: 38.0 g | Sugar: 20.3 g

Roasted Beets and Quinoa

This jarred salad is a great vegetarian option that's full of protein.
This dish keeps well in the refrigerator up to 5 days.

INGREDIENTS | SERVES 1

⅛ cup Simple Balsamic Dressing (see Chapter 10)

½ cup Oven-Roasted Beets (see Chapter 11)

½ cup Basic Steamed Quinoa (see Chapter 11)

½ cup cherry tomatoes

2 cups mixed greens

¼ cup chopped fresh cilantro

⅛ cup sliced almonds

1 teaspoon lemon zest

1. In a 32-ounce jar layer ingredients in the following order: dressing, beets, quinoa, tomatoes, greens, cilantro, almonds, and zest.

2. Close lid and refrigerate.

3. When ready to serve, shake it up and enjoy straight out of the jar or pour into a large bowl.

PER SERVING Calories: 268 | Fat: 10.6 g | Protein: 9.4 g | Sodium: 225 mg | Fiber: 7.6 g | Carbohydrates: 36.5 g | Sugar: 10.9 g

Nuts

You can also use crushed almonds or pine nuts if you don't have sliced almonds. To keep your nuts extra crunchy, keep them in separate smaller containers and only add to the salad right before serving.

Asian Zoodle Crunch

Love nutty Asian noodle take-out dishes? This is a great guilt-free option, and it's also calorie and carb friendly. This dish keeps well in the refrigerator up to 3 days.

INGREDIENTS | SERVES 1

⅛ cup Almond Butter Vinaigrette (see Chapter 10)

1 cup spiralized zucchini

½ cup shredded carrots

¼ cup cooked edamame beans

¼ cup diced bell peppers

⅔ cup Simple Oven-Baked Chicken Breasts (see Chapter 5)

¼ cup chopped fresh cilantro

1. In a 32-ounce jar layer ingredients in the following order: dressing, zucchini, carrots, beans, peppers, chicken, and cilantro.

2. Close lid and refrigerate.

3. When ready to serve, shake it up and enjoy straight out of the jar or pour into a large bowl.

PER SERVING Calories: 660 | Fat: 31.8 g | Protein: 55.3 g | Sodium: 571 mg | Fiber: 10.8 g | Carbohydrates: 36.2 g | Sugar: 16.5 g

Vegetarian Options

If you're vegetarian, you can substitute boiled eggs or steamed quinoa for the chicken. Alternatively, you can get creative and add mixed beans or even chickpeas to your salad. The flavors are complementary to almond butter.

Eggs and Pear Salad

You can also use walnuts, pine nuts, or pecans in this salad if you don't have almonds. Use an egg slicer to speed up the process of chopping the eggs. This salad keeps well in the refrigerator up to 5 days.

INGREDIENTS | SERVES 1

⅛ cup Simple Balsamic Dressing (see Chapter 10)

¼ cup diced onions

½ cup canned chickpeas

2 large hard-boiled eggs, chopped

¼ cup canned corn

⅛ cup chopped almonds

½ cup chopped pears

2 cups mixed greens

1. In a 32-ounce jar layer ingredients in the following order: dressing, onions, chickpeas, eggs, corn, almonds, pears, and mixed greens.

2. Close lid and refrigerate.

3. When ready to serve, shake it up and enjoy straight out of the jar or pour into a large bowl.

PER SERVING Calories: 489 | Fat: 19.5 g | Protein: 23.9 g | Sodium: 402 mg | Fiber: 11.7 g | Carbohydrates: 53.5 g | Sugar: 19.8 g

Pomegranate and Apple Crunch

Top this jar off with your favorite cheese if feta doesn't hit the spot. To make this vegan, omit the cheese. This will keep well in the refrigerator up to 5 days.

INGREDIENTS | SERVES 1

⅛ cup Lime Vinaigrette (see Chapter 10)

½ cup sliced green apples

½ cup Basic Steamed Quinoa (see Chapter 11)

2 cups baby spinach

¼ cup pomegranate seeds

¼ cup chopped walnuts

⅛ cup feta cheese

⅛ cup sliced black olives

¼ cup chopped fresh parsley

1. In a 32-ounce jar layer ingredients in the following order: dressing, apples, quinoa, spinach, pomegranate seeds, walnuts, cheese, olives, and parsley.

2. Close lid and refrigerate.

3. When ready to serve, shake it up and enjoy straight out of the jar or pour into a large bowl.

PER SERVING Calories: 479 | Fat: 28.1 g | Protein: 14.5 g | Sodium: 516 mg | Fiber: 9.6 g | Carbohydrates: 45.2 g | Sugar: 15.0 g

Mexican Shrimp Jar

If you love Mexican food but also want to stay on track with eating well, then try this dish. Not a fan of seafood or shellfish in general? You can replace it with pulled pork or chicken or even ground beef. This jar will keep in the refrigerator up to 5 days.

INGREDIENTS | SERVES 1

1 tablespoon coconut oil

½ cup wedged onions

1 cup bell pepper strips

⅛ teaspoon sea salt

¼ teaspoon freshly ground black pepper

½ medium avocado, pitted, flesh removed, and mashed

¼ cup seeded and diced tomatoes

¼ medium lime, juiced

¼ cup chopped fresh cilantro, divided

10 Pan-Seared Shrimp with Herbs (see Chapter 11)

½ cup Healthy Mexican Rice and Beans (see Chapter 11)

2 cups baby spinach

1. Heat a skillet over medium heat and add oil. Once oil is hot, add onions and stir 2 minutes. Add bell peppers, salt, and pepper and stir another 2–3 minutes or until peppers are soft. Remove and set aside.

2. In a medium bowl add avocado, tomatoes, lime juice, and half the cilantro. Use a fork to mash and mix everything together. Set aside.

3. In a 32-ounce jar layer ingredients in the following order: sautéed peppers and onions, shrimp, rice and beans, avocado mixture, spinach, and remaining half of the cilantro.

4. Close lid and refrigerate.

5. When ready to serve, shake it up and enjoy straight out of the jar or pour into a large bowl.

PER SERVING Calories: 560 | Fat: 28.3 g | Protein: 21.9 g | Sodium: 1,267 mg | Fiber: 13.3 g | Carbohydrates: 55.4 g | Sugar: 10.4 g

Chickpeas and Cucumber Salad

This salad is another vegetarian option for you that's filling and doesn't leave you wanting more. This salad keeps well in the refrigerator up to 5 days.

INGREDIENTS | SERVES 1

⅛ cup Lime Vinaigrette (see Chapter 10)

½ cup seeded and diced tomatoes

½ cup canned chickpeas

½ cup Basic Steamed Quinoa (see Chapter 11)

½ cup seeded and diced cucumbers

¼ cup canned corn

⅛ cup sliced olives

¼ cup chopped parsley

1. In a 32-ounce jar layer ingredients in the following order: dressing, tomatoes, chickpeas, quinoa, cucumbers, corn, olives, and parsley.

2. Close lid and refrigerate.

3. When ready to serve, shake it up and enjoy straight out of the jar or pour into a large bowl.

PER SERVING Calories: 327 | Fat: 7.5 g | Protein: 12.5 g | Sodium: 464 mg | Fiber: 10.5 g | Carbohydrates: 55.2 g | Sugar: 10.2 g

Chickpea Options

It is super convenient to buy chickpeas in cans soaked in water. However, you can also buy dry chickpeas and soak and cook them yourself. This is a more economical way of making large batches of chickpeas.

Spicy Asian Napa Salad

This salad will go well with chicken, pork, or beef. This dish will keep well in the refrigerator up to 5 days.

INGREDIENTS | SERVES 1

⅛ cup Lime Vinaigrette (see Chapter 10)
1 cup thinly sliced napa cabbage
½ cup shredded carrots
½ cup julienned red bell peppers
¾ cup Spicy Chicken Satay (see Chapter 5)
⅛ cup jalapeño rounds
¼ cup chopped fresh cilantro

1. In a 32-ounce jar layer ingredients in the following order: dressing, cabbage, carrots, bell peppers, chicken, jalapeños, and cilantro.

2. Close lid and refrigerate.

3. When ready to serve, shake it up and enjoy straight out of the jar or pour into a large bowl.

PER SERVING Calories: 382 | Fat: 16.7 g | Protein: 40.2 g | Sodium: 481 mg | Fiber: 5.6 g | Carbohydrates: 18.4 g | Sugar: 9.4 g

Napa Cabbage

Napa cabbage is widely available in most markets now, or you can look for it in an Asian market. It is light in flavor and usually a good base ingredient to use in slaws or salads.

Vietnamese Fresh Roll Jars

*If you love Vietnamese fresh rolls with shrimp, then you'll love this.
This jar will keep well in the refrigerator up to 5 days.*

INGREDIENTS | SERVES 1

⅛ cup Vietnamese Fish Sauce (see Chapter 10)
¼ cup shredded carrots
½ cup julienned red bell peppers
½ cup spiralized zucchini
½ cup cooked vermicelli noodles
1 tablespoon chopped fresh mint
1 tablespoon chopped fresh Thai basil
½ cup Pan-Seared Shrimp with Herbs (see Chapter 11)
½ cup chopped lettuce
⅛ cup chopped fresh cilantro
⅛ cup crushed raw cashews

1. In a 32-ounce jar layer ingredients in the following order: fish sauce, carrots, peppers, zucchini, noodles, mint, basil, shrimp, lettuce, cilantro, and cashews.

2. Close lid and refrigerate.

3. When ready to serve, shake it up and enjoy straight out of the jar or pour into a large bowl.

PER SERVING Calories: 334 | Fat: 10.1 g | Protein: 12.6 g | Sodium: 489 mg | Fiber: 4.1 g | Carbohydrates: 48.4 g | Sugar: 13.6 g

Figs and Apple Chicken Salad

If you like dried figs, you'll love fresh figs. They are such a great addition to salads. This dish keeps well in the refrigerator up to 5 days.

INGREDIENTS | SERVES 1

¼ cup Raspberry Vinaigrette (see Chapter 10)

¼ cup chopped raw sweet snap peas

½ cup chopped baby cucumbers

⅛ cup sliced radishes

¼ cup sliced green apples

1 medium fresh fig, wedged

¾ cup Simple Oven-Baked Chicken Breasts (see Chapter 5)

1 cup baby spinach

1. In a 32-ounce jar layer ingredients in the following order: dressing, peas, cucumbers, radish, apples, fig, chicken, and spinach.

2. Close lid and refrigerate.

3. When ready to serve, shake it up and enjoy straight out of the jar or pour into a large bowl.

PER SERVING Calories: 593 | Fat: 28.0 g | Protein: 40.8 g | Sodium: 887 mg | Fiber: 18.9 g | Carbohydrates: 47.9 g | Sugar: 23.4 g

Apples

Remember to soak apple slices in salted water for a few minutes to prevent them from turning brown. Rinse away salt under cold water after.

Beet Feta Salad

You can't go wrong with the combination of beets and feta. They complement each other well. This salad keeps well in the refrigerator up to 5 days.

INGREDIENTS | SERVES 1

¼ cup Beet Vinaigrette (see Chapter 10)

½ cup Oven-Roasted Beets (see Chapter 11)

½ cup chopped bell peppers

⅛ cup thinly sliced fennel

2 strawberries, tops removed and sliced

½ cup Basic Steamed Quinoa (see Chapter 11)

1 large hard-boiled egg, chopped

⅛ cup feta cheese

1 tablespoon chopped green onions

½ teaspoon orange zest

1. In a 32-ounce jar layer ingredients in the following order: dressing, beets, peppers, fennel, strawberries, quinoa, egg, feta, green onions, and orange zest.

2. Close lid and refrigerate.

3. When ready to serve, shake it up and enjoy straight out of the jar or pour into a large bowl.

PER SERVING Calories: 575 | Fat: 32.6 g | Protein: 17.2 g | Sodium: 798 mg | Fiber: 9.7 g | Carbohydrates: 53.6 g | Sugar: 24.5 g

Pink Quinoa

You can easily make your quinoa a little more visually appealing and add flavor to it with the addition of beets. To make your quinoa pink, mix ½ tablespoon Beet Vinaigrette (see Chapter 10) into your quinoa.

CHAPTER 9

Salads

Dill Tuna Salad

If you want something high in protein but low in fat, then this is an excellent option. This can be served on top of greens or roasted vegetables. This stores well up to 5 days in the refrigerator.

INGREDIENTS | SERVES 5

5 (5-ounce) cans tuna
½ cup finely diced red bell peppers
½ cup finely diced celery
¼ cup finely chopped fresh dill
1 medium lemon, juiced
¼ medium red onion, peeled and minced
1 teaspoon garlic powder
¼ teaspoon freshly ground black pepper
1 teaspoon dried parsley

1. In a large mixing bowl add tuna, bell pepper, celery, dill, lemon juice, onion, garlic powder, black pepper, and parsley and mix until well combined.

2. Place into food containers for storage.

PER SERVING Calories: 158 | Fat: 3.1 g | Protein: 27.3 g | Sodium: 436 mg | Fiber: 0.9 g | Carbohydrates: 3.0 g | Sugar: 1.3 g

Classic Greek Salad

This dish is a quick and easy salad to go with your main protein. Make extra and bring it to work for lunch the next day. This stores well up to 3 days in the refrigerator.

INGREDIENTS | SERVES 4

5 cups chopped romaine lettuce
2 cups mixed greens
3 Roma tomatoes, seeded and chopped
1 medium green bell pepper, seeded and thinly sliced
½ medium red onion, peeled and thinly sliced
1 cup seeded and chopped cucumber
½ cup pitted kalamata olives
¼ cup feta cheese
½ cup Classic Greek Dressing (see Chapter 10)

1. In a large mixing bowl add lettuce, greens, tomatoes, bell pepper, onions, cucumbers, and olives.

2. Divide salad evenly into food containers for storage.

3. Add 1 tablespoon feta cheese and 2 tablespoons Classic Greek Dressing to each salad right before serving.

PER SERVING Calories: 273 | Fat: 21.9 g | Protein: 3.8 g | Sodium: 752 mg | Fiber: 5.1 g | Carbohydrates: 14.7 g | Sugar: 7.8 g

Cauliflower Salad

Sick of cauliflower rice but love the taste of raw cauliflower? This is an easy salad to put together and stores well up to 5 days in the refrigerator.

INGREDIENTS | SERVES 5

½ medium cauliflower head, grated or processed

1 cup diced bell peppers

1 cup shredded carrots

1 cup finely diced celery

1 cup whole cherry tomatoes

1 tablespoon chopped green onions

2 tablespoons chopped fresh parsley

1 medium lemon, juiced

¼ medium red onion, peeled and finely diced

1 teaspoon garlic powder

¼ teaspoon sea salt

¼ teaspoon freshly ground black pepper

1 tablespoon extra-virgin olive oil

1. In a large mixing bowl add cauliflower, bell peppers, carrots, celery, tomatoes, green onion, parsley, lemon juice, red onion, garlic powder, salt, black pepper, and oil. Mix until well combined.

2. Place into food containers for storage.

PER SERVING Calories: 60 | Fat: 2.8 g | Protein: 1.7 g | Sodium: 137 mg | Fiber: 2.8 g | Carbohydrates: 8.1 g | Sugar: 4.2 g

Raw Cauliflower

If you're not a big fan of completely raw cauliflower, you can microwave it for 1 minute or parboil it quickly in boiling water to cook it slightly. If you parboil it, remember to completely drain it before making the salad.

Balsamic Cucumber and Tomato Salad

This is a classic Mediterranean salad that offers a punch of flavors. When you're meal prepping, avoid adding the dressing to the salad. Keep it separate to help the salad last longer. This salad is best served fresh or it can be stored in the refrigerator and kept up to 3 days.

INGREDIENTS | SERVES 5

1 clove garlic, peeled and minced

½ tablespoon dried oregano

1 tablespoon extra-virgin olive oil

1 tablespoon balsamic vinegar

¼ teaspoon freshly ground black pepper

½ cup whole kalamata olives, pitted

2 cups seeded and diced cucumbers

2 cups halved cherry tomatoes

¼ medium red onion, peeled and minced

2 tablespoons chopped fresh basil

1. In a medium mixing bowl whisk together garlic, oregano, oil, vinegar, and pepper. Set aside.

2. In a large bowl add olives, cucumbers, tomatoes, and onions, and mix until well combined.

3. If serving immediately, add dressing and top with fresh basil. If meal prepping, place into food containers for storage. Store dressing and basil separately. At time of serving, add 1 tablespoon of dressing and a pinch of basil; mix it up and then serve.

4. Add 1 tablespoon dressing and a pinch of basil at time of serving.

PER SERVING Calories: 77 | Fat: 4.9 g | Protein: 1.0 g | Sodium: 302 mg | Fiber: 2.5 g | Carbohydrates: 5.8 g | Sugar: 2.7 g

Roasted Beet and Apple Salad

Beet salads are so satisfying. The beets and apples in this salad complement each other very well. This dish stores well up to 5 days in the refrigerator.

INGREDIENTS | SERVES 5

4 cups Oven-Roasted Beets (see Chapter 11)

1 medium green apple, peeled, cored, and chopped

2 cups baby spinach

2 cups mixed greens

¼ cup plus 1 tablespoon chopped walnuts, divided

¼ cup Lime Vinaigrette (see Chapter 10)

1. In a large mixing bowl add beets, apple, spinach, mixed greens, and walnuts and toss.

2. Divide salad evenly into food containers for storage. Use a separate container for the dressing.

3. Add 1 tablespoon dressing and 1 tablespoon walnuts to each portion at time of serving.

PER SERVING Calories: 127 | Fat: 5.9 g | Protein: 3.3 g | Sodium: 179 mg | Fiber: 4.3 g | Carbohydrates: 17.3 g | Sugar: 11.8 g

Quinoa Israeli Salad

This is a classic salad in Middle Eastern cuisine, except there's quinoa added here for extra protein. This salad stores well up to 5 days in the refrigerator.

INGREDIENTS | SERVES 5

1 cup Basic Steamed Quinoa (see Chapter 11)

2 cups seeded and diced cucumbers

2 cups seeded and diced tomatoes

½ cup chopped fresh parsley

½ tablespoon sumac

¼ cup Lemon Vinaigrette (see Chapter 10)

1. In a large mixing bowl add quinoa, cucumbers, tomatoes, parsley, and sumac; mix until well combined.

2. Divide salad evenly into food containers for storage. To help the salad last longer, store the dressing separately, then add 1 tablespoon dressing to each portion at time of serving.

PER SERVING Calories: 77 | Fat: 1.9 g | Protein: 2.8 g | Sodium: 59 mg | Fiber: 2.5 g | Carbohydrates: 12.9 g | Sugar: 3.6 g

Smoked Salmon Mandarin Salad

The mandarin orange really adds a sweetness that complements the bitter arugula. This salad is best served fresh. If you are meal prepping this dish, prep and store up to 2 days in the refrigerator.

INGREDIENTS | SERVES 4

1 cup mandarin oranges, canned or fresh
6 cups baby arugula
½ cup crushed walnuts
16 (½-ounce) slices smoked salmon
¼ cup Simple Balsamic Dressing (see Chapter 10)

1. In each food container add mandarin pieces first, then arugula, walnuts, and salmon. Store salad separately without dressing.

2. Add 1 tablespoon dressing to each portion at time of serving.

PER SERVING Calories: 184 | Fat: 10.0 g | Protein: 13.1 g | Sodium: 437 mg | Fiber: 2.1 g | Carbohydrates: 10.9 g | Sugar: 7.6 g

Broccoli Cabbage Slaw

Bored of eating boiled broccoli? This twist will make it not only colorful but also flavorful. This slaw will keep well up to 5 days in the refrigerator.

INGREDIENTS | SERVES 5

4 cups grated or processed broccoli
1 cup grated red cabbage
½ medium red onion, peeled and diced
2 tablespoons pumpkin seeds
¼ cup Lime Vinaigrette (see Chapter 10)

1. In a large mixing bowl add broccoli, cabbage, onions, and pumpkin seeds and mix until well combined.

2. Store slaw in food containers and dressing in a separate container. Mix slaw and dressing just before serving.

PER SERVING Calories: 63 | Fat: 2.6 g | Protein: 3.4 g | Sodium: 72 mg | Fiber: 2.6 g | Carbohydrates: 8.1 g | Sugar: 3.0 g

Healthy Chicken Salad

Chicken salad is great to add on top of any green salad. This is a healthier version of the classic chicken salad. This dish will keep well up to 4 days in the refrigerator.

INGREDIENTS | SERVES 5

4 cups canned chicken breast in water, drained

½ cup finely diced celery

½ cup minced red onion

2 cloves garlic, peeled and minced

½ cup plain Greek yogurt

½ tablespoon Dijon mustard

¼ teaspoon freshly ground black pepper

¼ teaspoon sea salt

Mayonnaise and Chicken Options

Greek yogurt is a healthier choice than the traditional mayonnaise in a chicken salad, but you can also make this with mayonnaise for a richer taste. You can also boil chicken breasts and shred your own chicken. If you are buying canned chicken breasts, look for ones that are soaked in water only.

1. In a large mixing bowl add chicken, celery, onions, garlic, yogurt, mustard, pepper, and salt and mix until well combined.

2. Place into food containers for storage.

PER SERVING Calories: 330 | Fat: 12.8 g | Protein: 44.1 g | Sodium: 529 mg | Fiber: 0.5 g | Carbohydrates: 4.7 g | Sugar: 1.7 g

Thai Green Papaya Salad

This salad is very refreshing and spicy, so make sure you have a cold drink ready before eating this. This should keep well in the refrigerator up to 5 days.

INGREDIENTS | SERVES 5

1 medium jalapeño pepper, seeded and diced

1 medium red Thai chili, seeded and minced

2 cloves garlic, peeled and minced

1 tablespoon honey

½ tablespoon fish sauce

1 tablespoon lime juice

½ tablespoon rice vinegar

2 tablespoons warm water

4 cups thinly julienned or grated green papaya

1 cup shredded carrots

½ cup shredded green beans

¼ cup chopped fresh cilantro (for garnish)

1 tablespoon crushed raw cashews (for garnish)

1. In a small bowl whisk jalapeño peppers, chili, garlic, honey, fish sauce, lime juice, vinegar, and water until well combined. Set aside.

2. In a large mixing bowl add papaya, carrots, green beans, and prepared sauce and mix until well combined.

3. Divide evenly into storage containers and garnish with cilantro.

4. Store cashews separately and add at time of serving.

PER SERVING Calories: 84 | Fat: 0.8 g | Protein: 1.8 g | Sodium: 88 mg | Fiber: 3.6 g | Carbohydrates: 19.3 g | Sugar: 11.6 g

Green Papaya

If you are having a hard time finding green papaya in a supermarket near you, you can use green beans, cucumber, or green mango juliennes as substitutes.

Strawberry Pecan Spinach Salad

You'll love this salad especially when strawberries are in season. Store the dressing on the side until you serve it. This will help the spinach last. This salad will keep well in the refrigerator up to 4 days.

INGREDIENTS | SERVES 4

8 cups baby spinach

1 cup sliced strawberries

¼ medium red onion, peeled and thinly sliced

½ cup chopped pecans

¼ cup Simple Balsamic Dressing (see Chapter 10)

1. Evenly divide spinach, strawberries, onions, and pecans into each of 4 food containers.

2. Store dressing separately. Add to salad and mix at time of serving.

PER SERVING Calories: 143 | Fat: 10.9 g | Protein: 3.4 g | Sodium: 95 mg | Fiber: 3.6 g | Carbohydrates: 9.8 g | Sugar: 4.7 g

Asian Almond Slaw

Usually creamy slaw can be very calorie-dense and unhealthy, but this one can be enjoyed guilt-free. This should keep well in the refrigerator up to 5 days.

INGREDIENTS | SERVES 5

3 cups shredded cabbage

1 cup shredded carrots

1 cup julienned bell peppers

1 medium mango, peeled and julienned

1 medium red Thai chili, seeded and minced

2 cloves garlic, peeled and minced

½ cup Almond Butter Vinaigrette (see Chapter 10)

¼ cup chopped fresh cilantro (for garnish)

1 tablespoon crushed raw almonds (for garnish)

1. In a large mixing bowl add cabbage, carrots, peppers, mango, chili, garlic, and vinaigrette and mix until well combined.

2. Divide evenly into storage containers and garnish with cilantro.

3. Store almonds separately and add at time of serving.

PER SERVING Calories: 255 | Fat: 15.1 g | Protein: 6.0 g | Sodium: 100 mg | Fiber: 5.5 g | Carbohydrates: 24.9 g | Sugar: 17.3 g

Kale Pomegranate Salad

The mandarin orange and pomegranate seeds really add a nice sweetness to this salad. This should keep well in the refrigerator up to 5 days if dressing is stored separately.

INGREDIENTS | SERVES 4

10 black kale leaves, stems removed, chopped

1 cup chopped clementine or mandarin oranges

½ cup pomegranate seeds

1 medium avocado, pitted, flesh removed, and chopped

½ cup Lime Vinaigrette (see Chapter 10)

1. In your salad containers lay kale down first, then clementine on top; sprinkle on pomegranate seeds and top with avocado.

2. Pack ⅛ cup dressing per salad on the side. Mix dressing into salad at time of serving.

PER SERVING Calories: 153 | Fat: 7.6 g | Protein: 3.2 g | Sodium: 129 mg | Fiber: 5.6 g | Carbohydrates: 19.5 g | Sugar: 11.0 g

Ingredient Tips

Kale can be tough to eat, but you can soften it up by sprinkling a bit of sea salt on the leaves, then massaging them with your hands for about 30 seconds. It will wilt them down a bit. Avocados can go brown if you cut them open too far in advance of serving. Cut a quarter at a time and leave the rest in a tightly sealed zip-top bag. Rub some lemon juice on them to prevent browning.

Green Mango Salad

You should be able to find green mangoes in Asian markets, but if not, you can also use unripe regular mangoes. Red Thai chilies can also be replaced with jalapeño peppers. This salad keeps well in the refrigerator up to 5 days.

INGREDIENTS | SERVES 5

1 medium red Thai chili, seeded and minced

2 cloves garlic, peeled and minced

1 tablespoon honey

½ tablespoon fish sauce

1 tablespoon lime juice

2 tablespoons warm water

4 cups thinly julienned green mangoes

1 cup thinly julienned red bell peppers

½ cup thinly sliced green onions

¼ cup chopped fresh cilantro (for garnish)

5 lime wedges

1 tablespoon crushed peanuts

1. In a small bowl whisk chili, garlic, honey, fish sauce, lime juice, and water until well combined. Set aside.

2. In a large mixing bowl add mangoes, bell peppers, and green onions and toss until well combined. Add dressing and toss until well combined.

3. Divide evenly into storage containers and garnish with cilantro and lime wedges.

4. Store peanuts separately and add at time of serving.

PER SERVING Calories: 122 | Fat: 0.8 g | Protein: 2.0 g | Sodium: 74 mg | Fiber: 3.3 g | Carbohydrates: 29.2 g | Sugar: 23.9 g

Roasted Butternut Squash Kale Salad

This salad can be a complete meal with some boiled eggs or protein on top. This should keep well in the refrigerator up to 5 days if dressing is stored separately.

INGREDIENTS | SERVES 4

10 black kale leaves, stems removed, chopped

2 cups Cinnamon Roasted Butternut Squash (see Chapter 11)

1 cup halved cherry tomatoes

½ cup Lemon Vinaigrette (see Chapter 10)

1. In your salad containers lay kale down first, then squash, and then tomatoes.

2. Pack ⅛ cup dressing per salad on the side. Mix dressing into salad at time of serving.

PER SERVING Calories: 103 | Fat: 4.2 g | Protein: 2.8 g | Sodium: 135 mg | Fiber: 3.4 g | Carbohydrates: 16.2 g | Sugar: 5.6 g

Red Cabbage Slaw

This slaw is great alongside jerk chicken or pork. The sweetness of the slaw complements the spiciness of the jerk seasoning. This slaw will keep well in the refrigerator up to 5 days.

INGREDIENTS | SERVES 5

4 cups grated red cabbage
1 cup julienned red bell peppers
1 cup thinly sliced fennel
½ cup grated carrots
½ cup chopped fresh cilantro
¼ cup minced red onions
½ cup Lime Vinaigrette (see Chapter 10)
1 teaspoon apple cider

1. In a large mixing bowl add all ingredients and toss until well combined.

2. Divide evenly into food containers and store in the refrigerator.

PER SERVING Calories: 62 | Fat: 2.2 g | Protein: 1.5 g | Sodium: 121 mg | Fiber: 2.7 g | Carbohydrates: 10.5 g | Sugar: 6.1 g

Watermelon Feta Salad

This is great for entertaining or when it's summer and you need something refreshing for lunch. Keep the feta separate until you're ready to eat. This should keep well in the refrigerator up to 3 days.

INGREDIENTS | SERVES 2

2 cups cubed seedless watermelon
1 cup halved cherry tomatoes
1 tablespoon chopped fresh mint
1 tablespoon feta cheese

1. Place watermelon at the bottom of your containers, add cherry tomatoes, and top with mint.

2. Keep feta in a separate container or zip-top bag until time of serving. When ready to serve sprinkle it on top.

PER SERVING Calories: 71 | Fat: 1.2 g | Protein: 2.3 g | Sodium: 47 mg | Fiber: 1.6 g | Carbohydrates: 14.7 g | Sugar: 11.6 g

Quinoa Macaroni Salad

This salad is filling, light, healthy, and great to bring on a picnic. Quinoa pastas are much higher in protein than regular pastas, and this is gluten-free. This will store well in the refrigerator up to 5 days.

INGREDIENTS | SERVES 2

2 cups cooked quinoa macaroni

3 large hard-boiled eggs, chopped

1 cup diced bell peppers

½ cup diced celery

¼ cup sliced canned black olives, pitted

¼ cup minced red onions

1 cup halved cherry tomatoes

¼ cup light mayonnaise

1 tablespoon extra-virgin olive oil

1 tablespoon Dijon mustard

¼ teaspoon freshly ground black pepper

1. In large mixing bowl add macaroni, eggs, bell pepper, celery, olives, onions, and tomatoes and toss until well mixed.

2. In a small bowl add mayonnaise, oil, mustard, and black pepper and whisk until well blended. Pour mixture into macaroni bowl and mix until well combined.

3. Divide into food containers and store in the refrigerator.

PER SERVING Calories: 533 | Fat: 25.9 g | Protein: 15.2 g | Sodium: 636 mg | Fiber: 7.4 g | Carbohydrates: 54.5 g | Sugar: 8.8 g

Edamame Zoodle Salad

Raw zucchini is so sweet and almost tastes better than cooked. It also keeps a lot longer in the refrigerator than cucumbers. This salad should keep well up to 5 days. Serve it with baked chicken breasts or even seared shrimp.

INGREDIENTS | SERVES 5

1 medium lime, juiced

1 tablespoon Dijon mustard

¼ teaspoon freshly ground black pepper

1 tablespoon extra-virgin olive oil

½ tablespoon maple syrup

1 teaspoon garlic powder

1 teaspoon white wine vinegar

1 cup edamame beans

3 medium zucchini, spiralized

1 cup thinly sliced fennel

¼ cup chopped fresh basil

1. In a small bowl whisk together lime juice, mustard, black pepper, oil, syrup, garlic powder, and vinegar. Set aside.

2. Fill a medium pot halfway with water and bring to a boil over high heat. Add beans and boil 2 minutes. Strain and rinse under cold water. Dry beans completely.

3. Put beans into a large mixing bowl. Add zucchini, fennel, basil, and dressing and toss until well combined.

4. Divide evenly into food containers and store in refrigerator.

PER SERVING Calories: 223 | Fat: 9.8 g | Protein: 15.4 g | Sodium: 37 mg | Fiber: 5.3 g | Carbohydrates: 18.3 g | Sugar: 7.6 g

Cold Vermicelli Salad

Make this salad a complete meal by adding chicken or even shrimp on top. For extra fiber, add chickpeas or other beans to the salad. This should keep well up to 5 days.

INGREDIENTS | SERVES 4

2 cups cooked vermicelli noodles
3 cups chopped lettuce
2 tablespoons chopped fresh mint
2 tablespoons chopped fresh Thai basil
½ cup shredded carrots
½ cup bean sprouts
¼ cup chopped fresh cilantro
¼ cup Vietnamese Fish Sauce
(see Chapter 10)

1. In a large mixing bowl add all ingredients and toss until well combined.

2. Divide evenly into food containers and store in refrigerator.

PER SERVING Calories: 144 | Fat: 0.2 g | Protein: 2.4 g | Sodium: 138 mg | Fiber: 1.8 g | Carbohydrates: 32.9 g | Sugar: 5.7 g

Corn and Tomato Salad

When tomatoes and corn are at their peak (late summer), this salad is the perfect complement to your barbecue party. This salad should keep well up to 2–3 days.

INGREDIENTS | SERVES 4

1 tablespoon lime juice
¼ teaspoon freshly ground black pepper
⅛ teaspoon sea salt
¼ teaspoon garlic powder
⅛ cup minced red onions
4 cups cubed heirloom tomatoes
1½ cups canned corn or shaved fresh corn
⅛ cup chopped fresh cilantro

1. In a small mixing bowl add lime, pepper, salt, and garlic powder and whisk until combined. Set aside.

2. In a large mixing bowl add onions, tomatoes, corn, cilantro, and dressing and toss until well combined.

3. Divide evenly into food containers and store in refrigerator.

PER SERVING Calories: 97 | Fat: 0.6 g | Protein: 3.6 g | Sodium: 69 mg | Fiber: 3.9 g | Carbohydrates: 23.4 g | Sugar: 7.8 g

Dressings and Sauces

Olive Tapenade Dressing

Olives are a good part of a balanced diet, but don't overindulge on them because they're high in sodium and calories. This dressing lasts in the refrigerator up to 5 days.

INGREDIENTS | SERVES 5

10 kalamata olives, pitted
1 tablespoon olive oil
¼ cup red wine vinegar
¼ cup water
¼ teaspoon freshly ground black pepper
½ tablespoon honey (or maple syrup)

1. In a food processor add all ingredients and blend until smooth.

2. Store in a Mason jar or storage container.

PER SERVING Calories: 52 | Fat: 4.0 g | Protein: 0.0 g | Sodium: 187 mg | Fiber: 0.7 g | Carbohydrates: 2.5 g | Sugar: 1.7 g

Sumac Vinaigrette

This vinaigrette can be added to any summer salad. If you like sour and tart dressings, this is for you. This vinaigrette keeps in the refrigerator up to 5 days.

INGREDIENTS | SERVES 5

½ tablespoon ground sumac
1 tablespoon olive oil
¼ cup white wine vinegar
¼ cup water
1 medium lemon, juiced
¼ teaspoon freshly ground black pepper
¼ teaspoon sea salt

1. In a large bowl add all ingredients and whisk until well combined.

2. Store in a Mason jar or storage container.

PER SERVING Calories: 29 | Fat: 2.7 g | Protein: 0.1 g | Sodium: 96 mg | Fiber: 0.3 g | Carbohydrates: 0.6 g | Sugar: 0.2 g

Sumac

Ground sumac should be readily available in any grocery store. It is a very popular Middle Eastern spice used in many dishes in that region. Ground sumac is also very high in antioxidants.

Simple Balsamic Dressing

This vinaigrette is slightly sour so it is great on diced vegetables or leafy greens. This dressing keeps in the refrigerator up to 5 days.

INGREDIENTS | SERVES 5

1 tablespoon olive oil

¼ cup white wine vinegar

2 tablespoons water

1 medium lemon, juiced

¼ teaspoon freshly ground black pepper

¼ teaspoon sea salt

1 tablespoon balsamic vinegar

1 tablespoon maple syrup

1. In a large bowl add all ingredients and whisk until well combined.

2. Store in a Mason jar or storage container.

   PER SERVING Calories: 40 | Fat: 2.6 g | Protein: 0.1 g | Sodium: 95 mg | Fiber: 0.1 g | Carbohydrates: 3.8 g | Sugar: 3.1 g

Balsamic

There are many different types and price points of balsamic vinegar. The more aged balsamic is, the sweeter it gets. But also be mindful of how much aged balsamic you use due to its calories from sugar. Aged balsamic can be added onto salads as a glaze as well.

Almond Butter Vinaigrette

Almond butter is a great nut butter alternative to peanut butter. If you love peanut butter, you can use that as well. This vinaigrette keeps in the refrigerator up to 5 days.

INGREDIENTS | SERVES 5

¼ cup unsalted almond butter

¼ cup rice wine vinegar

1 tablespoon maple syrup

1 tablespoon olive oil

⅛ teaspoon sea salt

2 tablespoons water

Rice Wine Vinegar

Rice vinegar is made by fermenting the sugars from rice into an alcohol such as wine, then further fermenting the wine into acetic acid, which is vinegar. You can purchase rice vinegar in most supermarkets. If you do not have rice vinegar, you can replace it with white wine vinegar or lemon juice as well.

1. In a large bowl add all ingredients and whisk until well combined.

2. Store in a Mason jar or storage container.

   PER SERVING Calories: 113 | Fat: 8.9 g | Protein: 2.6 g | Sodium: 48 mg | Fiber: 1.3 g | Carbohydrates: 5.2 g | Sugar: 3.0 g

Lime Vinaigrette

Freshly squeezed lime juice is so refreshing and appetizing on salads. This Lime Vinaigrette is perfect on almost any salad. This vinaigrette keeps in the refrigerator up to 5 days.

INGREDIENTS | SERVES 5

1 tablespoon olive oil

3 medium limes, juiced

2 tablespoons water

¼ teaspoon freshly ground black pepper

¼ teaspoon sea salt

1 tablespoon Dijon mustard

½ tablespoon honey

1. In a large bowl add all ingredients and whisk until well combined.

2. Store in a Mason jar or storage container.

PER SERVING Calories: 33 | Fat: 2.6 g | Protein: 0.1 g | Sodium: 111 mg | Fiber: 0.1 g | Carbohydrates: 2.5 g | Sugar: 1.9 g

Lime

Add lime zest for an extra lime zing. Lime juice contains dietary vitamin C, antibiotic properties, and can help with detoxification. Lime zest also contains high levels of antioxidants.

Lemon Vinaigrette

To make your dressing extra zesty, add the lemon zest along with the juice. Citrus peels like lemon zest contain high levels of antioxidants. Lemon also aids with weight loss and digestion and is a good source of vitamin C. This dressing can last in the refrigerator up to 5 days.

INGREDIENTS | SERVES 5

1 tablespoon olive oil

3 medium lemons, juiced

2 tablespoons water

¼ teaspoon freshly ground black pepper

¼ teaspoon sea salt

½ tablespoon honey

1. In a large bowl add all ingredients and whisk until well combined.

2. Store in a Mason jar or storage container.

PER SERVING Calories: 34 | Fat: 2.6 g | Protein: 0.1 g | Sodium: 93 mg | Fiber: 0.1 g | Carbohydrates: 3.0 g | Sugar: 2.2 g

Vietnamese Fish Sauce

This sauce goes great on salads or as a dip for Vietnamese spring rolls. This sauce keeps in the refrigerator up to 5 days.

INGREDIENTS | SERVES 5

2 cloves garlic, peeled
1 red Thai chili, chopped with seeds
1 tablespoon fish sauce
⅓ cup water
3 tablespoons maple syrup
2 medium limes, juiced
1 tablespoon white wine vinegar

Fish Sauce

Fish sauce is a condiment made from fermented fish and salt. It is used as a staple ingredient in various cuisines in Southeast and East Asia. If you don't like the taste of fish sauce, you can replace it with ¼ teaspoon of salt. If this recipe is not salty enough for your taste, add an extra ½ tablespoon of fish sauce.

1. Pound garlic and Thai chili with a mortar and pestle until finely ground. If you do not have a mortar and pestle, use a grinder or food processor.

2. Pour garlic mixture into a medium bowl, then add fish sauce, water, maple syrup, lime juice, and white wine vinegar. Mix until well combined.

3. Store in a Mason jar or storage container.

PER SERVING Calories: 40 | Fat: 0.0 g | Protein: 0.6 g | Sodium: 140 mg | Fiber: 0.1 g | Carbohydrates: 10.0 g | Sugar: 7.5 g

Raspberry Vinaigrette

Raspberries are an excellent source of vitamin C, manganese, and dietary fiber. You can use frozen raspberries in this recipe if fresh ones aren't in season. This vinaigrette keeps in the refrigerator up to 5 days.

INGREDIENTS | SERVES 5

2 cups fresh raspberries

1 medium lemon, juiced

2 tablespoons white wine vinegar

2 tablespoons olive oil

¼ teaspoon freshly ground black pepper

¼ teaspoon sea salt

1. In a food processor add all ingredients and pulse until well mixed.

2. Store in a Mason jar or storage container.

PER SERVING Calories: 75 | Fat: 5.5 g | Protein: 0.6 g | Sodium: 94 mg | Fiber: 3.3 g | Carbohydrates: 6.4 g | Sugar: 2.3 g

Beet Vinaigrette

If you need to find a new way to use up your roasted beets, then try this recipe. This vinaigrette lasts in the refrigerator up to 5 days.

INGREDIENTS | SERVES 5

⅔ cup Oven-Roasted Beets (see Chapter 11)

⅓ cup orange juice

1 medium lemon, juiced

5 strawberries, tops removed

2 tablespoons olive oil

¼ teaspoon freshly ground black pepper

¼ teaspoon sea salt

1. In a food processor or blender add all ingredients and pulse until well mixed.

2. Store in a Mason jar or storage container.

PER SERVING Calories: 69 | Fat: 5.5 g | Protein: 0.5 g | Sodium: 113 mg | Fiber: 0.8 g | Carbohydrates: 4.9 g | Sugar: 3.4 g

Classic Greek Dressing

This is a basic vinaigrette that can be added to pretty much any salad.
This dressing keeps in the refrigerator up to 5 days.

INGREDIENTS | SERVES 5

2 medium lemons, juiced
3 tablespoons extra-virgin olive oil
1 teaspoon dried oregano
¼ teaspoon freshly ground black pepper
¼ teaspoon sea salt

1. In a medium bowl add all ingredients and whisk until well combined.

2. Store in a Mason jar or storage container.

PER SERVING Calories: 74 | Fat: 7.9 g | Protein: 0.1 g | Sodium: 93 mg | Fiber: 0.2 g | Carbohydrates: 1.1 g | Sugar: 0.3 g

Lemon Juice

You can use bottled lemon juice instead of fresh lemons to save time. Bottled lemon juice is convenient and has a longer shelf life than actual lemons. Fresh lemons are always the better choice, but sometimes we all need a shortcut.

Greek Yogurt Ranch

This is great as a dipping sauce on the side or to dress up any salad.
This dressing keeps in the refrigerator up to 5 days.

INGREDIENTS | SERVES 4

1 cup plain Greek yogurt
1 teaspoon garlic powder
½ teaspoon onion powder
¼ teaspoon freshly ground black pepper
¼ teaspoon sea salt
¼ teaspoon Worcestershire sauce
⅛ teaspoon ground cayenne pepper
½ teaspoon minced fresh dill
½ teaspoon minced fresh chives
¼ medium lemon, juiced

1. In a medium bowl add all ingredients and whisk until well combined.

2. Store in a Mason jar or storage container.

PER SERVING Calories: 46 | Fat: 1.2 g | Protein: 5.9 g | Sodium: 139 mg | Fiber: 0.2 g | Carbohydrates: 3.4 g | Sugar: 2.4 g

Cocktail Sauce

This is so easy to make at home that you won't want to buy another premade cocktail sauce again. This sauce keeps in the refrigerator up to 5 days.

INGREDIENTS | SERVES 4

¾ cup tomato paste
½ cup diced and crushed tomatoes
¼ cup minced horseradish
½ medium lemon, juiced
¼ teaspoon sea salt

1. In a medium bowl add all ingredients and whisk until well combined.

2. Store in a Mason jar or storage container.

PER SERVING Calories: 57 | Fat: 0.3 g | Protein: 2.8 g | Sodium: 627 mg | Fiber: 3.1 g | Carbohydrates: 13.5 g | Sugar: 8.7 g

Horseradish

Did you know that horseradish provides a number of health benefits, including protection against recurrent urinary tract infections and fighting off cancer cells?

Cranberry Sauce

This sauce is great to serve over Roasted Whole Chicken (see Chapter 5) or any other poultry dish. It will keep at least 5 days in the refrigerator.

INGREDIENTS | SERVES 4

3 cups fresh cranberries
⅔ cup coconut sugar
½ cup orange juice

1. Heat a medium saucepan over medium heat and add cranberries, sugar, and orange juice; bring to a boil.

2. Turn heat to low and simmer 12–15 minutes or until all cranberries have popped, making sure you're stirring occasionally.

3. Let cool before adding to a Mason jar for storage.

PER SERVING Calories: 173 | Fat: 0.1 g | Protein: 0.5 g | Sodium: 1 mg | Fiber: 3.5 g | Carbohydrates: 45.7 g | Sugar: 39.0 g

Coconut Sugar

Coconut sugar is made from the coconut palm. The flowers of the palm are cut and the sap is collected and then heated. It's still sugar regardless where it's from, so be careful with using too much if you're trying to lose weight. Also, it may be more cost-effective to replace the coconut sugar with regular sugar.

Spicy Chimichurri

This is one of those sauces that can go on any protein.
It keeps in the refrigerator up to 3 days.

INGREDIENTS | SERVES 8

1 cup chopped fresh curly parsley

½ cup chopped fresh cilantro

½ cup chopped fresh mint

1 medium jalapeño pepper, seeded and chopped

3 cloves garlic, peeled and chopped

¼ medium red onion, peeled and chopped

1 medium lemon, juiced

1 medium lime, juiced

1 tablespoon red wine vinegar

¼ teaspoon sea salt

¼ teaspoon freshly ground black pepper

⅛ teaspoon ground cayenne pepper

½ teaspoon red pepper flakes

3 tablespoons extra-virgin olive oil

1. In a food processor add all ingredients and pulse until smooth.

2. Store in a Mason jar or storage container.

PER SERVING Calories: 53 | Fat: 5.0 g | Protein: 0.5 g | Sodium: 63 mg | Fiber: 0.6 g | Carbohydrates: 2.1 g | Sugar: 0.4 g

Substitutions

If you don't like cilantro, simply use more parsley. Omit the jalapeño and red pepper flakes if you want a milder version. This sauce is great on chicken and especially great on grilled steaks.

Orange Vinaigrette

You can juice your own oranges (use two oranges for this recipe).
This vinaigrette keeps in the refrigerator up to 5 days.

INGREDIENTS | SERVES 4

¾ cup orange juice
2 tablespoons olive oil
1 tablespoon orange zest
1 tablespoon white wine vinegar
¼ teaspoon freshly ground black pepper
¼ teaspoon sea salt

1. In a medium bowl add all ingredients and whisk until well combined.

2. Store in a Mason jar or storage container.

PER SERVING Calories: 82 | Fat: 6.6 g | Protein: 0.4 g | Sodium: 117 mg | Fiber: 0.3 g | Carbohydrates: 5.3 g | Sugar: 3.9 g

Mint Pesto

This pesto goes great with any of the meatball recipes in Chapters 5 and 6 or even on lamb chops. This keeps in the refrigerator up to 5 days.

INGREDIENTS | SERVES 8

2 cups fresh mint leaves
¼ cup raw walnuts
2 tablespoons pine nuts
½ cup extra-virgin olive oil
1 tablespoon lemon juice
½ teaspoon salt
½ teaspoon freshly ground black pepper

1. In a food processor pulse mint leaves first, then add remaining ingredients and pulse until smooth.

2. Store in a Mason jar or storage container.

PER SERVING Calories: 158 | Fat: 16.4 g | Protein: 1.0 g | Sodium: 147 mg | Fiber: 0.8 g | Carbohydrates: 1.9 g | Sugar: 0.2 g

Mint Sauce

There are many varieties of mint sauce in the store, but be mindful of what goes into making them by reading the ingredients. You may notice lots of added sugar. Why not make your own and have healthier sauces available?

Garlic Chive Butter Dip

Your steaks and potatoes will love this dip, and so will you.
This keeps in the refrigerator up to 5 days.

INGREDIENTS | SERVES 2

⅛ cup unsalted butter
1 tablespoon chopped fresh chives
1 teaspoon minced garlic

Vegan Option

If you are vegan, try using coconut cream instead of the butter in this recipe. Coconut cream is available in cartons and cans, but whichever you choose, make sure it's 100% coconut cream with no additives.

1. In a small bowl add all ingredients and stir until well combined.

2. Serve immediately or store in a Mason jar or storage container.

PER SERVING Calories: 103 | Fat: 10.7 g | Protein: 0.3 g | Sodium: 91 mg | Fiber: 0.1 g | Carbohydrates: 0.5 g | Sugar: 0.1 g

Garlic Oil

Add this to your chicken noodle soup or anything that needs an extra
boost of flavor. This oil keeps in the refrigerator up to 5 days.

INGREDIENTS | SERVES 5

¼ cup coconut oil (odorless and flavorless)
5 cloves garlic, peeled and minced

Garlic Oil

Once the garlic turns light brown, you have to remove it and put it into a bowl or jar immediately. If you let it sit in the pan, the hot oil will continue to cook it and it will likely burn. Garlic oil keeps extremely well in the refrigerator for an extended period of time.

1. Heat a small saucepan over medium heat and add oil. Once oil is hot, add garlic and reduce heat to low.

2. Simmer on low heat until garlic turns light brown.

3. Remove immediately and serve or transfer into a Mason jar or storage container.

PER SERVING Calories: 98 | Fat: 10.3 g | Protein: 0.2 g | Sodium: 0 mg | Fiber: 0.1 g | Carbohydrates: 1.0 g | Sugar: 0.0 g

Mango Chutney

This sauce goes really well on white fish or even Seared Tuna (see Chapter 16). This chutney holds in the refrigerator up to 5 days.

INGREDIENTS | SERVES 4

1 tablespoon coconut oil

¼ cup chopped red onions

2 cloves garlic, peeled and minced

1 tablespoon grated fresh ginger

⅔ cup chopped red bell peppers

2 cups chopped ripe mangoes

1 teaspoon ground cinnamon

⅛ teaspoon ground cayenne pepper

1 tablespoon curry powder

½ teaspoon red pepper flakes

Mangoes

Did you know that there are over four hundred varieties of mangoes in the world? Some of the possible health benefits of eating mango include a decreased risk of macular degeneration, a decreased risk of colon cancer, improvement in digestion as well as bone health, and even benefits for the skin and hair.

1. Heat a large pan over medium heat and add oil. Once oil is hot, add onions and stir 2 minutes, then add garlic and ginger and stir 1 more minute.

2. Add bell peppers, mangoes, cinnamon, cayenne, curry, and red pepper flakes and stir 5 minutes or until mangoes soften.

3. Serve immediately or let cool for storage.

4. Store in a Mason jar or storage container.

PER SERVING Calories: 99 | Fat: 3.7 g | Protein: 1.4 g | Sodium: 2 mg | Fiber: 3.3 g | Carbohydrates: 17.0 g | Sugar: 12.8 g

Chili Drizzle

Drizzle this onto your stir-fry dishes for an extra kick of spice.
This can last up to 1 month in the refrigerator.

INGREDIENTS | SERVES 5

¼ cup coconut oil (odorless and flavorless)
1 teaspoon minced garlic
1 tablespoon red pepper flakes

Chili Drizzle

This also goes amazingly in noodle soups or stew dishes, and it keeps very well in the refrigerator for 1 month. You can make large batches and keep them for future use.

1. Heat a small saucepan over medium heat and add oil. Once oil is hot, add garlic and red pepper flakes and reduce heat to low.

2. Simmer on low heat until garlic turns light brown.

3. Remove immediately and serve or transfer into a Mason jar or storage container.

PER SERVING Calories: 94 | Fat: 10.3 g | Protein: 0.0 g | Sodium: 0 mg | Fiber: 0.0 g | Carbohydrates: 0.2 g | Sugar: 0.0 g

Italian Dressing

This dressing is great on grilled vegetables like asparagus or even steamed vegetables like broccoli, and it is exceptional on any leafy green salads. This dressing keeps in the refrigerator up to 5 days.

INGREDIENTS | SERVES 4

4 tablespoons extra-virgin olive oil
2 tablespoons white wine vinegar
2 tablespoons dried parsley
1 tablespoon fresh lemon juice
2 cloves garlic, peeled and minced
1 teaspoon dried basil
2 teaspoons dried oregano
½ teaspoon salt
½ teaspoon freshly ground black pepper

1. In a medium bowl add all ingredients and whisk until well combined.

2. Store in a Mason jar or storage container.

PER SERVING Calories: 127 | Fat: 13.2 g | Protein: 0.4 g | Sodium: 295 mg | Fiber: 0.6 g | Carbohydrates: 1.8 g | Sugar: 0.2 g

CHAPTER 11

Sides

Oven-Roasted Beets

Beets are high in vitamin C, fiber, and potassium. They're a great addition to a well-balanced diet. Beets store well in the refrigerator. Keep them in food containers and they can be refrigerated up to 5 days.

INGREDIENTS | SERVES 5

5 cups cubed beets
½ tablespoon coconut oil
¼ teaspoon freshly ground black pepper
⅛ teaspoon sea salt
½ teaspoon balsamic vinegar

Beets

Most people remove the skins of beets, but the skins are edible, and when the beets are roasted you won't taste the difference. Just make sure you use a potato brush to clean the skin really well before roasting.

1. Preheat oven to 400°F. Line an 18" baking pan with parchment paper.

2. In a large mixing bowl add beets, oil, pepper, salt, and vinegar and mix until well combined.

3. Transfer to prepared pan and bake 35–40 minutes.

4. Remove and store in food containers.

PER SERVING Calories: 70 | Fat: 1.4 g | Protein: 2.2 g | Sodium: 152 mg | Fiber: 3.8 g | Carbohydrates: 13.2 g | Sugar: 9.3 g

Oven-Roasted Brussels Sprouts

Brussels sprouts are the perfect side to any fish or meat dish. They are low in calories and high in nutrients. This dish stores well in the refrigerator up to 5 days.

INGREDIENTS | SERVES 5

5 cups halved Brussels sprouts
½ tablespoon coconut oil
¼ teaspoon freshly ground black pepper
⅛ teaspoon sea salt
½ teaspoon apple cider vinegar

1. Preheat oven to 400°F. Line an 18" baking pan with parchment paper.

2. In a large mixing bowl add Brussels sprouts, oil, pepper, salt, and vinegar and mix until well combined.

3. Transfer to prepared pan and bake 35–45 minutes.

4. Remove and store in food containers.

PER SERVING Calories: 49 | Fat: 1.5 g | Protein: 3.0 g | Sodium: 68 mg | Fiber: 3.4 g | Carbohydrates: 8.0 g | Sugar: 1.9 g

Oven-Baked Spaghetti Squash

This is the perfect option to pair with meatballs, and it's completely gluten-free, as well as paleo and Whole30 approved. Cooked spaghetti squash lasts really well in the refrigerator. Store it in a food container; it can be refrigerated up to 5 days.

INGREDIENTS | SERVES 8

2 medium spaghetti squash, halved

Spaghetti Squash

Spaghetti squash is a very versatile squash. It can serve as a side dish or on its own with sauce and protein as a complete meal. You can drizzle with coconut oil and sprinkle with salt once it's fully baked.

1. Preheat oven to 400°F. Line an 18" baking pan with parchment paper.

2. Place squash facedown in pan.

3. Bake 45–55 minutes, depending on size and thickness of squash, or until squash is soft.

4. Set aside to cool. Once cool, use a fork to shred.

5. Transfer into food containers for storage.

PER SERVING Calories: 78 | Fat: 0.6 g | Protein: 1.9 g | Sodium: 52 mg | Fiber: 4.1 g | Carbohydrates: 18.8 g | Sugar: 7.4 g

Caramelized Onions

These go great on top of burgers or any meat. Don't rush the process, though; caramelizing takes time. The browner the color, the better the taste. You can store these up to 5 days in the refrigerator.

INGREDIENTS | SERVES 5

2 tablespoons coconut oil
5 medium onions, peeled and thinly sliced

Onions

Don't slice the onions too thin because they will shrink quite a bit as they cook. Aim to cut them ⅛" thick.

1. Heat a large skillet over medium heat and add oil. Once oil is hot, add onions and cook 15–20 minutes depending on how brown you want them.

2. Make sure you turn every few minutes to ensure they don't burn.

3. Once cooked to desired brownness, remove and set aside to cool.

4. Place in food containers and refrigerate.

PER SERVING Calories: 85 | Fat: 5.2 g | Protein: 1.1 g | Sodium: 3 mg | Fiber: 1.7 g | Carbohydrates: 9.1 g | Sugar: 4.2 g

Cauliflower Fried "Rice"

If you're going grain-free but still crave rice, this is a great option to add to your meal-prepping arsenal. It works well as a side dish or on its own as a light meal. This keeps up to 5 days in the refrigerator.

INGREDIENTS | SERVES 5

1 large cauliflower head, chopped

1 tablespoon coconut oil

1 medium onion, peeled and diced

3 cloves garlic, peeled and minced

1 cup diced celery

1 teaspoon garlic powder

¼ teaspoon freshly ground black pepper

¼ teaspoon sea salt

Cauliflower

Make sure you pulse the food processor instead of blending it continuously when processing the cauliflower into rice. This will ensure you don't over-process the cauliflower, which may make it watery.

1. In a food processor pulse cauliflower to get it to rice consistency.

2. Heat a large wok or skillet over medium heat and add oil. Once oil is hot, add onion, stir 2 minutes, then add minced garlic and celery and stir 1 more minute.

3. Add cauliflower and stir 2–3 minutes.

4. Add garlic powder, pepper, and salt and stir another 2 minutes.

5. Remove from stove and set aside to cool. Once cool, store in food containers and refrigerate.

PER SERVING Calories: 62 | Fat: 2.8 g | Protein: 2.4 g | Sodium: 138 mg | Fiber: 2.6 g | Carbohydrates: 8.1 g | Sugar: 2.9 g

Cinnamon Roasted Butternut Squash

This can be a dessert or a side to your main dishes.
This dish keeps up to 5 days in the refrigerator.

INGREDIENTS | SERVES 5

5 cups cubed butternut squash (cut into 1½" cubes)

1 tablespoon coconut oil

⅛ teaspoon sea salt

¼ teaspoon freshly ground black pepper

¼ teaspoon ground cinnamon

Coconut Oil

Microwave coconut oil for about a minute to turn it from solid to liquid form. If you don't own a microwave, you can also heat it up in a saucepan over low heat.

1. Preheat oven to 400°F. Line an 18" baking pan with parchment paper.

2. In a large mixing bowl add squash, oil, salt, and pepper and mix until well combined. Transfer squash to prepared pan.

3. Bake 40 minutes.

4. Remove from oven and sprinkle cinnamon over squash. Turn and mix with tongs to ensure squash is well coated. Continue baking another 5 minutes.

5. Remove from oven and set aside to cool. Once cool, store in food containers and refrigerate.

PER SERVING Calories: 86 | Fat: 2.7 g | Protein: 1.4 g | Sodium: 52 mg | Fiber: 2.9 g | Carbohydrates: 16.5 g | Sugar: 3.1 g

Coconut Sweet Potato Smash

This will go perfectly as a side with a jerk meat and slaw.
Store this dish up to 5 days in the refrigerator.

INGREDIENTS | SERVES 5

4 large sweet potatoes, peeled and cut into large cubes

1 tablespoon coconut oil

½ cup coconut cream

1 tablespoon fresh parsley (for garnish)

Coconut Cream

There are so many types of coconut cream, so it can be confusing to understand which one is the best to buy. Just make sure you're selecting one without any added ingredients or sugar. If you prefer a lower-fat option, replace with coconut milk instead.

1. Fill a large pot halfway with water and bring to a boil over high heat. Add sweet potatoes, turn heat to medium, and boil 12–15 minutes or until potatoes are soft.

2. Drain and return potatoes to pot; add oil and coconut cream.

3. Using a potato masher or a large fork, mash potato, oil, and cream together until well mixed. Set aside to cool.

4. Once cool, garnish with parsley and place in food containers.

PER SERVING Calories: 192 | Fat: 10.4 g | Protein: 2.5 g | Sodium: 58 mg | Fiber: 3.7 g | Carbohydrates: 22.6 g | Sugar: 4.4 g

Cauliflower Potato Mash

This is a great lower-carb alternative to your regular mashed potatoes. Store up to 5 days in the refrigerator.

INGREDIENTS | SERVES 5

2 medium yellow potatoes, peeled and cut into large cubes

1 medium cauliflower head, cut into florets (4 cups)

1 tablespoon coconut oil

½ cup coconut cream

¼ teaspoon sea salt

¼ teaspoon freshly ground black pepper

3 cloves garlic, peeled and minced

½ cup vegetable broth

1 tablespoon chopped fresh parsley (for garnish)

1. Fill a large pot halfway with water and bring to a boil over high heat. Add potatoes and boil 12–15 minutes or until potatoes are soft. Drain and set aside.

2. Fill the same pot halfway with water and bring to a boil over high heat. Add cauliflower and boil 10 minutes or until soft.

3. Drain and transfer cauliflower and potatoes to a food processor. Add oil, cream, salt, pepper, garlic, and broth and process until smooth. Depending on the size of your processor, you may need to do this in batches.

4. Set aside to cool. Once cool, garnish with parsley and place in food containers.

PER SERVING Calories: 107 | Fat: 2.8 g | Protein: 3.2 g | Sodium: 227 mg | Fiber: 3.9 g | Carbohydrates: 18.7 g | Sugar: 2.8 g

Oven-Roasted Brussels Sprouts and Squash

Buttercup squash is quite starchy, and it's a great side for any of your main dishes. This dish stores up to 5 days in the refrigerator.

INGREDIENTS | SERVES 5

1 tablespoon coconut oil

¼ teaspoon sea salt

¼ teaspoon freshly ground black pepper

½ teaspoon garlic powder

1 large buttercup squash, cut into large cubes (4–5 cups)

1 large red onion, peeled and cut into 1" pieces

3 cups halved Brussels sprouts

2 medium bell peppers, seeded and cut into 1" pieces

Buttercup Squash

Buttercup squash skin is one of the hardest skins to peel. To save time, you can roast this squash with the skin on. This squash tastes exactly the same whether the skin is on or off when roasted.

1. Preheat oven to 400°F. Line an 18" baking pan with parchment paper.

2. In a small bowl whisk coconut oil, salt, pepper, and garlic powder until well combined. Set aside.

3. In a large mixing bowl add squash, onion, Brussels sprouts, and bell peppers. Add oil mixture and stir until well combined.

4. Transfer vegetable mixture to prepared pan.

5. Bake 45 minutes or until squash is soft; make sure you occasionally turn the vegetables with a pair of tongs.

6. Set aside to cool. Once cool, place in food containers.

PER SERVING Calories: 106 | Fat: 2.8 g | Protein: 3.6 g | Sodium: 113 mg | Fiber: 4.9 g | Carbohydrates: 19.4 g | Sugar: 6.2 g

Perfectly Roasted Japanese Sweet Potatoes

Japanese sweet potatoes are like nature's cake without the high amounts of sugar. These are much denser than the regular orange sweet potatoes, so a longer baking time is necessary. These keep up to 7 days in the refrigerator.

INGREDIENTS | SERVES 5

4 medium Japanese sweet potatoes

1. Preheat oven to 400°F. Line an 18" baking pan with parchment paper.

2. With a potato brush clean potatoes well. Leave the skin on. Cut ½" off the ends and cut 3 or 4 slits per side so potatoes can vent. Transfer potatoes to prepared pan.

3. Bake 1 hour and 15 minutes.

4. Remove and set aside to cool. Cut into rounds of desired thickness. Once cool, store in food containers and refrigerate.

PER SERVING Calories: 90 | Fat: 0.0 g | Protein: 1.6 g | Sodium: 0 mg | Fiber: 3.2 g | Carbohydrates: 21.6 g | Sugar: 4.0 g

Grilled Zucchini

Undressed and unseasoned zucchini are very tasty when grilled. Try grilling them whole to keep them extra juicy. This stores up to 5 days in the refrigerator.

INGREDIENTS | SERVES 5

1 tablespoon coconut oil
¼ teaspoon sea salt
¼ teaspoon freshly ground black pepper
5 medium zucchini, cut into halves lengthwise

1. In a large bowl drizzle coconut oil, salt, and pepper over the zucchini.

2. Grill over medium heat 3 minutes each side. Set aside to cool.

3. Once cool, place in food containers.

PER SERVING Calories: 55 | Fat: 2.9 g | Protein: 2.3 g | Sodium: 108 mg | Fiber: 1.9 g | Carbohydrates: 5.9 g | Sugar: 4.7 g

Stir-Fried Bok Choy

There are many varieties of bok choy in an Asian market. This recipe specifies baby bok choy, but it works with any variety. This dish stores up to 5 days in the refrigerator.

INGREDIENTS | SERVES 5

1 tablespoon coconut oil
1 tablespoon minced fresh ginger
3 cloves garlic, peeled and minced
6 cups chopped baby bok choy
¼ teaspoon sea salt
¼ teaspoon freshly ground black pepper

1. Heat a large wok over medium heat and add oil. Once oil is hot, add ginger and garlic and stir 30 seconds.

2. Add bok choy and stir until wilted, 2 minutes.

3. Add salt and pepper and stir 1 minute. Set aside to cool.

4. Once cool, place in food containers.

PER SERVING Calories: 37 | Fat: 2.7 g | Protein: 1.4 g | Sodium: 148 mg | Fiber: 0.9 g | Carbohydrates: 2.7 g | Sugar: 1.0 g

Spicy Pickled Cabbage Slaw

This is great to go with any grilled meat. If you don't have fresh basil, you can use dried. You can also add crushed almonds on top. This slaw will keep up to 5 days in the refrigerator.

INGREDIENTS | SERVES 5

1 tablespoon white wine vinegar
1 medium lime, juiced
⅛ teaspoon ground cayenne pepper
¼ teaspoon freshly ground black pepper
½ medium green cabbage, shredded (4–5 cups)
1 cup shredded carrots
⅓ cup finely chopped pickles
2 tablespoons chopped fresh basil

1. In a small bowl whisk vinegar, lime juice, cayenne, and black pepper until well combined. Set aside.

2. In a large bowl add cabbage, carrots, and pickles. Add vinegar mixture and toss until well mixed.

3. Top with basil and serve or store in food containers and refrigerate.

PER SERVING Calories: 28 | Fat: 0.1 g | Protein: 1.2 g | Sodium: 104 mg | Fiber: 2.5 g | Carbohydrates: 6.8 g | Sugar: 3.4 g

Coconut Cilantro Cauliflower Rice

There are many variations of cauliflower rice, but if you're a coconut fan, you'll love this one. This rice stores up to 5 days in the refrigerator.

INGREDIENTS | SERVES 5

1 medium cauliflower head, cut into florets (4–5 cups)
1 tablespoon coconut oil
½ cup coconut cream
¼ teaspoon sea salt
¼ teaspoon freshly ground black pepper
3 cloves garlic, peeled and minced
1 medium lime, juiced and zest
¼ cup chopped fresh cilantro
2 tablespoons unsweetened coconut flakes

1. In a food processor pulse cauliflower to get it to rice consistency.

2. Heat a large skillet over medium heat and add oil. Once oil is hot, add cauliflower and stir 5 minutes.

3. Add coconut cream, salt, pepper, garlic, lime juice, and lime zest and stir another 2–3 minutes.

4. Top with cilantro and coconut flakes, then remove and let cool. Once cool, place in food containers.

PER SERVING Calories: 145 | Fat: 11.9 g | Protein: 3.2 g | Sodium: 127 mg | Fiber: 3.1 g | Carbohydrates: 8.5 g | Sugar: 2.3 g

Coconut Flakes

You can also sauté coconut flakes briefly in a frying pan with coconut oil to brown them before you add them on top. Make sure you are getting flakes with no sugar added.

Broccoli and Carrot Stir-Fry

This quick and easy stir-fry is a great side dish to pair with any protein and rice. If you're craving Chinese takeout, but want to stay healthy, this will do the trick. This dish stores up to 5 days in the refrigerator.

INGREDIENTS | SERVES 5

1 tablespoon coconut oil

1 cup (1"-sliced) carrots

1 tablespoon minced fresh ginger

3 cloves garlic, peeled and minced

6 cups broccoli florets

1 tablespoon water

⅛ teaspoon sea salt

1 tablespoon oyster sauce

¼ teaspoon freshly ground black pepper

Oyster Sauce

Despite the name, oyster sauce isn't fishy tasting at all. It's a staple in Asian cooking. A little goes a long way for this sauce, so don't add too much because it will make your dish too salty.

1. Heat a large wok over medium heat and add oil. Once oil is hot, add carrots, ginger, and garlic and stir 1–2 minutes.

2. Add broccoli and water and stir 2 minutes.

3. Add salt, oyster sauce, and pepper and stir 1–2 minutes.

4. Set aside to cool. Once cool, place in food containers.

PER SERVING Calories: 76 | Fat: 2.7 g | Protein: 3.5 g | Sodium: 198 mg | Fiber: 3.7 g | Carbohydrates: 11.0 g | Sugar: 3.1 g

Oven-Roasted Plantains

Yellow plantains are a crowd favorite. They're great as sides to a main dish or even as desserts. These store up to 5 days in the refrigerator.

5 medium yellow plantains
1 tablespoon melted coconut oil
⅛ teaspoon sea salt

Turn It Into a Dessert

Plantains are so delicious when roasted. The sugar in them caramelizes and you can serve them as a dessert—just drizzle some of your favorite toppings on. To keep it healthy and simple, sprinkle ground cinnamon on top.

1. Preheat oven to 400°F. Line a baking sheet with parchment paper.

2. Slice plantains in half lengthwise, then slice into 1"-thick half rounds. Place plantains on prepared sheet. Brush melted coconut oil on both sides of the plantain slices.

3. Bake 15 minutes on each side.

4. Remove and let cool. Sprinkle salt on. Once cool, place in food containers.

PER SERVING Calories: 241 | Fat: 3.0 g | Protein: 2.3 g | Sodium: 53 mg | Fiber: 4.1 g | Carbohydrates: 57.1 g | Sugar: 26.9 g

Grilled Asparagus with Lemon Zest

Asparagus are packed with vitamins and minerals like vitamins A, C, E, K, and B_6, as well as folate, iron, copper, calcium, protein, and fiber. This dish stores up to 5 days in the refrigerator.

INGREDIENTS | SERVES 5

25 asparagus spears
1 tablespoon olive oil
⅛ teaspoon sea salt
¼ teaspoon freshly ground black pepper
Zest of 1 medium lemon

1. Preheat grill on medium or high heat.

2. Bend spears until asparagus naturally cracks; toss out bottom portions.

3. In a large bowl toss asparagus with oil, salt, and pepper.

4. Grill asparagus 2–3 minutes per side.

5. Remove and let cool. Sprinkle with lemon zest. Once cool, place in food containers.

PER SERVING Calories: 40 | Fat: 2.7 g | Protein: 1.8 g | Sodium: 48 mg | Fiber: 1.8 g | Carbohydrates: 3.4 g | Sugar: 1.6 g

Sautéed Purple Cabbage

Purple cabbage is not only colorful, but it's got a nice hint of sweetness as well. This dish stores up to 5 days in the refrigerator.

INGREDIENTS | SERVES 5

½ tablespoon coconut oil

1 tablespoon minced fresh ginger

2 cloves garlic, peeled and minced

½ medium head purple cabbage, sliced thinly (4–5 cups)

¼ teaspoon sea salt

¼ teaspoon freshly ground black pepper

Purple Cabbage

Purple cabbage is a good side to add to your diet. It has a low caloric density compared to other foods. A 1-cup serving of chopped raw purple cabbage contains only 28 calories.

1. Heat a large skillet or wok over medium heat and add oil. Once oil is hot, add ginger and garlic and stir 30 seconds.

2. Add cabbage, salt, and pepper and stir 3–4 minutes or until cabbage is wilted.

3. Remove from heat and let cool. Once cool, place in food containers.

PER SERVING Calories: 43 | Fat: 2.6 g | Protein: 1.0 g | Sodium: 106 mg | Fiber: 1.8 g | Carbohydrates: 4.7 g | Sugar: 2.3 g

Roasted Buttercup Squash

These squash can be steamed, boiled, or roasted. Roasting makes them extra sweet because the sugar inside caramelizes. These should last up to 5 days in the refrigerator.

INGREDIENTS | SERVES 5

1 large buttercup squash, seeded and chopped

5 teaspoons sea salt

1 tablespoon coconut oil

¼ teaspoon freshly ground black pepper

Buttercup Squash

How do you pick a good buttercup squash? Look for weight ranging between 3 and 5 pounds, dry vines, a dull or matte appearance to the skin, a smooth and firm texture, and a hollow sound when tapped.

1. Preheat oven to 400°F. Line an 18" baking pan with parchment paper.

2. In a large mixing bowl toss squash with salt, oil, and pepper.

3. Transfer squash to prepared pan. Bake 35–40 minutes; turn squash a couple of times to ensure all sides are evenly baked.

4. Remove from oven and let cool. Once cool, place in food containers for storage.

PER SERVING Calories: 102 | Fat: 2.8 g | Protein: 2.2 g | Sodium: 400 mg | Fiber: 3.5 g | Carbohydrates: 20.0 g | Sugar: 5.1 g

Cajun Sweet Potato Wedges

You can turn this recipe into Cajun fries by cutting the potatoes into thinner spears. You can also leave the skin on. Add extra oil for them to get crispier. These store up to 5 days in the refrigerator.

INGREDIENTS | SERVES 5

¼ teaspoon salt

¼ teaspoon freshly ground black pepper

1 teaspoon paprika

1 teaspoon garlic powder

1 teaspoon onion powder

¼ teaspoon ground cayenne pepper

3 large sweet potatoes, cut into wedges

2 tablespoons melted coconut oil

1. Preheat oven to 400°F. Line an 18" baking pan with parchment paper.

2. In a small bowl mix together salt, pepper, paprika, garlic powder, onion powder, and cayenne. Set aside.

3. In a large bowl add potato wedges and oil and toss to coat wedges.

4. Sprinkle prepared seasoning over wedges and toss until well coated. Transfer potatoes to prepared pan.

5. Bake 35–45 minutes, turning often with tongs.

6. Remove and let cool. Once cool, place in food storage containers.

PER SERVING Calories: 119 | Fat: 5.2 g | Protein: 1.5 g | Sodium: 159 mg | Fiber: 2.7 g | Carbohydrates: 16.9 g | Sugar: 3.4 g

Poached Spinach with Garlic

Tired of eating raw spinach? Try this recipe to switch things up.
This dish stores up to 5 days in the refrigerator.

INGREDIENTS | SERVES 3

1 tablespoon coconut oil
10 cups spinach leaves
⅛ cup sea salt
¼ teaspoon freshly ground black pepper
3 cloves garlic, mashed, peeled, and chopped
1 cup chicken broth

Spinach

Spinach is an excellent source of vitamins K and A. It also has lots of other vitamins and minerals including folate, iron, and calcium.

1. Heat a large skillet or wok over medium heat and add oil. Once oil is hot, add spinach and stir until spinach is wilted (1–2 minutes).

2. Add salt, pepper, garlic, and broth and lower heat to a simmer. Simmer 1 minute.

3. Remove and let cool. Once cool, place in food containers.

PER SERVING Calories: 71 | Fat: 4.5 g | Protein: 3.6 g | Sodium: 4,131 mg | Fiber: 2.3 g | Carbohydrates: 5.1 g | Sugar: 0.8 g

Herbed Grilled Eggplants

Did you know there are over ten varieties of eggplants? For this recipe use the traditional large black eggplants. Store this dish up to 5 days in the refrigerator.

INGREDIENTS | SERVES 4

2 large eggplants, sliced into rounds
1 tablespoon olive oil
⅛ cup sea salt
¼ teaspoon freshly ground black pepper
½ teaspoon herbes de Provence

Eggplants

Eggplant is a very good source of dietary fiber, vitamin B_1, and copper. It also contains manganese, vitamin B_6, niacin, potassium, folate, and vitamin K.

1. Preheat grill on medium-high heat.

2. In a large mixing bowl add eggplants, oil, salt, pepper, and herbes de Provence and toss to coat.

3. Grill 2–3 minutes per side or until eggplant is soft.

4. Remove and let cool. Once cool, place in food containers.

PER SERVING Calories: 85 | Fat: 3.5 g | Protein: 2.2 g | Sodium: 2,812 mg | Fiber: 6.7 g | Carbohydrates: 13.1 g | Sugar: 7.7 g

Sautéed Swiss Chard

Green chard is surprisingly sweet when steamed or sautéed. Swiss chard is extremely high in vitamins K and A, magnesium, and potassium. This dish stores up to 5 days in the refrigerator.

INGREDIENTS | SERVES 4

1 tablespoon coconut oil

3 cloves garlic, peeled and minced

6 cups chopped Swiss chard

⅛ cup sea salt

¼ teaspoon freshly ground black pepper

1. Heat a large wok over medium heat and add oil. Once oil is hot, add garlic and stir 30 seconds.

2. Add chard, salt, and pepper and stir until chard is wilted.

3. Remove and let cool. Once cool, place in food containers.

PER SERVING Calories: 43 | Fat: 3.3 g | Protein: 1.1 g | Sodium: 2,923 mg | Fiber: 1.0 g | Carbohydrates: 2.9 g | Sugar: 0.6 g

Steamed Mixed Vegetables

Steaming vegetables is the best way to retain their nutrients and vitamins. You can use the method in this recipe to steam almost any vegetable or leafy green. Steamed vegetables store well in the refrigerator up to 5 days.

INGREDIENTS | SERVES 5

2 cups broccoli florets

2 cups cauliflower florets

1 cup green beans

1 cup baby carrots

1. Fill large pot ⅓ of the way with water and bring to a boil over high heat.

2. Place vegetables in a steaming basket and steam on high 4–5 minutes.

3. Remove and let cool. Once cool, store in food containers.

PER SERVING Calories: 39 | Fat: 0.2 g | Protein: 2.5 g | Sodium: 43 mg | Fiber: 3.1 g | Carbohydrates: 8.4 g | Sugar: 3.3 g

Spicy Kale Chips

Kale chips are super trendy right now, but they're expensive to buy. Why not make your own? These chips should last a few days at room temperature.

INGREDIENTS | SERVES 4

1 bunch curly kale, stems removed, torn into bite-sized pieces
1 tablespoon coconut oil
⅛ cup sea salt
¼ teaspoon freshly ground black pepper
¼ teaspoon paprika
¼ teaspoon ground cayenne pepper
½ teaspoon garlic powder
¼ teaspoon onion powder

Kale

Kale is an amazing superfood. That's because it's full of antioxidants, nutrients, and vitamins. It is especially high in vitamin K.

1. Preheat oven to 350°F. Line an 18" baking pan with parchment paper.

2. In a large mixing bowl add kale, oil, and salt and gently massage kale with hands until salt and oil are thoroughly mixed into the kale.

3. Transfer kale to prepared pan. Bake 25–30 minutes; turn the chips a few times during cooking to ensure all sides are baked and crisped.

4. While kale is baking, in a small bowl combine pepper, paprika, cayenne, garlic powder, and onion powder.

5. When chips are finished baking, remove from oven and immediately sprinkle with seasoning mix; toss to ensure chips are well coated.

6. Let cool. Once cool, place in zip-top bags and store in a cool and dry place.

PER SERVING Calories: 72 | Fat: 3.6 g | Protein: 3.7 g | Sodium: 2,839 mg | Fiber: 3.2 g | Carbohydrates: 8.0 g | Sugar: 1.9 g

Curry Roasted Chickpeas

These are great as a healthy snack or can even be a side to a main dish or served on salads. These should last up to 3 days in a tightly sealed container in a cool place.

INGREDIENTS | SERVES 4

2 cups canned chickpeas
1 tablespoon melted coconut oil
¼ teaspoon freshly ground black pepper
¼ teaspoon paprika
¼ teaspoon ground cayenne pepper
½ teaspoon chili powder
1 teaspoon curry powder
1 teaspoon lemon juice

Chickpeas

Chickpeas are filled with protein and fiber, so they will keep you feeling satisfied for hours after eating. For more economical ways of making big batches of chickpeas, buy the dry peas and soak and cook them yourself.

1. Preheat oven to 400°F. Line a 17" baking pan with parchment paper.

2. Make sure the chickpeas are drained and completely dry. Use a paper towel to rub them together to absorb excess water. The drier they are, the crispier they will get.

3. In a large mixing bowl toss chickpeas, oil, pepper, paprika, cayenne, chili powder, curry, and lemon juice. Mix until well combined.

4. Transfer chickpeas to prepared pan. Bake 35–40 minutes or until crispy. Turn frequently to ensure even cooking.

5. Remove from oven and let cool.

6. These are best served immediately since they'll lose their crispiness when refrigerated. If you need to store them, they'll keep for up to 3 days in a tightly sealed container in a cool place.

PER SERVING Calories: 137 | Fat: 4.6 g | Protein: 5.5 g | Sodium: 170 mg | Fiber: 5.3 g | Carbohydrates: 18.2 g | Sugar: 3.1 g

Simple Sweet Potato Fries

Some restaurant sweet potato fries have almost 1,000 calories in one serving. They are also full of unhealthy oil. Make your own for a much healthier option. Store these in a tightly sealed container in a cool place. These are best served fresh but they will last 2–3 days if refrigerated.

INGREDIENTS | SERVES 5

3 medium sweet potatoes, cut into ½" spears (5 cups)
2 tablespoons melted coconut oil
¼ teaspoon salt
¼ teaspoon freshly ground black pepper
½ teaspoon garlic powder

1. Preheat oven to 400°F. Line a 17" baking pan with parchment paper.

2. Fill a large pot halfway with water and bring to a boil over high heat.

3. Place potatoes in boiling water 1–2 minutes. Strain and pat sweet potatoes dry with paper towels. The drier they are, the crispier they will get.

4. In a large mixing bowl toss potatoes, oil, salt, pepper, and garlic powder until well combined.

5. Transfer potatoes to prepared pan. Bake 35–40 minutes or until crispy. Turn frequently to ensure even cooking.

6. Remove from oven and let cool.

7. These are best served immediately since they'll lose their crispiness once refrigerated. If you need to store them, store in a tightly sealed container in a cool place.

PER SERVING Calories: 91 | Fat: 2.6 g | Protein: 1.3 g | Sodium: 159 mg | Fiber: 2.4 g | Carbohydrates: 16.0 g | Sugar: 3.3 g

Healthy Potato Salad with Dill

Potato salad can be very unhealthy if it is slathered with mayonnaise. This healthier version will let you enjoy it guilt-free. This salad will keep in the refrigerator up to 5 days.

INGREDIENTS | SERVES 5

5 cups (1" cubes, skins on) yellow potatoes

½ cup plain Greek yogurt

¼ teaspoon freshly ground black pepper

¼ teaspoon salt

½ teaspoon garlic powder

2 cloves garlic, peeled and minced

½ medium onion, peeled and minced

2 tablespoons Dijon mustard

3 large hard-boiled eggs, chopped

2 dill pickles, diced

1 tablespoon minced fresh dill

1. Fill a large pot halfway with water and bring to a boil over high heat.

2. Add potatoes and boil 8–10 minutes or until potatoes are soft. Strain until potatoes are completely dry.

3. In a large mixing bowl add potatoes, yogurt, pepper, salt, garlic powder, minced garlic, onion, mustard, eggs, pickles, and dill and mix well.

4. Store in food containers and refrigerate.

PER SERVING Calories: 181 | Fat: 3.3 g | Protein: 9.1 g | Sodium: 657 mg | Fiber: 4.4 g | Carbohydrates: 27.7 g | Sugar: 4.0 g

Paleo Substitutions

If you're looking for a paleo or Whole30 option, use sweet potatoes and add Whole30-approved mayonnaise instead of yogurt.

Rob's Roasted Potatoes

Roasted potatoes are always a great addition to any meal. You can also substitute colorful mini potatoes for the yellow potatoes—just cut them in half instead of cubing. This dish will keep in the refrigerator up to 5 days.

INGREDIENTS | SERVES 5

5 cups (1" cubes, skins on) yellow potatoes

½ teaspoon freshly ground black pepper

¼ teaspoon salt

1 teaspoon garlic powder

1 tablespoon apple cider vinegar

½ tablespoon dried rosemary

½ tablespoon dried parsley

½ tablespoon onion powder

1 teaspoon paprika

1 teaspoon red pepper flakes

2 tablespoons coconut oil (or olive oil)

1. Preheat oven to 400°F. Line an 18" baking pan with parchment paper.

2. In a large mixing bowl add potatoes, pepper, salt, garlic powder, vinegar, rosemary, parsley, onion powder, paprika, red pepper flakes, and oil. Mix until well combined.

3. Transfer to prepared pan. Bake 40 minutes, turning often to ensure all sides are brown.

4. Turn oven to broil and broil 2–3 minutes.

5. Remove from oven and let cool. Once cooled, store in food containers and refrigerate.

PER SERVING Calories: 158 | Fat: 5.3 g | Protein: 2.8 g | Sodium: 141 mg | Fiber: 4.2 g | Carbohydrates: 25.3 g | Sugar: 1.7 g

Smoky Cauliflower Nuggets

If you're craving chicken wings or nuggets, this is a healthy, paleo, and vegan option. Make it extra spicy by adding red pepper flakes on top. It will keep well up to 5 days.

INGREDIENTS | SERVES 4

1 medium cauliflower head, cut into florets
½ tablespoon olive oil
½ teaspoon freshly ground black pepper
⅛ teaspoon salt
1 teaspoon garlic powder
1 teaspoon smoked paprika

1. Preheat oven to 400°F. Line an 18" baking pan with parchment paper.

2. Place cauliflower in prepared pan in an even layer.

3. Drizzle with oil and sprinkle on half of each the black pepper, salt, garlic powder, and paprika.

4. Bake 15 minutes, remove from oven, turn cauliflower, and sprinkle on remaining seasoning. Bake another 15–20 minutes or until cauliflower is soft.

5. Remove from oven and let cool. Once cooled, store in food containers and refrigerate.

PER SERVING Calories: 39 | Fat: 1.9 g | Protein: 1.8 g | Sodium: 97 mg | Fiber: 2.0 g | Carbohydrates: 5.1 g | Sugar: 1.6 g

Basic Steamed Quinoa

This is the easiest way to cook your quinoa. It can be added to salads or used as a side dish to your proteins. This will keep well in the refrigerator up to 5 days.

INGREDIENTS | SERVES 6

6 cups water

3 cups uncooked quinoa

⅛ teaspoon salt

Ratio

The typical ratio of quinoa to water is 1 to 2. One cup uncooked quinoa typically yields 3 cups cooked. If you have a rice cooker, you can also cook the quinoa in that.

1. In a medium pot bring water and quinoa to a boil over medium heat.

2. Reduce heat to low, add salt, stir, cover, and simmer 15–20 minutes or until liquid has all been absorbed.

3. Remove from stove and let cool. Once cooled, store in food containers and refrigerate.

PER SERVING Calories: 208 | Fat: 3.2 g | Protein: 8.0 g | Sodium: 60 mg | Fiber: 4.0 g | Carbohydrates: 36.4 g | Sugar: 0.0 g

Rice and Peas

If you're craving Caribbean food but want a healthier version of rice and peas, this is it. This will keep well in the refrigerator up to 5 days.

INGREDIENTS | SERVES 6

5 cups water

2 cups parboiled/converted rice

⅛ teaspoon salt

1 tablespoon coconut oil

¼ cup coconut cream

1 cup frozen peas

1 tablespoon chopped fresh thyme

Thyme

If you don't have fresh thyme, dried or ground thyme will work fine. It's okay to be generous with the thyme because it is extra fragrant in this recipe.

1. In a medium pot bring water and rice to a boil over medium heat.

2. Reduce heat to low. Add salt, stir, cover, and simmer 15–20 minutes or until liquid has all been absorbed.

3. Once rice is fully cooked, add coconut oil, cream, peas, and thyme and stir 1 minute.

4. Remove from stove and let cool. Once cooled, store in food containers and refrigerate.

PER SERVING Calories: 300 | Fat: 6.0 g | Protein: 6.2 g | Sodium: 64 mg | Fiber: 2.4 g | Carbohydrates: 53.7 g | Sugar: 1.3 g

Basmati Rice with Turmeric

Having a rice side dish at a restaurant can add unwanted calories due to the amount of oil that's in prepared rice. You can make your own at home that is just as tasty but without the excess oil. This will keep well in the refrigerator up to 5 days.

INGREDIENTS | SERVES 6

4 cups water
2 cups basmati rice
⅛ teaspoon salt
¼ teaspoon ground turmeric
½ tablespoon coconut oil

Basmati Rice Trick

There may be a reason why some people can cook better rice than others. The secret is to soak your rice 30 minutes in water first. You'll notice a difference in the texture if you do this.

1. Rinse rice to wash and remove excess starch.

2. In a medium pot soak rice in 4 cups water 30 minutes.

3. Bring water and rice to a boil over medium heat.

4. Reduce heat to low. Add salt, turmeric, and coconut oil and stir well.

5. Cover and simmer 15–20 minutes or until liquid has all been absorbed.

6. Remove from stove and let cool. Once cooled, store in food containers and refrigerate.

PER SERVING Calories: 235 | Fat: 1.4 g | Protein: 4.4 g | Sodium: 51 mg | Fiber: 0.8 g | Carbohydrates: 49.4 g | Sugar: 0.1 g

Healthy Mexican Rice and Beans

This dish is so flavorful you can eat it alone or with your favorite protein. If your chicken broth is salted, you can omit the salt in this recipe. This dish will keep up to 5 days in the refrigerator.

INGREDIENTS | SERVES 6

2 cups brown rice

4 cups chicken broth

1 tablespoon coconut oil, divided

1 medium onion, peeled and diced

4 cloves garlic, peeled and minced

½ cup tomato paste

1 tablespoon paprika

1 tablespoon ground cumin

¼ teaspoon salt

¼ teaspoon freshly ground black pepper

1 cup canned black beans

2 tablespoons lime juice

1 teaspoon lime zest

½ cup chopped fresh cilantro

1. Rinse rice to wash and remove excess starch.

2. In a medium pot bring rice, broth, and ½ tablespoon oil to a boil.

3. Reduce heat to low. Cover and simmer 15–20 minutes or until liquid has all been absorbed.

4. While rice is cooking, in a medium pan over medium heat add remaining oil. Once oil is hot, add onions and stir 2 minutes or until onions are brown.

5. Add garlic and stir 1 more minute. Add tomato paste, paprika, cumin, salt, pepper, and black beans and stir 1 more minute. Set aside.

6. When rice is finished cooking, mix in bean mixture, lime juice, lime zest, and cilantro and stir until well combined. Remove from stove to cool.

7. Once cooled, store in food containers and refrigerate.

PER SERVING Calories: 330 | Fat: 4.2 g | Protein: 9.9 g | Sodium: 1,046 mg | Fiber: 6.8 g | Carbohydrates: 63.6 g | Sugar: 4.5 g

Coconut Jasmine Rice

This goes perfectly with the curry recipes in Chapter 5.
This will keep well in the refrigerator up to 5 days.

Rice Cooker

Invest in a rice cooker if you don't have one; it will allow you to multitask a lot more, which will save your prep time. When shopping for a rice cooker, look for one that has many different settings. It will allow you to keep cooked rice warm for an extended period of time.

1. Rinse rice to wash and remove excess starch. Repeat process a couple of times until the water runs clear.

2. In a medium pot bring rice, water, and coconut milk to a boil over medium heat.

3. Reduce heat to low. Cover and simmer 15–20 minutes or until liquid has all been absorbed.

4. Remove from stove and let cool. Once cooled, store in food containers and refrigerate.

PER SERVING Calories: 262 | Fat: 4.1 g | Protein: 4.8 g | Sodium: 5 mg | Fiber: 0.8 g | Carbohydrates: 49.8 g | Sugar: 0.1 g

Boiled Cassava

Cassavas are like potatoes, but even starchier. If you need another starchy vegetable option, this is it. It will keep well in the refrigerator up to 5 days.

INGREDIENTS | SERVES 5

1 large (2–3-pound) cassava, cut into 3 or 4 large rounds

Cassavas for Dessert

You can even turn cassavas into a dessert. Just cut them into bite-sized chunks, add a drizzle of maple syrup and some coconut cream on top, and voilà—a sweet and delicious treat.

1. Bring a large pot of water to boil over high heat.

2. Add cassava and boil 15–20 minutes or until soft. You can test this by inserting a steak knife or toothpick; it should smoothly enter the cassava.

3. Remove skin and center root, cut into smaller pieces, and place in food containers for storage.

PER SERVING Calories: 326 | Fat: 0.4 g | Protein: 2.8 g | Sodium: 28 mg | Fiber: 3.7 g | Carbohydrates: 77.7 g | Sugar: 3.5 g

Pan-Seared Shrimp with Herbs

Shrimp are an amazing protein to add to your diet. They are low in fat but high in protein, which will keep you full for a long time. These will keep well in the refrigerator up to 5 days.

INGREDIENTS | SERVES 4

3 cups shrimp, shells removed
¼ teaspoon freshly ground black pepper
1 teaspoon garlic powder
¼ teaspoon ground cayenne pepper
1 teaspoon herbes de Provence
1 tablespoon coconut oil

Shrimp

Shrimp naturally have a good amount of salt in them, so adding more salt is not necessary. Also, don't overcook shrimp; they are very tough when overcooked.

1. Rinse shrimp with water and pat dry with a paper towel.

2. In a large bowl add shrimp, black pepper, garlic powder, cayenne, and herbes de Provence and mix well.

3. Heat a large pan over medium heat and add oil. Once oil is hot, add shrimp one by one. Make sure shrimp are in an even layer to get a good sear on each.

4. Sear 30 seconds per side or longer depending on size. Remove shrimp when fully pink.

5. Place in food containers for storage.

PER SERVING Calories: 83 | Fat: 3.8 g | Protein: 10.0 g | Sodium: 407 mg | Fiber: 0.2 g | Carbohydrates: 1.6 g | Sugar: 0.0 g

Greek Potato Wedges

The Greeks really know how to bake their potatoes. This version is lemony and smooth.
This dish stores well; in food containers it will keep up to 5 days in the refrigerator.

INGREDIENTS | SERVES 5

½ cup fresh lemon juice

3 cloves garlic, peeled and minced

1 tablespoon dried oregano

1 tablespoon dried thyme

½ cup chicken broth

¼ teaspoon sea salt

¼ teaspoon freshly ground black pepper

2 tablespoons olive oil

6 large russet potatoes, peeled and wedged

Keep Them Poached

The secret to making sure these potatoes don't dry out is to keep them in the lemony oil broth until you're ready to serve them. Pack them separately if you're afraid of them leaking into other foods or use a divided container.

1. Preheat oven to 400°F.

2. In a bowl whisk lemon juice, garlic, oregano, thyme, broth, salt, pepper, and oil until well combined.

3. Put potatoes in a 2"-deep baking pan, making sure they don't overlap each other. Pour seasoning mixture over potatoes, making sure potatoes are well coated. Cover with foil and bake 1 hour and 15 minutes.

4. Turn potatoes at least once during cooking.

5. Remove and let cool; transfer into a deep food container along with cooking liquid. Keep potatoes soaking in the cooking liquid until ready to serve.

PER SERVING Calories: 345 | Fat: 5.6 g | Protein: 8.2 g | Sodium: 204 mg | Fiber: 5.3 g | Carbohydrates: 68.6 g | Sugar: 3.0 g

Guacamole

You can serve this with plantain chips or even sweet potato fries. This dish is best served fresh, or at most it can be stored 1 day in the refrigerator. If you are planning to store this, make sure the container is airtight. A Mason jar would be a great container to store it.

INGREDIENTS | SERVES 4

3 medium ripe avocados, pitted, flesh removed, and chopped

⅛ cup minced red onions

¼ cup seeded and diced tomatoes

1 medium jalapeño pepper, seeded and finely diced

1 clove garlic, peeled and minced

1 medium lime, juiced

⅛ cup chopped fresh cilantro

¼ teaspoon freshly ground black pepper

¼ teaspoon sea salt

⅛ teaspoon ground cayenne pepper

1. In a large bowl add avocados and use a fork to mash until smooth.

2. Add onion, tomatoes, jalapeño, garlic, lime juice, cilantro, black pepper, salt, and cayenne and mix until well combined.

3. Serve immediately or store 1 day in the refrigerator.

PER SERVING Calories: 177 | Fat: 14.0 g | Protein: 2.3 g | Sodium: 125 mg | Fiber: 7.4 g | Carbohydrates: 10.7 g | Sugar: 1.0 g

Pico de Gallo

Fresh salsas are so much healthier when they are homemade because there aren't any preservatives and additives, just wholesome ingredients. You can serve this immediately or store up to 3 days.

INGREDIENTS | SERVES 4

2 medium tomatoes, diced

½ medium red onion, chopped

⅛ cup chopped fresh cilantro

2 cloves garlic, peeled and minced

1 medium jalapeño pepper, seeded and finely diced

½ medium lime, juiced

⅛ teaspoon ground cayenne pepper

¼ teaspoon sea salt

⅛ teaspoon freshly ground black pepper

⅛ teaspoon ground cumin

¼ teaspoon paprika

In a large bowl add tomatoes, onion, cilantro, garlic, jalapeño, lime juice, cayenne, salt, black pepper, cumin, and paprika and mix until well combined. Store in food container and refrigerate up to 3 days.

PER SERVING Calories: 19 | Fat: 0.1 g | Protein: 0.9 g | Sodium: 120 mg | Fiber: 1.2 g | Carbohydrates: 4.6 g | Sugar: 2.4 g

Spice

For a milder version, omit the jalapeño and cayenne. Add ½ teaspoon paprika instead. For an even spicier version, add fresh serrano peppers.

Peach Salsa

This is amazing on fish or seafood. It even goes well with proteins like chicken or beef. Serve this immediately or store up to 3 days.

INGREDIENTS | SERVES 5

3 cups diced peaches

1 cup diced tomatoes

¼ cup finely diced red onion

⅛ cup chopped fresh cilantro

2 cloves garlic, peeled and minced

1 medium jalapeño pepper, seeded and finely diced

1 medium lime, juiced

⅛ teaspoon ground cayenne pepper

¼ teaspoon sea salt

In a large bowl add peaches, tomatoes, onions, cilantro, garlic, jalapeño, lime juice, cayenne, and salt and mix until well combined. Store in food containers and refrigerate up to 3 days.

PER SERVING Calories: 47 | Fat: 0.2 g | Protein: 1.4 g | Sodium: 95 mg | Fiber: 2.1 g | Carbohydrates: 11.6 g | Sugar: 9.1 g

Garlic Roasted Mushrooms

The mushrooms in this recipe come out juicy, meaty, and perfectly roasted. You'll want to eat them all in one sitting. These will keep well in the refrigerator up to 5 days.

INGREDIENTS | SERVES 5

3–4 cups white button whole mushrooms, cleaned and trimmed

3–4 cups cremini brown whole mushrooms, cleaned and trimmed

1 tablespoon melted butter

3 cloves garlic, peeled and minced

¼ teaspoon sea salt

½ teaspoon freshly ground black pepper

1. Preheat oven to 400°F. Line an 18" baking pan with parchment paper.

2. In a large bowl toss mushrooms, butter, garlic, salt, and pepper until well combined.

3. Transfer mushrooms to prepared pan. Bake 40–45 minutes, depending on the size of mushrooms. Make sure you turn the mushrooms a couple of times during cooking.

4. Put aside to cool, then store in food containers.

PER SERVING Calories: 48 | Fat: 2.3 g | Protein: 3.3 g | Sodium: 118 mg | Fiber: 1.0 g | Carbohydrates: 5.1 g | Sugar: 2.1 g

Grill Them

These mushrooms are amazing on the barbecue grill. Wrap them tightly with foil to make sure the juices don't leak out. If you're vegan, substitute coconut oil for the butter.

Cajun Shrimp

Shrimp are a healthy protein. A 3-ounce portion of shrimp has almost 18 grams of protein and 1 gram of fat. This dish will keep well in the refrigerator up to 5 days.

INGREDIENTS | SERVES 4

3 cups shrimp, shells removed
¼ teaspoon freshly ground black pepper
1 teaspoon garlic powder
¼ teaspoon ground cayenne pepper
½ teaspoon paprika
½ teaspoon red pepper flakes
½ teaspoon ground cumin
½ teaspoon dried basil
⅛ teaspoon salt
1 tablespoon coconut oil

1. Rinse shrimp with water and pat dry with paper towels.

2. In a large bowl add shrimp and seasonings and mix well.

3. Heat a large pan over medium heat and add oil. Once oil is hot, add shrimp one by one. Make sure shrimp are in an even layer to get a good sear on each.

4. Sear 30 seconds per side or longer depending on size. Remove when shrimp are fully pink.

5. Place in food containers for storage.

PER SERVING Calories: 84 | Fat: 3.8 g | Protein: 10.0 g | Sodium: 480 mg | Fiber: 0.2 g | Carbohydrates: 1.7 g | Sugar: 0.1 g

Steamed Brown Rice

You can steam any rice using this recipe, just follow the rice-to-water ratio of one part rice to two parts water. Some rice like parboiled/converted might need a little more water. This will keep well up to 5 days.

INGREDIENTS | SERVES 6

4 cups water
2 cups brown rice

1. In a medium pot bring water and rice to a boil over medium heat.

2. Reduce heat to low. Cover and simmer 15–20 minutes or until liquid has all been absorbed.

3. Once rice is fully cooked, remove and let cool. Once cooled, store in food containers and refrigerate.

4. If you're finding it a bit dry the next day, just put a couple of drops of water into the rice before microwaving to reheat.

PER SERVING Calories: 229 | Fat: 1.6 g | Protein: 4.8 g | Sodium: 8 mg | Fiber: 2.2 g | Carbohydrates: 48.2 g | Sugar: 0.0 g

CHAPTER 12

Soups

Butternut Squash Soup

This soup is so creamy without even a drop of cream being added.
This soup will store well up to 5 days in the refrigerator.

INGREDIENTS | SERVES 6

1 medium butternut squash, peeled and cubed

3 medium yellow potatoes, skins on and cubed

1 leek stalk, cleaned and chopped

¼ teaspoon sea salt

¼ teaspoon freshly ground black pepper

¼ teaspoon paprika

1 tablespoon melted coconut oil, divided,

1 medium Spanish onion, peeled and sliced thinly

½ teaspoon ground cinnamon

4 cups low-sodium chicken broth

⅛ teaspoon ground cayenne pepper

3 tablespoons coconut milk (optional)

Butternut Squash

When picking the right squash, look for one that's heavy for its size with firm skin and free of bruises. The fall is the best time to make this soup because that's when squash are in season and will make the soup extra sweet.

1. Preheat oven to 400°F. Line an 18" baking pan with parchment paper.

2. In a large mixing bowl add squash, potatoes, leeks, salt, pepper, paprika, and ½ tablespoon oil and combine well.

3. Transfer mixture to prepared pan. Bake 40–45 minutes or until squash and potatoes are soft.

4. While baking, in a small saucepan over medium heat add remaining ½ tablespoon oil. When oil is hot reduce heat to low and add onions. Stir onions periodically to caramelize without burning and cook 15 minutes or until onions are light brown. Add cinnamon and stir 1 more minute. Set aside.

5. In a blender (you may have to do this in batches depending on the size of your blender), add squash mixture, onions, and broth (1 cup at a time) and blend until smooth. Don't let the consistency get too watery. You may not need all 4 cups of broth depending on the size of your vegetables.

6. Divide evenly into food containers and store (this is best in Mason jars).

7. When ready to serve, sprinkle cayenne and add ½ tablespoon coconut milk on top of each serving.

PER SERVING (with coconut milk) Calories: 177 | Fat: 3.8 g | Protein: 5.5 g | Sodium: 472 mg | Fiber: 5.2 g | Carbohydrates: 32.4 g | Sugar: 4.9 g

Spicy Kale and Broccoli Soup

You can use either black kale or curly kale for this.
This soup will store well up to 5 days in the refrigerator.

INGREDIENTS | SERVES 5

3 cups low-sodium chicken broth

2 medium yellow potatoes, skins on and cubed

1 medium carrot, peeled and chopped (1 cup)

4 cups broccoli florets

1 bunch (stems and leaves) kale, chopped (about 5 cups)

½ medium onion, peeled and chopped

1 medium jalapeño pepper, seeded and chopped

¼ teaspoon sea salt

¼ teaspoon freshly ground black pepper

⅛ teaspoon ground cayenne pepper

½ teaspoon red pepper flakes

1. In a large stockpot bring chicken broth to a boil over high heat.

2. Add potatoes and carrots and boil on medium heat 8–10 minutes or until potatoes and carrots are soft.

3. Add broccoli, kale, and onions and cook 2–3 minutes or until kale is wilted.

4. Pour vegetable mixture into a blender; add jalapeño, salt, black pepper, cayenne, and red pepper flakes and blend until smooth. Add broth 1 cup at a time and blend, making sure that the consistency does not get too watery. You may not need all 3 cups of broth depending on the size of your vegetables.

5. Divide evenly into food containers and store (this is best in Mason jars).

PER SERVING Calories: 116 | Fat: 0.2 g | Protein: 6.5 g | Sodium: 487 mg | Fiber: 5.5 g | Carbohydrates: 23.8 g | Sugar: 4.7 g

Cauliflower Potato Leek Soup

If you love potato soups, you'll love this low-carbohydrate version.
This soup will store well up to 5 days in the refrigerator.

INGREDIENTS | SERVES 6

4 medium yellow potatoes, skins on and cubed

1 leek stalk, cleaned and chopped

1 medium cauliflower head, chopped (3–4 cups)

1 medium white Spanish onion, peeled and chopped

¼ teaspoon sea salt

¼ teaspoon freshly ground black pepper

1 tablespoon melted coconut oil

4 cups low-sodium chicken broth

Vegan or Vegetarian?

Use vegetable broth to make this dish vegan. You can also use water. The flavors won't be as pronounced, but it will still work.

1. Preheat oven to 400°F. Line an 18" baking pan with parchment paper.

2. In a large mixing bowl add potatoes, leeks, cauliflower, onions, salt, pepper, and oil and mix until well combined.

3. Add vegetables to prepared pan and bake 40–45 minutes or until potatoes are soft.

4. Remove from oven and transfer vegetable mixture to a blender; add broth 1 cup at a time and blend, making sure that the consistency does not get too watery. You may not need all 4 cups of broth depending on the size of your vegetables.

5. Divide evenly into food containers and store (this is best in Mason jars).

PER SERVING Calories: 153 | Fat: 2.4 g | Protein: 6.1 g | Sodium: 493 mg | Fiber: 5.1 g | Carbohydrates: 28.1 g | Sugar: 3.8 g

Tomato Gazpacho

This soup is great on the go because you can eat it cold. This is best refrigerated overnight, but you can refrigerate it a minimum of 1 hour if you don't have time. Also, do not process everything at once; it will get too mushy. This is best served immediately, however it can be refrigerated up to 3 days.

INGREDIENTS | SERVES 4

2 medium English cucumbers, peeled and chopped

5 medium tomatoes, peeled, seeded, and chopped

1 medium red bell pepper, seeded and chopped

1 medium Spanish onion, peeled and chopped

3 cloves garlic, peeled and minced

1 (26-ounce) can crushed tomatoes

1 medium lemon, juiced

1 teaspoon red wine vinegar

1 tablespoon extra-virgin olive oil

½ teaspoon sea salt

½ teaspoon freshly ground black pepper

1 tablespoon minced fresh mint

1. In a food processor process ingredients one at a time in following order, then transfer to a large bowl: cucumbers, chopped tomatoes, red pepper, and onions.

2. Return processed vegetables to the food processor; add garlic, crushed tomatoes, lemon juice, vinegar, oil, salt, black pepper, and mint and blend until smooth.

3. Divide evenly into food containers and refrigerate overnight for best results.

PER SERVING Calories: 149 | Fat: 3.9 g | Protein: 5.7 g | Sodium: 588 mg | Fiber: 7.1 g | Carbohydrates: 26.7 g | Sugar: 15.7 g

Cucumber and Basil Gazpacho

This soup is so refreshing and it definitely beats the summer heat. This is best refrigerated overnight, but if you are pressed for time you can refrigerate it a minimum of 1 hour. This is best served immediately, but can be refrigerated up to 3 days.

INGREDIENTS | SERVES 5

2 medium English cucumbers, peeled and chopped

1 medium tomato, peeled, seeded, and chopped

2 medium green bell peppers, seeded and chopped

1 medium Spanish onion, peeled and chopped

2 cloves garlic, peeled and minced

¼ cup chopped green onions

½ medium lime, juiced

1 tablespoon extra-virgin olive oil

½ teaspoon sea salt

½ teaspoon freshly ground black pepper

½ cup chopped fresh basil

1. In a food processor process the following ingredients one at a time, then transfer to a large bowl: cucumbers, tomato, green pepper, and onions.

2. Return processed vegetables to the food processor; add garlic, green onions, lime juice, oil, salt, black pepper, and basil and blend until smooth.

3. Divide evenly into food containers and refrigerate overnight for best results.

PER SERVING Calories: 53 | Fat: 2.7 g | Protein: 1.3 g | Sodium: 191 mg | Fiber: 1.8 g | Carbohydrates: 6.5 g | Sugar: 3.2 g

Thai Pumpkin Soup

If you like pumpkin, you might be obsessed with this. To make the pumpkin seeds extra tasty and flavorful, you can roast them quickly in a pan over low heat and add to the soup right before serving. This soup will last up to 5 days in the refrigerator.

INGREDIENTS | SERVES 5

1 tablespoon extra-virgin olive oil

1 medium Spanish onion, peeled and chopped

1 tablespoon tomato paste

3 cups pumpkin purée

1 cup sweet potatoes, peeled, chopped, and boiled

1 tablespoon chopped fresh ginger

2 cloves garlic, peeled and chopped

3 cups chicken broth

1 green Thai chili, seeded and chopped

½ cup coconut cream

1 cup coconut milk

1 medium lemon, juiced

½ teaspoon sea salt

½ teaspoon freshly ground black pepper

¼ cup pumpkin seeds (for garnish)

1. Heat a large skillet over medium heat and add oil and onions. Sauté onions until lightly brown, 2 minutes. Add tomato paste, pumpkin, sweet potatoes, ginger, and garlic and stir 3–4 minutes.

2. Transfer mixture to blender, then add broth, chili, cream, milk, lemon juice, salt, and pepper and blend until smooth.

3. Divide evenly into food containers (best kept in Mason jars).

4. Garnish with pumpkin seeds before serving.

PER SERVING Calories: 312 | Fat: 22.9 g | Protein: 7.2 g | Sodium: 604 mg | Fiber: 5.9 g | Carbohydrates: 21.7 g | Sugar: 7.3 g

Sweet Pea Soup

Consuming green peas is a great way to get your protein from a plant source. This soup will last up to 5 days in the refrigerator.

INGREDIENTS | SERVES 5

1 tablespoon coconut oil

1 Spanish onion, peeled and chopped

3 medium yellow potatoes, skins on and cubed

1 cup chopped carrots

2 cloves garlic, peeled and chopped

1 cup frozen green peas

½ teaspoon sea salt

½ teaspoon freshly ground black pepper

4 cups low-sodium chicken broth

Fresh Peas

For an even fresher taste, use fresh green peas instead of frozen ones. These are seasonal, though, and may also be very expensive. If you are using frozen peas, you do not need to thaw before using.

1. Heat a large skillet over medium heat and add oil and onions. Sauté onions until lightly brown, 2 minutes. Add potatoes, carrots, and garlic and stir another 5–6 minutes. Add peas, salt, pepper, and chicken broth.

2. Simmer over low heat 10–15 minutes or until potatoes are soft.

3. Transfer everything into a blender and blend until smooth.

4. Divide evenly into food containers (best kept in Mason jars).

PER SERVING Calories: 165 | Fat: 2.8 g | Protein: 6.7 g | Sodium: 698 mg | Fiber: 5.4 g | Carbohydrates: 29.3 g | Sugar: 5.3 g

Zucchini Soup

This soup is one of the tastiest ways to eat zucchini, and it's also very sweet and refreshing too. If you're not a fan of sweet potatoes, you can use one yellow potato. You can also leave the skin on for regular potatoes. This will last up to 5 days in the refrigerator.

INGREDIENTS | SERVES 5

1 tablespoon coconut oil

1 medium onion, peeled and chopped

1 medium sweet potato, skin on and chopped

1 cup chopped carrots

2 cloves garlic, peeled and chopped

½ cup diced celery

1 medium green bell pepper, seeded and chopped

2 medium zucchini, chopped

½ teaspoon sea salt

½ teaspoon freshly ground black pepper

3 cups low-sodium chicken broth

½ cup coconut milk

1. Heat a large skillet over medium heat and add oil and onions. Sauté onions until lightly brown, 2 minutes. Add potatoes, carrots, and garlic and stir another 5–6 minutes. Add celery, bell pepper, zucchini, salt, pepper, and chicken broth.

2. Simmer over low heat 8–10 minutes or until potatoes and carrots are soft.

3. Transfer everything into a blender, add coconut milk, and blend until smooth.

4. Divide evenly into food containers (best kept in Mason jars).

PER SERVING Calories: 137 | Fat: 7.3 g | Protein: 4.5 g | Sodium: 569 mg | Fiber: 3.1 g | Carbohydrates: 14.6 g | Sugar: 5.8 g

Healthy Mixed Vegetables Soup

This is a great way to get rid of all of your leftover vegetables in the refrigerator. You can add just about anything to a minestrone like this one. This soup will last up to 5 days in the refrigerator.

INGREDIENTS | SERVES 8

1 tablespoon coconut oil

1 medium onion, peeled and chopped

½ cup diced sweet potatoes

½ cup diced carrots

2 cloves garlic, peeled and minced

½ cup diced celery

½ cup canned chickpeas

½ cup canned red kidney beans

½ cup canned corn kernels

2 tablespoons tomato paste

2 cups canned diced tomatoes

½ teaspoon sea salt

1 teaspoon freshly ground black pepper

½ teaspoon dried oregano

½ teaspoon dried basil

½ teaspoon ground thyme

2 cups low-sodium chicken broth

1. Heat a large skillet over medium heat and add oil and onions. Sauté onions until lightly brown, 2 minutes. Add sweet potatoes, carrots, and garlic and stir 5–6 minutes.

2. Add celery, chickpeas, beans, corn, tomato paste, diced tomatoes, salt, pepper, oregano, basil, and thyme and stir 2–3 minutes.

3. Add chicken broth and simmer over low heat 8–10 minutes or until potatoes and carrots are soft.

4. Divide evenly into food containers (best kept in Mason jars).

PER SERVING Calories: 87 | Fat: 2.0 g | Protein: 3.8 g | Sodium: 368 mg | Fiber: 3.7 g | Carbohydrates: 15.1 g | Sugar: 4.8 g

Chicken Zoodles Soup

This is a paleo and gluten-free twist to your classic chicken noodle soup. This soup can be refrigerated up to 5 days.

INGREDIENTS | SERVES 4

1 tablespoon coconut oil

½ cup chopped onions

2 cloves garlic, peeled and minced

3 cups cubed skinless, boneless chicken breasts

½ teaspoon sea salt

1 teaspoon freshly ground black pepper

½ teaspoon dried basil

1 teaspoon dried oregano

1 cup diced carrots

1 cup diced celery

½ cup frozen green peas

5 cups chicken broth

2 medium zucchini, spiralized

1. Heat a large skillet over medium heat and add oil and onions. Sauté onions until lightly brown, 2 minutes. Add garlic, chicken, salt, pepper, basil, and oregano and stir 5–6 minutes.

2. Add carrots, celery, and frozen peas and stir another 3 minutes. Add chicken broth and bring to a boil. Reduce heat to a simmer and add zucchini. Simmer 3–4 minutes, then remove from stove.

3. Divide evenly into food storage containers.

PER SERVING Calories: 241 | Fat: 5.5 g | Protein: 30.4 g | Sodium: 1,507 mg | Fiber: 3.6 g | Carbohydrates: 13.3 g | Sugar: 7.2 g

Lamb Stew

This stew is perfect for a cold fall evening. Your home will be filled with the aroma of rosemary and all of the herbs. This stew keeps in the refrigerator up to 5 days.

INGREDIENTS | SERVES 5

4 cups lamb stew chunks

2 cups chopped leeks

4 cloves garlic, peeled and minced

5 sprigs fresh thyme

3 sprigs fresh rosemary

½ teaspoon sea salt

1 teaspoon freshly ground black pepper

½ teaspoon dried basil

1 teaspoon dried oregano

3 cups diced carrots

2 cups diced celery

5 cups chicken broth

1. Put lamb in the bottom of a slow cooker, then add remaining ingredients into the pot.

2. Cook on high 8 hours.

3. To store for the week, let cool before transferring to storage containers.

PER SERVING Calories: 514 | Fat: 31.1 g | Protein: 34.8 g | Sodium: 1,308 mg | Fiber: 3.7 g | Carbohydrates: 16.0 g | Sugar: 6.7 g

Cream of Asparagus Soup

Contrary to this recipe's name, this soup does not actually contain any cream. It is, however, a creamy and healthy choice. This soup will last up to 5 days in the refrigerator.

INGREDIENTS | SERVES 6

1 tablespoon coconut oil

1 medium Spanish onion, peeled and chopped

1 cup chopped yellow potatoes

2 cloves garlic, peeled and minced

4 cups chopped asparagus

½ cup canned chickpeas

½ teaspoon sea salt

1 teaspoon freshly ground black pepper

4 cups low-sodium chicken broth

½ teaspoon dried basil

Looking for Low Carb?

If you're going on a low-carb diet, then omit the potatoes and chickpeas in this soup. Substitute more asparagus and add an extra 2 cups of another favorite leafy vegetable like spinach.

1. Heat a large skillet over medium heat and add oil and onions. Sauté onions until lightly brown, 2 minutes. Add potatoes and garlic and stir 5–6 minutes.

2. Add asparagus, chickpeas, salt, pepper, and stir another 2–3 minutes.

3. Add chicken broth, cover, and simmer over low heat 8–10 minutes or until potatoes and carrots are soft.

4. Transfer everything into a food processor or blender and blend until smooth.

5. Divide evenly into food containers (best kept in Mason jars). Garnish with basil and refrigerate.

PER SERVING Calories: 91 | Fat: 2.5 g | Protein: 5.8 g | Sodium: 558 mg | Fiber: 3.7 g | Carbohydrates: 13.0 g | Sugar: 3.5 g

Oatmeal Chicken Soup

Add a cup of coconut milk to make this extra creamy. Or consider drizzling some coconut cream or regular cream on top when serving. This soup can be refrigerated up to 5 days.

INGREDIENTS | SERVES 5

1 tablespoon coconut oil

¼ cup rolled oats

1 cup chopped onions

3 cloves garlic, peeled and minced

3 cups cubed skinless, boneless chicken breasts

½ teaspoon sea salt

1 teaspoon freshly ground black pepper

½ teaspoon dried basil

1 teaspoon dried oregano

1 cup diced carrots

1 cup diced celery

2 cups cubed butternut squash

5 cups chicken broth

1. Heat a large skillet over medium heat and add oil. Once oil is hot, add oats and stir until they turn slightly brown, 1 minute.

2. Add onions and garlic and sauté another 1–2 minutes. Add chicken, salt, pepper, basil, and oregano and stir 5–6 minutes.

3. Add carrots, celery, and squash and stir another 3 minutes.

4. Add chicken broth and bring to a boil. Then turn heat to low and simmer 20 minutes or until squash is soft. Make sure you stir it occasionally.

5. Store in food containers and refrigerate.

PER SERVING Calories: 217 | Fat: 4.6 g | Protein: 24.0 g | Sodium: 1,188 mg | Fiber: 3.4 g | Carbohydrates: 17.4 g | Sugar: 5.3 g

Classic Tomato Soup

This is not your basic tomato soup. It is creamy and aromatic, and the basil adds a sweet and warm taste to this dish. It's also a vegan dish. This soup can be refrigerated up to 5 days.

INGREDIENTS | SERVES 5

8 medium ripe tomatoes, chopped
1 cup chopped carrots
1 tablespoon olive oil
¼ teaspoon sea salt, divided
½ teaspoon freshly ground black pepper, divided
1 teaspoon coconut oil
½ cup chopped onions
4 cloves garlic, peeled and minced
½ teaspoon dried basil
1 teaspoon dried oregano
⅓ cup tomato paste
4 cups chicken broth
½ cup thinly sliced basil leaves

1. Preheat oven to 350°F. Line an 18" baking pan with parchment paper.

2. In a large mixing bowl add tomatoes, carrots, olive oil, and half the salt and pepper; stir to combine.

3. Pour tomato mixture onto prepared pan and bake 30 minutes.

4. Heat a large pot over medium heat and add coconut oil. Once oil is hot, add onions and stir 2 minutes. Then add garlic, tomato mixture, dried basil, oregano, and tomato paste. Stir 3–4 minutes.

5. Add chicken broth and the remaining salt and pepper and bring to a boil. Reduce heat to low, cover, and simmer 25–30 minutes.

6. Transfer soup to blender or food processor and blend until smooth.

7. Garnish with fresh basil and serve. To store for the week, let cool and transfer to Mason jars.

PER SERVING Calories: 112 | Fat: 3.9 g | Protein: 4.4 g | Sodium: 999 mg | Fiber: 4.2 g | Carbohydrates: 16.6 g | Sugar: 9.9 g

Homemade Chicken Broth

If you roast a lot of whole chicken, make sure you save and freeze the carcasses. Once you accumulate two or more, you can make your own chicken stock. This broth will last in the refrigerator up to 5 days or can be frozen to last longer.

INGREDIENTS | SERVES 5

3 chicken carcasses

1 cup chopped carrots

1 cup chopped celery

1 cup wedged onions

4 cloves garlic, peeled and whole

2 sprigs fresh rosemary

3 sprigs fresh thyme

3 bay leaves

16 cups water

1 teaspoon sea salt

1 teaspoon freshly ground black pepper

1. In a large stockpot, add chicken carcasses, carrots, celery, onions, garlic, rosemary, thyme, bay leaves, and water.

2. Bring to a boil over high heat, then reduce heat and simmer 2 hours.

3. Add salt and pepper. Strain out bones and vegetables, leaving only the broth. Let cool and store in Mason jars. If you are going to freeze it, make sure you don't fill containers all the way to the top as broth will expand when frozen.

PER SERVING Calories: 79 | Fat: 4.4 g | Protein: 4.8 g | Sodium: 376 mg | Fiber: 0.7 g | Carbohydrates: 4.2 g | Sugar: 1.2 g

Mom's Lemongrass Fish Soup

This one should be served fresh, or at most the next day. This dish can be served with some rice and steamed vegetables. This soup can be refrigerated up to 2 days or frozen to last over 2 weeks.

INGREDIENTS | SERVES 3

5 cups chicken broth

2 cups water

½ lemongrass stalk, roughly chopped

3 lime leaves

2 cups (2" pieces) tilapia

1 teaspoon fish sauce

1 teaspoon freshly ground black pepper

1 tablespoon chopped fresh basil

1. In a large pot bring broth and water to boil over high heat. Add lemongrass and lime leaves and lower heat to a simmer. Simmer 30 minutes.

2. Add tilapia, fish sauce, and pepper and cook 5–7 minutes or until fish is cooked thoroughly.

3. Serve with basil.

4. If you want to meal prep this, pour into Mason jars.

PER SERVING Calories: 173 | Fat: 2.3 g | Protein: 33.4 g | Sodium: 1,694 mg | Fiber: 0.2 g | Carbohydrates: 3.4 g | Sugar: 1.8 g

Lime Leaves

You can usually find lime leaves in the frozen food section of an Asian supermarket. If not, then replace with 1 teaspoon lime zest.

Vietnamese Hot and Sour Soup

This soup is typically served as a part of a Vietnamese meal. It's tangy and sweet and has a kick to it as well. Serve this with rice. This will store well in the refrigerator up to 3 days.

INGREDIENTS | SERVES 5

2 tablespoons tamarind pulp/paste

2 tablespoons hot water

5 cups low-sodium chicken broth

3 lime leaves

1 cup halved mushrooms

1 cup sliced fresh pineapples

1 cup wedged tomatoes

1 tablespoon fish sauce

1 tablespoon honey

2 cups bean sprouts

2 cups shrimp, shells removed and deveined

2 red Thai chilies, chopped with seeds

1 tablespoon chopped fresh basil

1 tablespoon Garlic Oil (see Chapter 10)

1. In a small bowl add tamarind and water and mix to melt the paste.

2. In a large pot bring broth and lime leaves to boil over high heat.

3. Add mushrooms, pineapple, tomatoes, fish sauce, and honey. Boil 2 minutes.

4. Add bean sprouts, shrimp, and chilies and turn heat to low.

5. Simmer until shrimp turn pink, 2–3 minutes.

6. Garnish with basil and Garlic Oil. Store in food containers and refrigerate.

PER SERVING Calories: 165 | Fat: 3.4 g | Protein: 18.1 g | Sodium: 1,213 mg | Fiber: 1.6 g | Carbohydrates: 16.1 g | Sugar: 10.9 g

Tamarind Paste

You can usually find tamarind paste in an Asian market in brick form. You'll need to soften it up by either warming in the microwave or breaking a piece off and mixing it in hot water.

CHAPTER 13

One-Pot Meals

Sausage and Potato Skillet

For a healthier option, you can replace regular potatoes with sweet potatoes and sausages with ground turkey. This dish will last in the refrigerator up to 5 days.

INGREDIENTS | SERVES 4

1 tablespoon coconut oil, divided

3 hot Italian pork sausages, chopped (2 cups)

1 medium red onion, peeled and diced

3 cloves garlic, peeled and minced

1 cup diced carrots, boiled

5 medium Yukon gold potatoes, skin on and boiled

1 cup chopped red bell peppers

1 cup chopped zucchini

½ tablespoon herbes de Provence

¼ teaspoon freshly ground black pepper

¼ cup shredded Cheddar cheese (optional)

Herbes de Provence

You can make your own herbes de Provence if you can't find it at the store. Just add equal amounts of dried rosemary and fennel seeds and mix with equal amounts of these dried herbs: thyme, savory, basil, marjoram, lavender, parsley, oregano, and tarragon.

1. Heat a large skillet over medium heat and add ½ tablespoon oil. Once oil is hot, add sausages and stir until well cooked, 7–8 minutes depending on the size of your sausage chunks. Transfer to a medium bowl and set aside.

2. In the same skillet add the remaining oil and onions. Stir 2–3 minutes or until onions start to turn light brown.

3. Add garlic and boiled carrots and potatoes and stir 3–4 minutes or until potatoes are soft. Add bell peppers and zucchini and stir 2–3 more minutes.

4. Add cooked sausages back into the skillet along with herbes de Provence and black pepper. Stir everything together 2 more minutes.

5. Add cheese on top (optional) and cook 1 more minute.

6. Remove from stove and serve or store in food containers.

PER SERVING (with cheese) Calories: 727 | Fat: 30.8 g | Protein: 23.9 g | Sodium: 736 mg | Fiber: 9.4 g | Carbohydrates: 83.5 g | Sugar: 10.3 g

Chicken Fried "Rice"

If you love Chinese chicken fried rice, you'll love this healthier low-carb option. This dish can be refrigerated up to 5 days.

INGREDIENTS | SERVES 6

1 medium cauliflower head, cut into florets

1 tablespoon coconut oil, divided

5 cups diced skinless, boneless chicken thighs

1 tablespoon soy sauce or tamari

1 teaspoon freshly ground black pepper, divided

½ cup diced onions

3 cloves garlic, peeled and minced

½ cup diced carrots

½ cup diced celery

¼ teaspoon salt

2 tablespoons chopped green onions

Chicken Thighs

If you're watching your calories and fat intake, opt for chicken breast instead. You can even use lean pork for a more tender type of meat.

1. In a food processor pulse cauliflower until processed to a rice consistency. Use pulse function instead of continuous blending to avoid overprocessing (this can make it mushy and watery).

2. Heat a large skillet over medium heat and add ½ tablespoon oil. Once oil is hot, add chicken and stir until well cooked, 7–8 minutes; season with soy sauce and ½ teaspoon pepper. Remove and pour into a large bowl.

3. In the same skillet add remaining ½ tablespoon oil and onions. Stir 2–3 minutes or until onions start to turn light brown.

4. Add garlic and carrots and stir 3–4 minutes or until carrots are soft. Add celery, cauliflower, salt, and remaining pepper and stir 3–4 more minutes.

5. Add cooked chicken back into the skillet and stir everything together 2–3 minutes.

6. Garnish with green onions, then remove from stove to let cool. Store in food containers.

PER SERVING Calories: 274 | Fat: 8.9 g | Protein: 38.4 g | Sodium: 451 mg | Fiber: 1.9 g | Carbohydrates: 6.2 g | Sugar: 2.3 g

Kale Coconut Fried Rice

To make fried rice that's not mushy, refrigerate steamed rice overnight and stir-fry the next day. This will remove excess moisture from the rice. This dish will store in refrigerator up to 5 days.

INGREDIENTS | SERVES 5

3 cups sliced skinless, boneless chicken breasts

1 teaspoon freshly ground black pepper, divided

2 tablespoons soy sauce or tamari, divided

2 tablespoons coconut oil, divided

½ cup diced onions

3 cloves garlic, peeled and minced

½ cup julienned carrots

½ cup julienned red bell peppers

¼ teaspoon salt

10 kale leaves, stems removed, chopped

3 large eggs

4 cups Coconut Jasmine Rice (see Chapter 11)

2 tablespoons unsweetened coconut flakes

2 tablespoons chopped green onions

1. In a large bowl add chicken, ¼ teaspoon black pepper, and 1 tablespoon soy sauce. Stir to combine and let marinate 30 minutes.

2. Heat a large skillet over medium heat and add ½ tablespoon oil. Once oil is hot add chicken and stir until well cooked, 7–8 minutes. Remove and place in a large bowl.

3. In the same skillet add another ½ tablespoon oil and onions. Stir 2–3 minutes or until onions turn light brown. Add garlic and carrots and stir 3–4 minutes or until carrots are soft.

4. Add bell peppers and stir another 2–3 minutes. Add salt, remaining black pepper, and kale and stir until kale is wilted, 1–2 minutes. Pour mixture into chicken mixture and set aside.

5. Wipe off skillet with a paper towel, then add ½ tablespoon oil. Crack in eggs and scramble 1 minute. Add rice and 1 tablespoon soy sauce and stir until soy sauce is well mixed into rice. Add chicken and vegetable mixture and stir 2–3 more minutes.

6. Remove from stove and set aside.

7. Heat a small saucepan over medium heat and add remaining ½ tablespoon oil. Once oil is hot, add coconut flakes. Stir until flakes turn light brown. Remove and pour onto rice mixture. Finish by garnishing with green onions.

8. Once cooled, divide evenly into food containers.

PER SERVING Calories: 510 | Fat: 14.8 g | Protein: 40.5 g | Sodium: 596 mg | Fiber: 3.1 g | Carbohydrates: 48.0 g | Sugar: 2.8 g

Slow Cooker Chicken and Leeks

This recipe is super easy and flavorful. Leeks make the entire pot super sweet. Serve this dish with rice or a side of vegetables. You can refrigerate this dish up to 5 days.

INGREDIENTS | SERVES 4

3 cups chopped leeks

2 cups chopped carrots

4 cloves garlic, peeled and minced

2 cups chopped parsnips

1 teaspoon salt

1 teaspoon freshly ground black pepper

1 tablespoon olive oil

1 teaspoon garlic powder

1 tablespoon herbes de Provence

8 bone-in, skin-on chicken thighs

1. In a large mixing bowl add leeks, carrots, garlic, parsnips, salt, pepper, oil, garlic powder, and herbs and mix until well combined.

2. Put chicken thighs in a slow cooker and top with leek mixture. Cook on high 7–8 hours.

3. Cool and store in food containers.

PER SERVING Calories: 1,018 | Fat: 62.4 g | Protein: 66.6 g | Sodium: 377 mg | Fiber: 6.9 g | Carbohydrates: 30.9 g | Sugar: 8.9 g

Chicken

You can also replace the chicken thighs with a whole chicken or chicken breasts as well or alternately skinless, boneless chicken thighs.

Beef and Potato Stew

Slow cooker recipes save time and work, and you'll come home to a delicious meal. Serve this dish with rice. Try this recipe with pork shoulder as well. You can refrigerate this stew up to 5 days.

INGREDIENTS | SERVES 5

2 cups chopped parsnips
3 cups chopped Yukon gold potatoes
1 cup chopped carrots
4 cloves garlic, peeled and minced
1 teaspoon salt
1 teaspoon freshly ground black pepper
1 tablespoon olive oil
1 teaspoon garlic powder
1 tablespoon herbes de Provence
½ tablespoon paprika
½ tablespoon ground cumin
1 teaspoon red pepper flakes
5 cups stew beef chunks

1. In a large mixing bowl add parsnips, potatoes, carrots, minced garlic, salt, pepper, oil, garlic powder, herbes de Provence, paprika, cumin, and red pepper flakes and mix until well combined.

2. Put beef in a slow cooker and top with vegetable mixture. Cook on high 7–8 hours.

3. Cool and store in food containers.

PER SERVING Calories: 435 | Fat: 13.1 g | Protein: 51.8 g | Sodium: 685 mg | Fiber: 5.6 g | Carbohydrates: 29.3 g | Sugar: 5.1 g

Butternut Squash and Pork Stew

Try adding a tablespoon of coconut cream on top of this stew before serving. It really puts it over the top. You can refrigerate this stew up to 5 days.

INGREDIENTS | SERVES 5

2 medium sweet potatoes, chopped
3 cups chopped butternut squash
1 cup chopped celery
1 cup chopped onions
4 cloves garlic, peeled and minced
1 teaspoon salt
1 teaspoon freshly ground black pepper
1 tablespoon olive oil
1 teaspoon garlic powder
1 tablespoon herbes de Provence
5 cups stewing pork chunks

1. In a large mixing bowl add potatoes, squash, celery, onion, minced garlic, salt, pepper, oil, garlic powder, and herbes de Provence and mix until well combined.

2. Put pork in a slow cooker and top with potato mixture. Cook on high 7–8 hours.

3. Cool and store in food containers.

PER SERVING Calories: 658 | Fat: 39.0 g | Protein: 41.0 g | Sodium: 660 mg | Fiber: 4.6 g | Carbohydrates: 25.8 g | Sugar: 5.7 g

Chicken Tomato Stew

This one-pot meal is perfect served alone, but you can also serve it over rice or even cauliflower rice. You can refrigerate this stew up to 5 days.

INGREDIENTS | SERVES 4

2 tablespoons coconut oil, divided

4 bone-in, skin-on chicken drumsticks

4 bone-in, skin-on chicken thighs

1 cup chopped onions

4 cloves garlic, peeled and minced

2 cups chopped zucchini

1 cup diced red bell peppers

¼ teaspoon salt

½ teaspoon freshly ground black pepper

1 (26-ounce) can fire-roasted diced tomatoes

1 cup chicken broth

1 tablespoon herbes de Provence

2 tablespoons chopped fresh basil (for garnish)

Chicken

You can also use skinless, boneless chicken breasts or thighs in this recipe. They will be easier to pack for lunch too. Instead of pan-searing the chicken, you can also grill it on the barbecue first.

1. Heat a large wok or skillet over medium heat and add 1 tablespoon oil. Once oil is hot, pan-sear drumsticks and thighs until skin is golden brown, 3–4 minutes each side. Remove and transfer to a plate.

2. In the same skillet add 1 tablespoon oil and onions. Stir 2 minutes; then add garlic, zucchini, bell peppers, salt, and black pepper and stir 2 more minutes.

3. Add chicken back into the skillet. Pour in tomatoes and broth. Add herbes de Provence and lower heat to a simmer.

4. Cover and simmer 20 minutes.

5. Garnish with basil and serve or store in food containers.

PER SERVING Calories: 786 | Fat: 46.5 g | Protein: 61.5 g | Sodium: 1,203 mg | Fiber: 5.6 g | Carbohydrates: 19.4 g | Sugar: 9.6 g

Roasted Turmeric Chicken

While it's true that roasting the chicken adds another pan to this recipe you can forgo that step if you buy precooked rotisserie chicken for this recipe. This dish will be amazing over any of the steamed rice recipes in Chapter 11. This dish can be refrigerated up to 5 days.

INGREDIENTS | SERVES 5

4 cups cubed, skinless, boneless chicken thighs

½ tablespoon ground turmeric

1 teaspoon sea salt, divided

1 teaspoon garlic powder

½ teaspoon freshly ground black pepper, divided

½ teaspoon paprika

¼ teaspoon ground cayenne pepper

1 tablespoon coconut oil

1 cup chopped onions

4 cloves garlic, peeled and minced

3 cups cubed, skin-on sweet potatoes

2 cups chopped cauliflower florets

4 cups chicken broth

1 tablespoon lime juice

1 cup coconut milk

2 tablespoons chopped fresh cilantro

Chicken

Tired of chicken? Try this recipe with shrimp or even white fish! Just make sure you don't meal prep too much fish in advance because they don't keep well in the refrigerator precooked.

1. Preheat oven to 350°F. Line an 18" baking pan with parchment paper.

2. In a large mixing bowl add chicken, turmeric, ½ teaspoon salt, garlic powder, ¼ teaspoon black pepper, paprika, and cayenne and mix until well combined.

3. Transfer chicken to prepared pan and bake 30 minutes.

4. Heat a large skillet over medium heat and add oil and onions. Stir 2 minutes; then add garlic, sweet potatoes, remaining salt and pepper, and stir 5 minutes. Add cauliflower and stir 2 more minutes.

5. Add chicken back into the skillet. Pour in broth and lime juice and lower heat to a simmer.

6. Cover and simmer 20 minutes. Then pour in coconut milk, stir, and turn heat off.

7. Garnish with cilantro and serve or store in food containers.

PER SERVING Calories: 442 | Fat: 18.2 g | Protein: 40.3 g | Sodium: 1,347 mg | Fiber: 4.3 g | Carbohydrates: 25.8 g | Sugar: 6.5 g

Roasted Cajun Pork Loins

If you don't like pork, replace it with ground turkey or even chicken breast chunks. Roasting the pork does add another pan but the flavor it imparts is worth it. This will be amazing over any of the steamed rice recipes in Chapter 11. This will keep in the refrigerator up to 5 days.

INGREDIENTS | SERVES 5

4 cups cubed boneless pork center loin

1 tablespoon paprika

½ teaspoon sea salt, divided

1 teaspoon garlic powder

½ teaspoon freshly ground black pepper, divided

1 tablespoon ground cumin

½ teaspoon ground cayenne pepper

½ tablespoon red pepper flakes

1 tablespoon coconut oil

1 cup chopped onions

4 cloves garlic, peeled and minced

3 cups cubed, skin-on buttercup squash

1 cup diced celery

1 cup diced carrots

4 cups chicken broth

2 tablespoons chopped fresh parsley

1. Preheat oven to 350°F. Line an 18" baking pan with parchment paper.

2. In a large mixing bowl add pork, paprika, ¼ teaspoon salt, garlic powder, black pepper, cumin, cayenne, and red pepper flakes and mix until well combined.

3. Transfer pork to prepared pan and bake 20 minutes.

4. Heat a large wok or skillet over medium heat and add oil. Once oil is hot, add onions. Stir 2 minutes; then add garlic, squash, celery, carrots, and remaining salt and pepper and stir another 4–5 minutes.

5. Add pork back into the skillet. Pour in broth and lower to a simmer. Cover and simmer 20 minutes.

6. Garnish with parsley and serve or store in food containers.

PER SERVING Calories: 341 | Fat: 8.3 g | Protein: 43.0 g | Sodium: 1,072 mg | Fiber: 4.1 g | Carbohydrates: 19.6 g | Sugar: 5.8 g

Chicken Primavera

This dish is a complete meal alone or can be served over cauliflower rice. You can store this dish in the refrigerator up to 5 days.

INGREDIENTS | SERVES 5

4 cups cubed skinless, boneless chicken thighs

1 teaspoon dried oregano

½ teaspoon dried basil

½ teaspoon sea salt

1 teaspoon garlic powder

½ teaspoon freshly ground black pepper

1 teaspoon ground thyme

½ teaspoon ground cayenne pepper

1 tablespoon coconut oil

1 cup chopped onions

4 cloves garlic, peeled and minced

3 cups peeled, cubed butternut squash

1 cup diced celery

1 (26-ounce) can crushed tomatoes

1 cup chicken broth

10 kale leaves, stems removed, chopped

2 tablespoons chopped fresh basil

1. In a large mixing bowl add chicken, oregano, basil, salt, garlic powder, black pepper, thyme, and cayenne and mix until well combined.

2. Heat a large wok or skillet over medium heat and add oil. Once oil is hot, add onions. Stir 2 minutes; add chicken and garlic and stir 4–5 minutes.

3. Add squash and celery and stir 2 minutes. Add tomatoes and broth, bring to a boil, then add kale and lower heat to a simmer. Cover and simmer 15 minutes.

4. Garnish with basil and serve or store in food containers.

PER SERVING Calories: 363 | Fat: 9.5 g | Protein: 40.7 g | Sodium: 664 mg | Fiber: 6.9 g | Carbohydrates: 28.7 g | Sugar: 10.8 g

Slow Cooker Roast Beef

Roast beef cooked in a slow cooker tastes amazing. You can add this meat to sandwiches or serve with your favorite sides. You can refrigerate this up to 5 days.

INGREDIENTS | SERVES 5

2 pounds roast beef

2 teaspoons salt

1 teaspoon freshly ground black pepper

2 cups sliced onions

1 cup chopped carrots

1 cup diced celery

3 cups peeled and cubed butternut squash

4 cloves garlic, peeled and minced

6 sprigs fresh thyme

3 sprigs fresh rosemary

3 cups beef broth

1. Season roast with salt and pepper.

2. Place roast in slow cooker, then add onions, carrots, celery, squash, garlic, thyme, rosemary, and broth.

3. Cook on high 8 hours. Remove rosemary and thyme sprigs and let rest about 10 minutes. Use two forks to shred the meat.

4. Store in food containers.

PER SERVING Calories: 410 | Fat: 21.2 g | Protein: 38.4 g | Sodium: 1,651 mg | Fiber: 3.7 g | Carbohydrates: 18.3 g | Sugar: 5.3 g

Fresh Herbs

Fresh herbs are always better to roast and cook with, but if you don't have any on hand, use ground or dried herbs. They will work just fine.

Sweet Potato Shepherd's Pie

If you prefer, you can replace the sweet potatoes with regular potatoes. They work just as well as sweet potatoes. This can be refrigerated up to 5 days.

INGREDIENTS | SERVES 4

2 medium sweet potatoes, peeled and cubed (4 cups)

2 tablespoons coconut oil, divided

¼ tablespoon coconut cream

1 cup diced onions

3 cups (1½ pounds) ground beef

3 cloves garlic, peeled and minced

1 cup diced celery

1 cup diced carrots

½ cup canned corn

½ cup green peas

1 teaspoon salt

½ teaspoon freshly ground black pepper

½ teaspoon ground thyme

1 teaspoon dried oregano

1. Preheat oven to 350°F.

2. Fill a large pot halfway with water and bring to a boil over high heat. Add sweet potatoes and boil 8–10 minutes or until potatoes are soft.

3. Drain completely, then add 1 tablespoon coconut oil and coconut cream and use a potato masher to mash sweet potatoes. Set aside.

4. Heat a large skillet over medium heat and add remaining 1 tablespoon oil. Once oil is hot, add onions and stir 2 minutes or until onions are light brown.

5. Add beef and garlic, and stir 3–5 minutes. Add celery, carrots, corn, peas, salt, pepper, thyme, and oregano and stir 3–4 more minutes.

6. Transfer meat mixture to a deep casserole dish or 9" × 12" baking pan. Make sure mixture is spread evenly. Add mashed sweet potatoes on top and spread evenly.

7. Bake 25–30 minutes.

8. Remove, let cool, then cut into desired serving sizes. Store in food containers.

PER SERVING Calories: 385 | Fat: 11.8 g | Protein: 41.2 g | Sodium: 774 mg | Fiber: 5.7 g | Carbohydrates: 29.6 g | Sugar: 8.3 g

Roasted Chicken and Potatoes

Who doesn't love chicken and potatoes? Squash or sweet potatoes are good substitutes for regular potatoes as well. This dish can be refrigerated up to 5 days.

INGREDIENTS | SERVES 4

8 skin-on, bone-in chicken thighs
1 cup chopped onions
2 cups chopped carrots
4 cups halved baby potatoes
4 cloves garlic, peeled and chopped
2 tablespoons olive oil
½ teaspoon salt
1 teaspoon garlic powder
½ teaspoon freshly ground black pepper
½ tablespoon herbes de Provence

1. Preheat oven to 350°F. Line a large baking pan with parchment paper.

2. In a large mixing bowl add chicken, onions, carrots, potatoes, and garlic. Drizzle oil over top and add salt, garlic powder, pepper, and herbes de Provence. Mix until well combined.

3. Pour mixture into prepared pan; make sure to arrange chicken between vegetables.

4. Bake 1 hour and 15 minutes or until chicken skin turns light brown. Check to make sure the temperature of chicken reaches 165°F and potatoes are soft.

5. Let cool and store in food containers.

PER SERVING Calories: 1,067 | Fat: 64.4 g | Protein: 68.0 g | Sodium: 676 mg | Fiber: 5.3 g | Carbohydrates: 36.5 g | Sugar: 6.7 g

Lemon Rosemary Chicken Skillet

This dish is very satisfying, and you can prepare it in about 30 minutes. Add 1 cup of squash or potatoes to make it a complete meal. This dish stores well in the refrigerator and will last up to 3 days.

INGREDIENTS | SERVES 2

2 (4-ounce) halved skinless, boneless chicken breasts
½ teaspoon salt, divided
½ teaspoon freshly ground black pepper, divided
1 tablespoon coconut oil
1 cup chopped onions
2 cups chicken broth
2 cloves garlic, peeled and minced
1 teaspoon garlic powder
1 teaspoon minced fresh rosemary
½ cup coconut cream
1 tablespoon lemon juice
1 tablespoon chopped parsley (for garnish)

1. Preheat oven to 375°F.

2. In a large mixing bowl add chicken, ¼ teaspoon salt, and ¼ teaspoon pepper and mix well.

3. Heat a large cast-iron skillet over medium heat and add oil. Once oil is hot, sear chicken 3–4 minutes per side. Remove and set aside on a plate.

4. In the same skillet add onions and sauté 2 minutes or until onions turn light brown. Add broth, minced garlic, garlic powder, rosemary, coconut cream, and remaining salt and pepper and reduce heat to low.

5. Stir and simmer 10 minutes.

6. Stir in lemon juice and add chicken back into the skillet. Let simmer 2 more minutes.

7. Transfer entire skillet to the oven and bake 10 minutes or until chicken reaches an internal temperature of 165°F. Use a meat thermometer to check before removing.

8. Remove and garnish with parsley.

9. Serve or let cool and store in food containers.

PER SERVING Calories: 451 | Fat: 28.0 g | Protein: 30.8 g | Sodium: 1,562 mg | Fiber: 3.2 g | Carbohydrates: 15.8 g | Sugar: 4.7 g

One-Skillet Chicken Curry Rice

This one-skillet meal is perfect for those lazy nights when you just want to throw everything together in one pan and forget about it. This dish stores well in the refrigerator up to 3 days.

INGREDIENTS | SERVES 4

2 (4-ounce) skinless, boneless chicken breasts, cut into chunks

½ teaspoon salt, divided

½ teaspoon freshly ground black pepper, divided

1 tablespoon coconut oil

1 cup chopped onions

3 cloves garlic, peeled and minced

1 cup chopped red bell peppers

2 cups canned crushed tomatoes

1 cup parboiled/converted rice

1½ cups chicken broth

1 tablespoon curry powder

1 tablespoon lime juice

½ cup coconut milk

½ cup frozen peas

1 tablespoon chopped fresh cilantro (for garnish)

Chicken Broth

Cooking rice with chicken broth makes it extra tasty, but you can also just use water to eliminate the sodium and fat from the broth. This dish is flavorful enough without the broth.

1. In a large mixing bowl add chicken, ¼ teaspoon salt, and ¼ teaspoon pepper and mix well.

2. Heat a large skillet over medium heat and add oil. Once oil is hot, add chicken and cook 4–5 minutes. Remove and set aside on a plate.

3. In the same skillet add onions and sauté 2 minutes or until onions turn light brown. Add garlic, red pepper, tomatoes, rice, broth, curry powder, lime juice, and remaining salt and pepper and stir until well mixed.

4. Bring to a boil, then reduce heat to low, cover, and simmer 20 minutes.

5. Add coconut milk and frozen peas and put the cover on to simmer 2–3 more minutes.

6. Remove and garnish with cilantro. Serve or let cool and store in food containers.

PER SERVING Calories: 422 | Fat: 10.6 g | Protein: 21.2 g | Sodium: 912 mg | Fiber: 6.2 g | Carbohydrates: 59.1 g | Sugar: 10.0 g

One-Skillet Spanish Rice and Chicken

This dish is packed with wholesome ingredients, and it's filling and healthy as well. You can replace long-grain rice with brown or parboiled/converted rice, or you can use quinoa instead of the rice. This dish stores well in the refrigerator and will keep up to 3 days.

INGREDIENTS | SERVES 4

2 (5–6-ounce) skinless, boneless chicken breasts, cut into chunks

½ teaspoon salt, divided

½ teaspoon freshly ground black pepper, divided

1 tablespoon coconut oil

1 cup chopped onions

3 cloves garlic, peeled and minced

1 cup chopped red bell peppers

2 tablespoons tomato paste

½ cup tomato sauce

1 cup uncooked long-grain white rice

1½ cups chicken broth

1 tablespoon paprika

1 tablespoon chili powder

1 tablespoon ground cumin

¼ cup sliced black olives

1 tablespoon chopped fresh cilantro

1 medium lemon, cut into wedges

1. In a large mixing bowl add chicken, ¼ teaspoon salt, and ¼ teaspoon pepper and mix well.

2. Heat a large skillet over medium heat and add oil. Once oil is hot, add chicken and cook 4–5 minutes. Remove and set aside on a plate.

3. In the same skillet add onions and sauté 2 minutes or until onions turn light brown. Add garlic, red pepper, tomato paste, tomato sauce, rice, broth, paprika, chili powder, cumin, and remaining salt and pepper and stir until well mixed.

4. Bring to a boil, then reduce heat to low, cover, and simmer 20 minutes.

5. Add olives and cilantro, mix, and turn off heat.

6. Remove and garnish with a squeeze of lemon wedge.

7. Serve or let cool and store in food containers.

PER SERVING Calories: 371 | Fat: 6.6 g | Protein: 25.4 g | Sodium: 1,023 mg | Fiber: 4.6 g | Carbohydrates: 49.8 g | Sugar: 6.1 g

Pineapple Chicken Fried Rice

This dish is sweet and savory. Cook your rice the night before and chill it overnight. This will take out excess moisture from the rice. This dish will store in refrigerator up to 3 days.

INGREDIENTS | SERVES 5

3 cups sliced skinless, boneless chicken breasts

1 teaspoon freshly ground black pepper, divided

2 tablespoons soy sauce or tamari, divided

1½ tablespoons coconut oil, divided

½ cup diced onions

3 cloves garlic, peeled and minced

1 cup (1"-diced) red bell peppers

1 cup sliced fresh pineapples

½ cup green frozen peas

¼ teaspoon salt

3 large eggs, whisked

5 cups cooked and chilled Steamed Brown Rice (see Chapter 11)

¼ cup chopped fresh cilantro

1. In a large bowl add chicken, ¼ teaspoon black pepper, and 1 tablespoon soy sauce and stir to combine; let marinate 30 minutes.

2. Heat a large skillet over medium heat and add ½ tablespoon oil.

3. Once oil is hot, add chicken and stir until well cooked, 7–8 minutes. Remove and put into a large bowl.

4. In the same skillet add another ½ tablespoon oil and onions. Stir 2–3 minutes or until onions turn light brown.

5. Add garlic, red peppers, pineapple, and peas and stir 2–3 minutes. Add salt and remaining ¾ teaspoon black pepper, and stir 1 more minute. Pour mixture into the same bowl as chicken and set aside.

6. Wipe off skillet with a paper towel, then add remaining ½ tablespoon oil. Add eggs and scramble 30 seconds, then add rice and remaining 1 tablespoon soy sauce and stir until soy sauce is well mixed into rice. Add chicken mixture and stir 2–3 minutes.

7. Remove from stove and garnish with cilantro.

8. Once cooled, divide evenly into food containers.

PER SERVING Calories: 570 | Fat: 11.2 g | Protein: 50.9 g | Sodium: 615 mg | Fiber: 4.4 g | Carbohydrates: 59.1 g | Sugar: 6.0 g

Oxtail Potato Stew

Oxtail is one of those proteins that you cannot rush when cooking. The meat will just fall off the bones and the potatoes will be nice and soft in this slow-cooked stew. Serve this over rice or other sides. This will keep in the refrigerator up to 5 days.

INGREDIENTS | SERVES 4

2 pounds chopped oxtail

2 cups sliced onions

3 cups chopped carrots

3 cups chopped yellow potatoes

2 bay leaves

4 cloves garlic, peeled and minced

3 sprigs fresh thyme

3 sprigs fresh rosemary

½ teaspoon salt

1 teaspoon freshly ground black pepper

3 cups beef broth

1. In a slow cooker, add oxtail, onions, carrots, potatoes, bay leaves, garlic, thyme, rosemary, salt, pepper, and broth.

2. Cook on high 8 hours. Once finished, let rest about 15 minutes and remove rosemary, bay leaves, and thyme sprigs. Use two forks to shred the meat.

3. Store in food containers.

PER SERVING Calories: 1,327 | Fat: 122.2 g | Protein: 19.9 g | Sodium: 1,090 mg | Fiber: 7.0 g | Carbohydrates: 35.8 g | Sugar: 9.3 g

CHAPTER 14

Appetizers and Snacks

Rob's Fried Plantains

These are great for entertaining or even added to your breakfast with eggs and avocados.
Best served immediately, or you can store them up to a day in the refrigerator.

INGREDIENTS | SERVES 2

2 tablespoons coconut oil

2 medium green plantains, peeled and sliced into ½" rounds

⅛ teaspoon sea salt

Baking or Frying?

If you're trying to lose weight, you can bake these instead of frying in oil. Bake 30 minutes (15 minutes on each side) at 400°F.

1. Heat a large pan over medium-low heat and add oil. Once oil is hot, add plantains one by one, ensuring they do not overlap. Fry 3–4 minutes per side or until light brown.

2. Remove, place on a plate, and sprinkle with salt.

PER SERVING Calories: 229 | Fat: 1.7 g | Protein: 2.3 g | Sodium: 124 mg | Fiber: 4.1 g | Carbohydrates: 57.1 g | Sugar: 26.9 g

Vegetable Sticks with Ranch

These are great for your midday snack or when you need something small to tide
you over to the next meal. Refrigerate this and it will store well up to 5 days.

INGREDIENTS | SERVES 1

¼ cup broccoli florets

¼ cup cauliflower florets

¼ cup baby carrots

¼ cup celery sticks

¼ cup Greek Yogurt Ranch (see Chapter 10)

Broccoli and Cauliflower

Many grocery stores now sell broccoli and cauliflower florets. This will save you lots of prep time!

Combine vegetables; store vegetables and dip in separate food containers.

PER SERVING Calories: 75 | Fat: 1.4 g | Protein: 7.5 g | Sodium: 195 mg | Fiber: 2.6 g | Carbohydrates: 9.9 g | Sugar: 5.1 g

Fresh Spring Rolls

If you're hosting a party, these will be a hit. They are so delicious and light. They will store well up to 2 days in the refrigerator.

INGREDIENTS | SERVES 5 (YIELDS 10 ROLLS)

20 shrimp (26–30 count)

5 lettuce leaves, torn into small pieces (3 or 4 per leaf), center rib removed

1 cup uncooked vermicelli noodles

10 (8") round rice papers

1 cup fresh Thai basil leaves

1 cup fresh mint leaves

1 cup julienned carrots

1 cup seeded and julienned cucumber

¼ cup Vietnamese Fish Sauce (see Chapter 10)

Rice Paper

You can find rice papers at an Asian market. They might be labeled as spring roll wraps, and they come in all sizes and shapes. Get the large circle ones (8") for this recipe.

1. Boil shrimp in a small pot with water 2–3 minutes or until cooked. Drain, then run under cold water and pat dry. Remove shells and tails and cut in half lengthwise. Place on a plate.

2. Place lettuce on a large serving plate.

3. Bring a medium pot of water to bowl over high heat; then remove from stove, add noodles, and let sit 8–10 minutes or until soft. Drain and run under cold water. Remove excess water and place noodles into a separate bowl.

4. Fill a large shallow bowl with warm water. On a counter or big work area, form an assembly line with plate of rice papers, bowl of water, large round plate for wet rice sheets, basil, mint, carrots, cucumbers, noodles, lettuce, and shrimp.

5. Roll one at a time. Start by dipping one rice sheet into the bowl of water and fully submerge 1 second. Remove and place on a plate. Let sit on plate until soft and sticky.

6. Lay ingredients down across the width of the sheet 2½" from the top in this order: 2 or 3 basil leaves, 2 or 3 mint leaves, 4 or 5 carrot and cucumber juliennes, 2 tablespoons noodles, 2 lettuce pieces, and 4 shrimp halves. Pull the bottom of the sheet up over the filling, fold the sides into the center, and roll up tightly. Place on plate and cover with damp cloth. Repeat for remaining rice sheets.

7. Serve immediately with fish sauce. If you want to meal prep these, rub rolls with oil, then keep covered with a damp cloth. Store in food containers and refrigerate.

PER SERVING Calories: 225 | Fat: 1.1 g | Protein: 8.0 g | Sodium: 208 mg | Fiber: 2.6 g | Carbohydrates: 45.0 g | Sugar: 1.6 g

Sautéed Calamari

Calamari doesn't have to be heavily breaded and deep-fried to taste good. Try this healthier option. These will not store well in the refrigerator. They are best served immediately.

INGREDIENTS | SERVES 4

½ tablespoon coconut oil
2 cloves garlic, peeled and minced
2 cups calamari rings
1 teaspoon soy sauce or tamari
¼ teaspoon fish sauce
½ teaspoon red pepper flakes
½ teaspoon onion powder
½ tablespoon chopped fresh parsley (for garnish)

1. Heat a medium pan over medium heat and add oil.

2. Add garlic and stir 15–30 seconds. Add calamari rings and stir 1 minute.

3. Add soy sauce, fish sauce, red pepper flakes, and onion powder and stir 2–3 minutes or until calamari turns opaque.

4. Remove and place on plate, garnish with parsley, and serve immediately.

PER SERVING Calories: 141 | Fat: 2.7 g | Protein: 20.0 g | Sodium: 812 mg | Fiber: 0.1 g | Carbohydrates: 7.3 g | Sugar: 0.0 g

Shrimp Cocktail

Don't overcook shrimp, as the meat turns very tough when you do. Watch and wait till the entire shrimp turns pink, then remove and run under cold water right away. This is best served immediately. However, you can still store this up to 3 days in a container in the refrigerator.

INGREDIENTS | SERVES 4

16 jumbo shrimp, shells removed
1 medium lemon, cut into wedges
½ cup Cocktail Sauce (see Chapter 10)

1. Fill a large pot halfway with water and bring to a boil over high heat. Add shrimp and boil until shrimp rise to the surface and turn pink.

2. Drain in colander and run under cold water.

3. Serve immediately with wedges of lemon and Cocktail Sauce.

PER SERVING Calories: 99 | Fat: 0.9 g | Protein: 16.4 g | Sodium: 850 mg | Fiber: 1.0 g | Carbohydrates: 5.5 g | Sugar: 2.9 g

Bacon-Wrapped Scallops

Scallops are an amazing appetizer, but make sure you don't overcook them. Most seafood dishes like this one are best cooked fresh. If you are meal prepping this recipe, then you can store it up to 2 days in the refrigerator.

INGREDIENTS | SERVES 4

12 large scallops
¼ teaspoon freshly ground black pepper
½ teaspoon paprika
½ teaspoon garlic powder
6 bacon strips

Grill Them

These are even better on the grill because the bacon crisps up nicely. Grilling gets rid of the fat from the bacon because it drips out.

1. Preheat oven to 425°F. Line a 17" baking pan with parchment paper.

2. In a large bowl toss scallops, pepper, paprika, and garlic powder until well combined.

3. Cut bacon in half, then use one bacon half to wrap around each scallop. Skewer with a toothpick to hold together.

4. Put scallops in prepared pan and bake 8–10 minutes. Flip scallops over and bake 8–10 more minutes.

5. Remove and serve immediately.

PER SERVING Calories: 181 | Fat: 15.7 g | Protein: 6.3 g | Sodium: 307 mg | Fiber: 0.1 g | Carbohydrates: 1.1 g | Sugar: 0.5 g

Asian-Style Chicken Wings

Chicken wings are a must on game nights or even when you're hosting your next barbecue. These will keep up to 3 days in the refrigerator.

25 chicken wings

3 cloves garlic, peeled and minced

1 teaspoon garlic powder

1 tablespoon soy sauce or tamari

½ tablespoon honey

½ teaspoon sea salt

½ teaspoon freshly ground black pepper

Substitutions

If you don't consume soy products, you can use coconut aminos as a substitute. Traditional Asian cooking includes a lot of regular sugar, so you can add sugar instead of honey as well. However, honey is a more natural source of sugar and is less refined than store-bought granulated sugar.

1. Preheat oven to 350°F. Line an 18" baking pan with parchment paper.

2. In a large mixing bowl toss wings, garlic, garlic powder, soy sauce, honey, salt, and pepper and mix until well combined.

3. Transfer wings to prepared pan. Bake 40–45 minutes or until wings are light brown.

4. For extra crispiness, turn oven on broil the last 2–3 minutes of cooking, then remove from oven.

5. Serve immediately or store in food containers.

PER SERVING Calories: 1,034 | Fat: 70.3 g | Protein: 94.2 g | Sodium: 812 mg | Fiber: 0.2 g | Carbohydrates: 3.1 g | Sugar: 1.8 g

Zucchini Chips

These are easy to make, super thin, crispy, and delicious. They are also healthy too! These should last up to 3 days.

INGREDIENTS | SERVES 4

2 large zucchini, thinly sliced
2 tablespoons melted coconut oil
⅛ teaspoon sea salt
⅛ teaspoon freshly ground black pepper

Coconut Oil

You'll need to microwave the coconut oil to turn it from solid to liquid form. You can also use olive oil instead. If you don't use a microwave, you can heat the oil over low heat in a small saucepan.

1. Preheat oven to 225°F. Line an 18" baking pan with parchment paper.

2. Lay zucchini one by one in the pan, making sure slices don't overlap. Use a brush to dab melted coconut oil onto each chip. Make sure to cover both sides.

3. Bake 2 hours or until crispy and brown. Turn slices every 15 minutes to ensure even cooking.

4. Remove from oven and sprinkle with salt and pepper. Let cool.

5. Store in an airtight container and keep in a cool place.

PER SERVING Calories: 84 | Fat: 6.7 g | Protein: 1.9 g | Sodium: 70 mg | Fiber: 1.6 g | Carbohydrates: 4.8 g | Sugar: 3.8 g

Cajun Sweet Potato Chips

These chips are crispy and tasty either alone or served with chicken salad. Best of all, they are healthy so you can enjoy them guilt-free. These should last up to 3 days.

INGREDIENTS | SERVES 4

2 large sweet potatoes, thinly sliced
2 tablespoons melted coconut oil
⅛ teaspoon sea salt
⅛ teaspoon freshly ground black pepper
½ teaspoon paprika
¼ teaspoon ground cayenne pepper
½ teaspoon ground cumin
½ teaspoon chili powder
½ teaspoon garlic powder

Crispiness

The thinner you can slice the sweet potatoes, the crispier they will be. Use a mandoline if you are not experienced with using a knife. It will make it easier and faster to slice. You can also skip all of the spices and just add salt for plain chips.

1. Preheat oven to 375°F. Line an 18" baking pan with parchment paper.

2. Lay potato slices in the pan one by one, making sure they don't overlap. Use a brush to dab melted coconut oil onto each chip. Make sure to cover both sides.

3. Bake 15 minutes per side or until crispy and light brown.

4. While chips are baking, in a small bowl mix salt, pepper, paprika, cayenne, cumin, chili powder, and garlic powder until well combined.

5. Remove chips from oven, place in a large bowl, and sprinkle with seasoning. Toss to ensure chips are well coated. Let cool.

6. Store in an airtight container and keep in a cool place.

PER SERVING Calories: 118 | Fat: 6.6 g | Protein: 1.2 g | Sodium: 104 mg | Fiber: 2.3 g | Carbohydrates: 13.9 g | Sugar: 2.8 g

Healthy No-Bake Protein Bars

Protein bars can have a lot of sugar and unnecessary additives, so to avoid those you should make your own. These will keep in the refrigerator up to 5 days or in the freezer up to 1 month.

INGREDIENTS | SERVES 5

¾ cup almond meal

¼ cup milled flaxseed

2 tablespoons chia seeds

3 tablespoons unsweetened coconut flakes

¾ cup vanilla whey protein powder

2 tablespoons raisins

⅓ cup almond butter

¼ cup rice syrup (or maple syrup)

Add Chocolate

You can very easily add chocolate on top of your bars. Just melt ¼ cup dark chocolate and drizzle over the bars.

1. In a large bowl add almond meal, flaxseed, chia seeds, coconut, protein powder, and raisins and mix until well combined.

2. In a small bowl add almond butter and syrup and mix until well blended.

3. Add syrup mixture to almond meal mixture and stir to combine.

4. Line a 9" × 5" loaf pan with parchment paper.

5. Pour mixture into pan and press firmly with a spatula until the surface is even and mixture is tightly pressed.

6. Refrigerate overnight or at least 6 hours. Remove and cut evenly into long bars.

7. Store in food containers.

PER SERVING Calories: 357 | Fat: 20.6 g | Protein: 16.9 g | Sodium: 28 mg | Fiber: 7.4 g | Carbohydrates: 25.2 g | Sugar: 12.7 g

Healthy Granola Bars

Need some extra energy in your mornings or late afternoon? These nutty, tasty bars will get you through those low-energy funks. They store well in the fridge up to 5 days.

INGREDIENTS | SERVES 12

1½ cups rolled oats

¼ cup chopped cashews

¼ cup chopped almonds

¼ cup chia seeds

¼ cup uncooked quinoa

⅔ cup natural creamy peanut butter

⅓ cup maple syrup

1 teaspoon vanilla extract

1 teaspoon ground cinnamon

¼ teaspoon sea salt

½ cup chopped dates

Dates

Dates are very high in sugar, so consume them in moderation. If you want to replace the dates with something that has a lower sugar content, use dried unsweetened cranberries or dried goji berries instead.

1. Preheat oven to 350°F. Line a 15" baking pan with parchment paper.

2. In a mixing bowl add oats, nuts, seeds, and quinoa and mix until well combined.

3. Pour oat mixture into prepared pan and bake 10 minutes. Set aside.

4. In a large bowl add peanut butter and maple syrup and microwave 1 minute or until mixture softens. Add vanilla, cinnamon, salt, dates, and oat mixture and mix until well combined.

5. Transfer into an 8" × 8" baking pan and press firmly with a spatula until evenly spread.

6. Refrigerate 3 hours, then cut into 12 bars. Store in containers.

PER SERVING Calories: 188 | Fat: 10.4 g | Protein: 5.4 g | Sodium: 102 mg | Fiber: 3.2 g | Carbohydrates: 19.8 g | Sugar: 11.0 g

CHAPTER 15

Healthy Desserts

Roasted Plantains with Coconut Cream

This is a perfect treat as it features natural sugars and good fat. These are best served immediately. However, you can still store these in the refrigerator up to 3 days.

INGREDIENTS | SERVES 2

2 Oven-Roasted Plantains (see Chapter 11)
2 tablespoons coconut cream
⅛ teaspoon ground cinnamon
¼ cup vanilla ice cream (optional)

Plantains

Make sure that the plantains are very ripe before you make this recipe. Look for plantains with lots of dark spots. The darker it is, the riper it is.

1. Place plantains in a shallow bowl and drizzle with coconut cream. Sprinkle with cinnamon.

2. Pair with ice cream if desired.

   PER SERVING (with ice cream) Calories: 307 | Fat: 8.7 g | Protein: 3.1 g | Sodium: 60 mg | Fiber: 4.6 g | Carbohydrates: 60.2 g | Sugar: 28.7 g

Grilled Peach and Pineapple with Coconut Cream

Make sure that the peaches are very soft before grilling. This makes the juice caramelize, making the peaches even sweeter. These will store well in food containers and can be refrigerated up to 3 days.

INGREDIENTS | SERVES 2

2 medium peaches, halved and pitted
4 slices pineapple
⅛ teaspoon ground cinnamon
½ tablespoon unsweetened coconut flakes
2 tablespoons coconut cream
¼ cup ice cream (optional)

1. Preheat grill on medium-high heat.

2. Grill peaches and pineapple 2–3 minutes per side or until you get good grill marks on each.

3. Transfer fruit to a shallow bowl; sprinkle with cinnamon, coconut flakes, and coconut cream. Add ice cream on the side if you desire.

   PER SERVING (with ice cream) Calories: 217 | Fat: 6.9 g | Protein: 3.2 g | Sodium: 8 mg | Fiber: 5.2 g | Carbohydrates: 39.8 g | Sugar: 31.0 g

Protein Coconut Chia Seed Pudding

If you don't like coconut milk, use regular milk or almond milk. Any type of milk will work. This will store well in Mason jars and will keep up to 5 days in the refrigerator.

INGREDIENTS | SERVES 4

1 scoop vanilla whey protein powder

2 cups coconut milk

½ cup chia seeds

½ tablespoon vanilla extract

½ cup blueberries

½ cup sliced strawberries

½ tablespoon unsweetened coconut flakes

1. In a shaker add protein powder and coconut milk and shake until well blended.

2. Pour milk mixture into large bowl or storage container, add chia seeds and vanilla, and mix with a spoon until well blended.

3. Cover and refrigerate at least 2–3 hours.

4. Top with berries and coconut flakes and serve. Close jars with lids and store in the refrigerator up to 5 days.

PER SERVING Calories: 371 | Fat: 29.4 g | Protein: 10.2 g | Sodium: 44 mg | Fiber: 7.7 g | Carbohydrates: 18.3 g | Sugar: 3.2 g

Coconut Macaroons

These Coconut Macaroons bring a taste of the tropics into your kitchen. This recipe is so simple, you'll want to keep making more. These will store well in a cool place in a tightly sealed container up to 5 days.

INGREDIENTS | SERVES 4

6 large egg whites

1 teaspoon vanilla extract

½ cup maple syrup

3 cups unsweetened coconut flakes

Maple Syrup

You can replace the maple syrup with rice syrup or honey. Honey might be a lot stickier in texture. This dessert is fairly high in sugar and fat, so enjoy in moderation if you are watching your weight.

1. Preheat oven to 325°F. Line a baking sheet with parchment paper.

2. Beat egg whites with a mixer until stiff. Add vanilla, syrup, and coconut and mix well.

3. Form mixture into 1" balls and place on prepared sheet.

4. Bake 15–18 minutes or until the top of the macaroons become light brown.

PER SERVING Calories: 530 | Fat: 40.0 g | Protein: 9.4 g | Sodium: 106 mg | Fiber: 8.0 g | Carbohydrates: 42.9 g | Sugar: 28.3 g

No-Bake Coconut Fudge Brownies

Six ingredients and no baking involved—it doesn't get easier than this to make brownies. Pack these in food containers and they will store well in a cool place up to 5 days.

INGREDIENTS | SERVES 4

1 cup melted coconut butter
¼ cup cocoa powder
2 tablespoons honey
1 teaspoon vanilla extract
⅛ teaspoon sea salt
½ cup unsweetened coconut flakes

Options for Replacements

You can replace the honey with rice syrup or maple syrup. Use unsweetened coconut flakes as there is enough sugar in the recipe that it won't need the extra added sugar from sweetened coconut flakes.

1. In a large bowl add coconut butter, cocoa, honey, vanilla, salt, and coconut flakes and mix until well combined.

2. Transfer mixture into a medium-sized food container and use flat side of a spatula or spoon to press firmly down until evenly spread in container.

3. Refrigerate at least 2 hours or overnight and then serve.

PER SERVING Calories: 537 | Fat: 45.7 g | Protein: 5.6 g | Sodium: 82 mg | Fiber: 11.0 g | Carbohydrates: 29.7 g | Sugar: 13.2 g

Coconut Gelatin Squares

These squares are light and healthy, so you can enjoy them guilt-free, and they will keep well in the refrigerator up to 5 days.

INGREDIENTS | SERVES 5

1 cup coconut water
2½ cups coconut milk
1 cup coconut cream
4 tablespoons gelatin powder

Coconut Cream

Coconut cream is much higher in fat content than milk. If you are weight conscious, replace the cream with coconut water.

1. In a medium pot bring coconut water, milk, and cream to a boil over high heat.

2. Lower heat to a simmer, add gelatin powder, and stir until well combined. Simmer 2–3 minutes.

3. Pour mixture into an 8" × 8" cake pan and set aside to cool.

4. Once cool, refrigerate overnight or at least 3 hours.

5. Cut into 2" squares and serve.

PER SERVING Calories: 408 | Fat: 38.3 g | Protein: 8.9 g | Sodium: 39 mg | Fiber: 1.1 g | Carbohydrates: 8.4 g | Sugar: 1.9 g

Dark Chocolate–Covered Strawberries

These are a great ending to a dinner date or a super way to impress your guests when you host a dinner party. These are meant to be served same day but they can also be stored in the refrigerator up to 3 days.

INGREDIENTS | SERVES 4

16 medium strawberries, stem on
1 cup dark chocolate chips

Dark Chocolate

The darker the chocolate, the less the sugar. There are many benefits to eating chocolate, including the high level of magnesium found in chocolate. If you're not a big fan of dark chocolate, you can use semisweet chocolate instead.

1. Fill a medium pot halfway with water and bring to a boil over high heat.

2. Lower heat to a simmer and place a metal mixing bowl that's bigger than the pot on top.

3. Pour chocolate chips into the mixing bowl and stir with a whisk until completely melted.

4. Line an 18" baking pan with parchment paper. Dip strawberries into melted chocolate one by one and place on parchment paper.

5. Refrigerate entire pan until chocolate hardens, then serve.

PER SERVING Calories: 335 | Fat: 20.1 g | Protein: 1.9 g | Sodium: 39 mg | Fiber: 5.0 g | Carbohydrates: 35.7 g | Sugar: 23.4 g

No-Bake Chocolate Protein Bites

These chocolate bites are tasty and good for you. Store these in a tightly sealed food container and keep in a cool place. These can be stored up to 5 days.

INGREDIENTS | SERVES 8

½ cup almond butter

⅓ cup maple syrup

2 tablespoons coconut oil

1 teaspoon vanilla extract

1 cup rolled oats

3 tablespoons unsweetened cocoa

⅓ plus ¼ cup unsweetened coconut flakes, divided

⅓ cup finely chopped dates

1 tablespoon chia seeds

¼ cup dark chocolate chips

⅛ teaspoon sea salt

1 scoop chocolate whey protein powder

⅓ cup chopped raw almond slivers

Preworkout Snack

These protein bites are the perfect snack for an afternoon energy boost or even before a workout. They're easy to make and also to pack to take with you.

1. In a medium bowl melt almond butter, syrup, and oil in the microwave 30 seconds. Add vanilla, oats, cocoa, ⅓ cup coconut flakes, dates, chia seeds, chocolate, salt, and protein powder. Mix with hands until well combined.

2. On a shallow plate combine almond slivers and remaining ¼ cup coconut flakes.

3. Roll dough into 1" balls, then roll balls through almond-coconut mixture to coat.

4. Place in food container and store in the refrigerator to harden.

PER SERVING Calories: 344 | Fat: 21.2 g | Protein: 9.0 g | Sodium: 49 mg | Fiber: 6.1 g | Carbohydrates: 32.5 g | Sugar: 16.5 g

Banana Nut Rolls

With natural sugars and carbohydrates as well as potassium, bananas are a great snack to have on hand. Make sure you freeze them on a plate first until they turn solid, then transfer them to a zip-top bag or storage container.

INGREDIENTS | SERVES 2

⅓ cup finely crushed raw almonds

½ tablespoon chia seeds

⅛ teaspoon sea salt

¼ cup unsalted almond butter

2 medium ripe bananas, peeled and cut into 1" rounds

1. In a shallow bowl add crushed almonds, chia seeds, and salt and mix until combined. Place almond butter in a separate shallow bowl.

2. Roll bananas first in almond butter then in nut mixture until fully coated with both mixtures.

3. Enjoy immediately or freeze to last longer.

PER SERVING Calories: 400 | Fat: 24.3 g | Protein: 11.6 g | Sodium: 120 mg | Fiber: 9.1 g | Carbohydrates: 37.3 g | Sugar: 16.5 g

Coconut Berry Ice Pops

These are perfect for a summer treat. Experiment with a variety of fruits and add coconut milk if you want a creamier treat. These can be stored in the freezer up to 1 month.

INGREDIENTS | SERVES 6

½ cup fresh blueberries

½ cup fresh raspberries

½ cup sliced fresh strawberries

3 cups coconut water

1. Divide berries evenly into ice pop molds.

2. Fill molds with coconut water. Add sticks, cover, and freeze overnight.

3. When ready to serve, run mold briefly under warm water to free pops.

PER SERVING Calories: 38 | Fat: 0.1 g | Protein: 0.6 g | Sodium: 31 mg | Fiber: 1.2 g | Carbohydrates: 9.3 g | Sugar: 7.2 g

Chickpea Peanut Butter Chocolate Cookies

Gluten-free pastries and cookies are expensive to buy, so it's cost-effective to make your own. It's also much healthier because you know exactly what's in them. These will refrigerate up to 5 days. You can also freeze them up to 1 month.

INGREDIENTS | SERVES 16

1 teaspoon coconut oil (for greasing)

2 cups canned chickpeas, drained and rinsed

¼ cup quick-cooking oats

½ cup natural peanut butter

¼ cup maple syrup

½ tablespoon vanilla extract

¼ teaspoon sea salt

¼ teaspoon baking powder

¼ teaspoon baking soda

⅓ cup dark chocolate chips, divided

Pure Protein

Chickpeas are full of fiber and protein. Peanut butter also has protein in it too. Just make sure you pick an all-natural one without added sugars.

1. Preheat oven to 350°F. Grease an 8" × 8" cake pan with coconut oil.

2. In a food processor add chickpeas, oats, peanut butter, syrup, vanilla, ¼ teaspoon salt, baking powder, and baking soda and blend until smooth.

3. Pour mixture into large mixing bowl and add ⅔ of the chocolate chips. Mix until well combined.

4. Pour mixture into prepared pan; pat down with spatula until the surface is even and smooth. Sprinkle remaining chocolate chips over the surface.

5. Bake 20–25 minutes or until toothpick comes out clean or the edges start to turn light brown.

6. Remove from oven and let cool. Cut into 16 squares and store in food containers.

7. Microwave 30–45 seconds before serving. They're extra delicious when they're warm.

PER SERVING Calories: 119 | Fat: 6.3 g | Protein: 3.6 g | Sodium: 97 mg | Fiber: 2.3 g | Carbohydrates: 12.6 g | Sugar: 6.3 g

Weekend Gourmet Meals

Shakshuka

Shakshuka consists of eggs poached in a spicy, herbed tomato sauce. It is a popular dish in Middle Eastern cuisine. This is meant to be served immediately or the next day and can be stored up to 2 days in the refrigerator.

INGREDIENTS | SERVES 2

1 tablespoon coconut oil

½ cup diced onions

1 cup diced red bell peppers

3 cloves garlic, peeled and minced

5 medium tomatoes, chopped

½ teaspoon sea salt

1 teaspoon freshly ground black pepper

½ teaspoon dried oregano

½ teaspoon fresh thyme

½ teaspoon ground cumin

½ teaspoon paprika

¼ teaspoon ground cayenne pepper

½ teaspoon red pepper flakes

¼ teaspoon onion powder

6 large eggs

2 tablespoons chopped fresh cilantro

Substitutions

You can also use canned crushed tomatoes in this recipe. Add ground beef or turkey for an extra punch of protein. Serve this dish with some diced avocados sprinkled on top as well.

1. Preheat oven to 400°F.

2. Heat a large oven-safe skillet over medium heat and add oil. When oil is hot, add onions and sauté until lightly brown, 2 minutes. Add bell peppers and garlic and stir 2–3 minutes or until peppers are soft.

3. Add tomatoes and spices and reduce heat to a simmer. Stir 6–7 minutes until the water from the tomatoes is gone and sauce starts to thicken.

4. With a spatula create 6 holes in the sauce and crack an egg into each hole.

5. Transfer skillet to oven and bake 5 minutes or until egg whites are cooked.

6. Remove and garnish with cilantro and serve or store in food containers.

PER SERVING Calories: 376 | Fat: 20.1 g | Protein: 23.2 g | Sodium: 700 mg | Fiber: 6.6 g | Carbohydrates: 23.7 g | Sugar: 13.0 g

Lamb Chops

These lamb chops are simple yet perfect for a special occasion or weekend where you feel like having something a little extra special. Lamb chops are best served immediately and are not recommended for extended storage. They will keep well up to 2 days in the refrigerator.

INGREDIENTS | SERVES 2

2 cloves garlic, peeled and mined
½ tablespoon minced fresh rosemary
1 tablespoon olive oil
⅛ teaspoon sea salt
¼ teaspoon freshly ground black pepper
6 (3–4-ounce) lamb chops

Lamb Chops

Make sure you let meat sit at room temperature 30 minutes before preparing. This ensures that the meat doesn't turn out tough or chewy.

1. Preheat grill on high.

2. In a small bowl whisk garlic, rosemary, oil, salt, and pepper until combined.

3. Rub marinade over lamb and marinate 15–20 minutes.

4. Grill on high until desired doneness. Check temperature with a thermometer for doneness: 145°F for medium rare (8–10 minutes) and 160°F for medium to well done (10–12 minutes), depending on thickness of chops.

5. Remove and serve or store in food storage containers.

PER SERVING Calories: 775 | Fat: 43.4 g | Protein: 64.5 g | Sodium: 321 mg | Fiber: 0.2 g | Carbohydrates: 1.7 g | Sugar: 0.0 g

Grilled Steak with Spicy Chimichurri

Steaks are one of those meats that you cannot meal prep; you must serve them the same day. The meat will just not taste the same.

INGREDIENTS | SERVES 2

2 (10-ounce) grilling steaks

⅛ teaspoon sea salt

¼ teaspoon freshly ground black pepper

¼ cup Spicy Chimichurri (see Chapter 10)

Steaks

Make sure you let meat sit at room temperature 30 minutes before preparing. This ensures that the meat doesn't turn out tough or chewy.

1. Preheat grill on high.

2. Pat steaks dry and place on a plate. Sprinkle with salt and pepper.

3. Grill on high until desired doneness. Check temperature with a thermometer for doneness: 145°F for medium rare (8–10 minutes) and 160°F for medium to well done (10–12 minutes), depending on thickness of steaks.

4. Serve each portion with ⅛ cup Spicy Chimichurri on the side.

PER SERVING Calories: 487 | Fat: 20.1 g | Protein: 63.2 g | Sodium: 338 mg | Fiber: 0.7 g | Carbohydrates: 2.3 g | Sugar: 0.4 g

Pan-Seared Salmon Fillet

Fish is one type of protein that is hard to prep in advance. It's better cooked and served on the spot. Serve with rice, a salad, or your favorite sides. These will last up to 3 days in the refrigerator.

INGREDIENTS | SERVES 2

2 (3-ounce) salmon fillets
⅛ teaspoon sea salt
¼ teaspoon freshly ground black pepper
¼ teaspoon garlic powder
⅛ teaspoon onion powder
¼ teaspoon paprika
1 tablespoon coconut oil

Salmon

Wild salmon has fewer calories and fat compared to farmed salmon. That's the reason why wild salmon is meatier and denser to cook with.

1. Pat fish dry and place on a plate. Sprinkle salt, pepper, garlic powder, onion powder, and paprika evenly over fillets.

2. Heat a medium frying pan over medium heat and add oil. Once oil is hot, add fillets. Cook 3–4 minutes per side, depending on thickness of fillets and doneness preference. Store in food containers and refrigerate up to 3 days.

PER SERVING Calories: 168 | Fat: 9.0 g | Protein: 17.6 g | Sodium: 180 mg | Fiber: 0.2 g | Carbohydrates: 0.7 g | Sugar: 0.1 g

Seared Tuna

Make sure you get sashimi-grade tuna for this recipe since you'll be eating most of it rare. This recipe is meant to be enjoyed immediately. If you want to meal prep this, then instead of only searing, cook it thoroughly (5–6 minutes per side) and it can be stored in the refrigerator up to 2 days.

INGREDIENTS | SERVES 2

2 (3-ounce) tuna fillets
⅛ teaspoon sea salt
¼ teaspoon freshly ground black pepper
¼ teaspoon garlic powder
¼ teaspoon ground ginger
1 tablespoon coconut oil

1. Pat fillets dry with paper towels and place on a plate.

2. Sprinkle salt, pepper, garlic powder, and ginger over all sides of the fish.

3. Heat a large frying pan over medium heat and add oil. Once oil is hot, add fillets. Sear each side 2–3 minutes (including the sides).

4. Let rest on cutting board 3–4 minutes. Cut into ½" pieces and serve.

PER SERVING Calories: 153 | Fat: 6.8 g | Protein: 20.9 g | Sodium: 155 mg | Fiber: 0.1 g | Carbohydrates: 0.6 g | Sugar: 0.0 g

Cilantro Lime Tilapia

This dish is very appetizing and refreshing, and it is also light and healthy. Serve with rice, salad, or your favorite sides. This dish will store well in the refrigerator up to 3 days.

INGREDIENTS | SERVES 2

½ tablespoon Dijon mustard

¼ teaspoon freshly ground black pepper

¼ teaspoon garlic powder

1 medium jalapeño pepper, seeded and minced

2 tablespoons finely chopped fresh cilantro

½ medium lime, juiced

2 (4-ounce) tilapia fillets

Substitutions

If you don't like tilapia, replace with another white fish or even salmon. Dijon mustard can be an acquired taste, so if you don't like it, you can omit it and this recipe will still taste great.

1. Preheat oven to 400°F.

2. In a food processor add mustard, pepper, garlic powder, jalapeño, cilantro, and lime juice and blend until smooth.

3. Place fillets on a large piece of tinfoil (large enough to wrap the fillets). Scoop 1 tablespoon cilantro mixture on top of each fillet. Fold foil over and seal to create a pouch.

4. Bake 15–20 minutes, depending on the thickness of your fish.

PER SERVING Calories: 114 | Fat: 1.7 g | Protein: 23.0 g | Sodium: 81 mg | Fiber: 0.4 g | Carbohydrates: 1.6 g | Sugar: 0.4 g

Parchment Paper Baked Salmon

If possible, use wild-caught salmon instead of farm raised. Wild salmon is lower in fat and typically has 100 fewer calories per fillet than farmed salmon. This is best served immediately. You can store this in the refrigerator up to 3 days.

INGREDIENTS | SERVES 2

½ cup julienned carrots

½ cup julienned zucchini

2 (5-ounce) salmon fillets

1 clove garlic, peeled and minced

⅛ teaspoon salt

¼ teaspoon freshly ground black pepper

2 slices lemon

1 tablespoon chopped fresh dill

1. Preheat oven to 400°F.

2. Cut 2 large sheets of parchment paper (large enough to fit one fillet with space to fold over and twist into a bag). On each sheet, layer ¼ cup carrots and ¼ cup zucchini; then place a fillet on top.

3. Sprinkle each fillet with half of the garlic, salt, and pepper; then top with a slice of lemon and ½ tablespoon dill.

4. Fold each sheet over, then make small, tight overlapping folds down the outside edge to close pocket. Twist the ends to seal. If this is too hard, you can always use parchment baking bags or tinfoil.

5. Bake 20–25 minutes, depending on the thickness of your fish.

PER SERVING Calories: 127 | Fat: 2.6 g | Protein: 18.2 g | Sodium: 231 mg | Fiber: 1.3 g | Carbohydrates: 4.5 g | Sugar: 2.2 g

Sautéed-Onion Sliders

If the eggs aren't enough to hit the spot, try adding canned sardines or even canned salmon on top. They're great additions to these sliders and will store well up to 3 days.

INGREDIENTS | SERVES 2

1 medium sweet potato, cut into ¼" slices
1 tablespoon coconut oil, divided
1 large white Spanish onion, peeled and sliced thinly
¼ teaspoon freshly ground black pepper
4 large hard-boiled eggs, chopped
⅛ teaspoon sea salt

1. Microwave the sweet potatoes covered 1 minute to precook them. Remove and pat dry with a paper towel.

2. Heat a large pan over medium heat and add ½ tablespoon oil.

3. Add potato slices to the pan one by one, making sure they don't overlap each other. Fry until lightly brown, 3–4 minutes per side. Remove and set aside on a plate.

4. In the same pan add remaining ½ tablespoon oil and onions. Sauté, stirring occasionally until brown, 6–8 minutes.

5. Add pepper and stir another 30 seconds. Divide onions evenly over potato slices.

6. Sprinkle chopped eggs on top of the onions. Sprinkle with salt and serve. Store in food containers and refrigerate.

PER SERVING Calories: 296 | Fat: 15.2 g | Protein: 14.4 g | Sodium: 279 mg | Fiber: 3.2 g | Carbohydrates: 20.6 g | Sugar: 6.7 g

Steamed Egg with Green Onions

When you're not feeling well, this dish is a great pick-me-up. Serve with rice, other sides, or as a great appetizer to your dinner. This will store well in the refrigerator up to 3 days.

INGREDIENTS | SERVES 1

3 large eggs, at room temperature

1 cup warm water

¼ teaspoon salt

¼ teaspoon soy sauce or tamari

¼ teaspoon sesame oil (or coconut oil)

1 teaspoon chopped green onions

Sesame Oil

Using sesame oil gives the dish a strong sesame scent, but if you don't like sesame, opt for odorless coconut oil or even olive oil instead. For some extra zing, add a few drops of Chili Drizzle (see Chapter 10).

1. Crack eggs into a large bowl and beat 1 minute.

2. Add water and salt and beat 1 more minute.

3. Scoop and discard excess bubbles or foam with a spoon.

4. Pour eggs into a large heat-safe shallow bowl. Cover with plastic wrap.

5. Fill a large wok halfway with water and bring to a boil over high heat.

6. Place egg bowl into a steamer and into the wok, cover the wok, and steam on low 8 minutes.

7. Remove egg bowl from steamer and wok and remove plastic wrap; pour soy sauce and sesame oil on top, then sprinkle green onions all over to garnish. Divide into desired portions and store in food containers. Can be refrigerated up to 3 days.

PER SERVING Calories: 223 | Fat: 14.1 g | Protein: 19.0 g | Sodium: 866 mg | Fiber: 0.1 g | Carbohydrates: 1.3 g | Sugar: 0.6 g

Arugula Mandarin Smoked Salmon Salad

If you want to have a quiet date night at home, this dish is perfect as a starter. The salad will last up to 3 days.

INGREDIENTS | SERVES 2

½ cup mandarin oranges (fresh or canned)

4 cups baby arugula

6 (½-ounce) slices smoked salmon, cut into 1½" pieces

¼ cup chopped walnuts

½ teaspoon extra-virgin olive oil

⅛ teaspoon sea salt

⅛ teaspoon freshly ground black pepper

1. If using fresh oranges, remove peel and outer membrane from all of the wedges. Cut wedges into halves.

2. On two large salad plates, add arugula, then layer oranges, salmon, then walnuts. Drizzle oil and sprinkle salt and pepper on top.

3. Serve immediately.

PER SERVING Calories: 190 | Fat: 12.1 g | Protein: 11.4 g | Sodium: 413 mg | Fiber: 2.5 g | Carbohydrates: 10.1 g | Sugar: 6.4 g

Cajun Shrimp Zoodle Bowl

Looking for a big bowl of salad for lunch? Try this out. It's tasty, flavorful, filling, and healthy as well.

INGREDIENTS | SERVES 1

1 medium zucchini, spiralized

2 cups baby spinach

¼ cup shredded carrots

½ cup Cajun Shrimp (see Chapter 11)

⅓ cup Guacamole (see Chapter 11)

⅓ cup Pico de Gallo (see Chapter 11)

½ cup chopped bell peppers

⅛ cup chopped fresh cilantro

1. In a large bowl layer the following: spiralized zucchini at the bottom, then spinach, carrots, shrimp, Guacamole, Pico de Gallo, bell pepper, and cilantro.

2. Mix and serve or store in a large food container and refrigerate up to 3 days.

PER SERVING Calories: 235 | Fat: 12.3 g | Protein: 12.4 g | Sodium: 596 mg | Fiber: 9.4 g | Carbohydrates: 21.0 g | Sugar: 7.4 g

Dressing

There is no need for additional dressing on this bowl because the Guacamole and Pico de Gallo are already very flavorful.

Salmon Salad Bowl

This bowl is perfect if you're looking for something low-carb but filling and flavorful. The berries, salmon, and almonds in this will give you all of the satisfaction you need in a salad. This can be stored in the refrigerator up to 3 days.

INGREDIENTS | SERVES 1

2 cups baby spinach

2 cups chopped lettuce

¼ cup chopped almonds

¼ cup sliced strawberries

½ cup raspberries

¼ medium avocado, pitted, flesh removed, and sliced

1 Pan-Seared Salmon Fillet (see recipe in this chapter)

1 teaspoon balsamic vinegar

1. In a large bowl layer the following: spinach and lettuce at the bottom, then almonds, berries, avocado, and salmon; drizzle vinegar on top.

2. Mix and serve or store in large food container and refrigerate up to 3 days.

PER SERVING Calories: 446 | Fat: 26.6 g | Protein: 26.8 g | Sodium: 231 mg | Fiber: 13.4 g | Carbohydrates: 26.4 g | Sugar: 9.4 g

Goji Berry, Shrimp, and Egg Salad Bowl

If you're looking for a different type of salad, then the unique flavor combinations in this salad make it one you'll want to try. The subtle hint of sweetness in the goji berries will freshen up your meal. This salad will last in the refrigerator up to 3 days.

INGREDIENTS | SERVES 1

2 cups baby spinach

2 cups chopped lettuce

2 large hard-boiled eggs, chopped

1 tablespoon dried goji berries

¼ medium avocado, pitted, flesh removed, and sliced

½ cup Pan-Seared Shrimp with Herbs (see Chapter 11)

1 tablespoon Lemon Vinaigrette (see Chapter 10)

1. In a large bowl layer the following: spinach and lettuce at the bottom, then eggs, berries, avocado, shrimp, and dressing.

2. Mix and serve or store in food container and refrigerate up to 3 days.

PER SERVING Calories: 334 | Fat: 17.5 g | Protein: 23.7 g | Sodium: 519 mg | Fiber: 8.2 g | Carbohydrates: 18.2 g | Sugar: 5.8 g

Easy Gluten-Free Protein Pancakes

Protein pancakes are the perfect postworkout meal. This dish is great for muscle recovery and also very satisfying. You can also add fresh berries on top. These are best made fresh daily. However, you can meal prep these and they will keep up to 3 days.

INGREDIENTS | SERVES 1

1 medium banana, peeled

2 large eggs, whisked

2 tablespoons vanilla whey protein powder

1 tablespoon coconut flour

⅛ teaspoon baking powder

⅛ teaspoon vanilla extract

½ tablespoon coconut oil

1 teaspoon maple syrup (optional)

⅛ teaspoon ground cinnamon (optional)

Coconut Flour

You can replace the coconut flour with any flour or even milled flaxseed for extra-healthy fats. Coconut flour adds a nice fragrance to the pancakes.

1. In a medium bowl mash banana with a fork until well mashed.

2. Add eggs, protein powder, flour, baking powder, and vanilla and whisk until well combined.

3. Heat a medium pan over low heat and add a couple of drops of oil and ⅛ pancake mixture. Cook 30 seconds, then flip and cook another 30 seconds. Repeat until mix is used up.

4. This should yield 6 or 7 (4") pancakes.

5. Store as is in food storage containers and refrigerate, or drizzle with maple syrup, sprinkle with ground cinnamon, and serve.

PER SERVING (with maple syrup) Calories: 396 | Fat: 16.5 g | Protein: 24.3 g | Sodium: 236 mg | Fiber: 6.1 g | Carbohydrates: 37.3 g | Sugar: 19.3 g

Blueberry Chocolate Protein Pancakes

If chocolate pancakes are more your thing, then this recipe is right up your alley. These are chocolaty but also healthy for you, so you can enjoy them guilt-free. These will last up to 3 days.

INGREDIENTS | SERVES 2

1 cup quick-cooking oats
1 medium banana, peeled
4 large eggs, whisked
4 tablespoons chocolate whey protein powder
1 teaspoon baking powder
1 cup fresh blueberries
2 tablespoons dark chocolate chips
½ tablespoon coconut oil
1 teaspoon maple syrup

1. In a food processor blend oats until smooth.

2. In a large bowl mash banana with a fork until well mashed.

3. Add oats, eggs, protein powder, and baking powder and whisk until well combined.

4. Add blueberries and chocolate chips and stir to combine.

5. Heat a medium pan over low heat and add a couple of drops of oil and ⅛ cup pancake mixture. Cook 30 seconds, then flip and cook another 30 seconds. Repeat until mix is used up.

6. Store as is in food storage containers and refrigerate, or drizzle with ma-ple syrup and serve.

PER SERVING Calories: 481 | Fat: 18.8 g | Protein: 26.6 g | Sodium: 409 mg | Fiber: 6.7 g | Carbohydrates: 50.6 g | Sugar: 23.3 g

Savory Buckwheat Pancakes

These are perfect served with eggs and grilled tomatoes for a weekend brunch.
They are also gluten-free. They will last up to 3 days in the refrigerator.

INGREDIENTS | SERVES 2

2 cups raw buckwheat groats
5 cups plus 1½ cups water, divided
2 tablespoons coconut oil
⅛ teaspoon sea salt

Taco Shells

You can use this recipe to make gluten-free buckwheat taco shells. Just use less batter when frying. They are chewy and actually hold well.

1. Soak groats in a large bowl with 5 cups water overnight. The next morning drain and rinse thoroughly.

2. Pour groats into a blender, add 1½ cups water, and blend on high until well blended.

3. Heat a medium pan over low heat and add a couple drops of oil and ¼ pancake mixture. Cook 1–2 minutes, then flip and cook another 1–2 minutes. Repeat until mix is used up.

4. Sprinkle sea salt on top and serve.

PER SERVING Calories: 684 | Fat: 16.5 g | Protein: 19.2 g | Sodium: 135 mg | Fiber: 16.9 g | Carbohydrates: 122.9 g | Sugar: 0.0 g

Salmon Quinoa Burgers

These are a great option if you're staying away from meat but still craving a burger. They will keep in the refrigerator 2–3 days but no longer.

INGREDIENTS | SERVES 5

¾ cup canned chickpeas

¾ cup Basic Steamed Quinoa (see Chapter 11)

1 large egg, whisked

1 cup finely chopped black kale

2 cups diced raw salmon fillet

½ cup minced shallots or red onions

2 cloves garlic, peeled and minced

1 teaspoon garlic powder

½ teaspoon paprika

½ teaspoon ground cumin

½ teaspoon onion powder

½ teaspoon dried parsley

½ teaspoon dried basil

1 tablespoon Dijon mustard

⅛ teaspoon sea salt

¼ teaspoon freshly ground black pepper

1½ cups water

Tip

Though it seems like this recipe calls for a lot of blending, the blending does serve a purpose. Blending a third of the mixture acts like a natural binder, allowing the patties to stick together more easily.

1. Cut 5 (4" × 4") pieces of parchment paper and set aside.

2. In a food processor process chickpeas until smooth and pour into large mixing bowl.

3. Add remaining ingredients except water to bowl and mix until well combined.

4. Take ⅓ of the mixture and put it back into the food processor and blend until smooth.

5. Pour the processed mixture back into the bowl and mix everything together.

6. Pour back into a blender, add 1½ cups water, and blend on high until blended.

7. Form patties 3½" in diameter and place each on a parchment square.

8. Grill immediately or freeze up to a month. If you are planning to freeze them, you can store them in freezer-safe zip-top bags, stacking one on top of another with parchment paper in between each one. You can also pan-sear in a frying pan over medium-high heat 3–4 minutes per side.

PER SERVING Calories: 168 | Fat: 3.5 g | Protein: 16.5 g | Sodium: 182 mg | Fiber: 3.0 g | Carbohydrates: 15.1 g | Sugar: 2.4 g

Gluten-Free Fish Tacos

You can substitute the tilapia with pan-seared salmon or even scallops. You could also add sour cream or Greek yogurt as a garnish. These are best served fresh.

INGREDIENTS | SERVES 2

2 cups chopped tilapia fillets

¼ teaspoon sea salt

¼ teaspoon freshly ground black pepper

½ tablespoon coconut oil

½ cup canned pinto beans

4 Savory Buckwheat Pancakes (see recipe in this chapter)

½ cup Guacamole (see Chapter 11)

½ cup Pico de Gallo (see Chapter 11)

1 cup grated red cabbage

2 cups chopped baby spinach

¼ cup chopped fresh cilantro

4 lime wedges

1. Add fish to a small bowl and sprinkle with salt and pepper. Stir to combine.

2. Heat a medium pan over medium heat and add oil. Once oil is hot, add fish and pan-sear each side 2 minutes or until fish is no longer translucent. Remove and place on a plate.

3. In a medium bowl mash pinto beans with a fork or process in a food processor.

4. To put together the tacos, grab a pancake and spread with beans then add Guacamole, Pico de Gallo, cabbage, spinach, fish, and top with cilantro. Repeat for remaining pancakes.

5. Serve with a wedge of lime and store in food containers and refrigerate.

PER SERVING Calories: 1,045 | Fat: 29.4 g | Protein: 59.7 g | Sodium: 736 mg | Fiber: 25.1 g | Carbohydrates: 144.7 g | Sugar: 4.1 g

Two-Week Meal Plan

WEEK 1

Monday through Friday

Breakfast	Berry Delicious Oats (Chapter 3) (1 serving per day × 5 days)
Morning snack	Vegetable Sticks with Ranch (Chapter 14) (1 serving per day × 5 days)
Lunch	Taco in a Jar (Chapter 8) (1 serving per day × 5 days)
Afternoon snack	Healthy No-Bake Protein Bars (Chapter 14) (1 serving per day × 5 days)
Dinner	Mix and Match style: Easy BBQ Chicken Drumsticks (Chapter 5), Cauliflower Fried "Rice" (Chapter 11), and Stir-Fried Bok Choy (Chapter 11)

Saturday

Breakfast	Shakshuka (Chapter 16)
Morning snack	piece of fruit (apple or orange)
Lunch	Arugula Mandarin Smoked Salmon Salad (Chapter 16)
Afternoon snack	Rob's Fried Plantains (Chapter 14)
Dinner	Goji Berry, Shrimp, and Egg Salad Bowl (Chapter 16)

Sunday

Breakfast	Omelette with a Kick (Chapter 2)
Morning snack	¼ cup raw almond nuts
Lunch	Sausage and Potato Skillet (Chapter 13)
Afternoon snack	Protein Coconut Chia Seed Pudding (Chapter 15)
Dinner	Chicken Primavera (Chapter 13) with Basic Steamed Quinoa (Chapter 11)

WEEK 2

Monday through Friday

Breakfast	2 Egg Whites and Chicken Muffins (Chapter 2) (1 serving per day × 5 days)
Morning snack	Healthy Granola Bars (Chapter 14) (1 serving per day × 5 days)
Lunch	Kale Coconut Fried Rice (Chapter 13) (1 serving per day × 5 days)
Afternoon snack	No-Bake Chocolate Protein Bites (Chapter 15) (1 serving per day × 5 days)
Dinner	Mix and Match style: Chinese Five-Spice Pork Chops (Chapter 7), Oven-Roasted Brussels Sprouts and Squash (Chapter 11), and Sautéed Purple Cabbage (Chapter 11)

Saturday

Breakfast	Coconut Milk Scrambled Eggs with Chives (Chapter 2)
Morning snack	¼ cup raw cashew nuts with 1 cup strawberries
Lunch	Cilantro Lime Tilapia (Chapter 16), Oven-Roasted Beets (Chapter 11), and Grilled Zucchini (Chapter 11)
Afternoon snack	Oven-Roasted Plantains (Chapter 11)
Dinner	Grilled Steak with Spicy Chimichurri (Chapter 16), Cajun Sweet Potato Wedges (Chapter 11), and Grilled Asparagus with Lemon Zest (Chapter 11)

Sunday

Breakfast	Spicy Spinach and Tomato Frittata (Chapter 2)
Morning snack	1 cup mixed berries
Lunch	Cajun Shrimp Zoodle Bowl (Chapter 16)
Afternoon snack	Banana Nut Rolls (Chapter 15)
Dinner	Lamp Chops (Chapter 16), Spicy Pickled Cabbage Slaw (Chapter 11), and Perfectly Roasted Japanese Sweet Potatoes (Chapter 11)

Standard US/Metric Measurement Conversions

VOLUME CONVERSIONS

US Volume Measure	Metric Equivalent
⅛ teaspoon	0.5 milliliter
¼ teaspoon	1 milliliter
½ teaspoon	2 milliliters
1 teaspoon	5 milliliters
½ tablespoon	7 milliliters
1 tablespoon (3 teaspoons)	15 milliliters
2 tablespoons (1 fluid ounce)	30 milliliters
¼ cup (4 tablespoons)	60 milliliters
⅓ cup	80 milliliters
½ cup (4 fluid ounces)	125 milliliters
⅔ cup	160 milliliters
¾ cup (6 fluid ounces)	180 milliliters
1 cup (16 tablespoons)	250 milliliters
1 pint (2 cups)	500 milliliters
1 quart (4 cups)	1 liter (about)

WEIGHT CONVERSIONS

US Weight Measure	Metric Equivalent
½ ounce	15 grams
1 ounce	30 grams
2 ounces	60 grams
3 ounces	85 grams
¼ pound (4 ounces)	115 grams
½ pound (8 ounces)	225 grams
¾ pound (12 ounces)	340 grams
1 pound (16 ounces)	454 grams

OVEN TEMPERATURE CONVERSIONS

Degrees Fahrenheit	Degrees Celsius
200 degrees F	95 degrees C
250 degrees F	120 degrees C
275 degrees F	135 degrees C
300 degrees F	150 degrees C
325 degrees F	160 degrees C
350 degrees F	180 degrees C
375 degrees F	190 degrees C
400 degrees F	205 degrees C
425 degrees F	220 degrees C
450 degrees F	230 degrees C

BAKING PAN SIZES

American	Metric
8 × 1½ inch round baking pan	20 × 4 cm cake tin
9 × 1½ inch round baking pan	23 × 3.5 cm cake tin
11 × 7 × 1½ inch baking pan	28 × 18 × 4 cm baking tin
13 × 9 × 2 inch baking pan	30 × 20 × 5 cm baking tin
2 quart rectangular baking dish	30 × 20 × 3 cm baking tin
15 × 10 × 2 inch baking pan	38 × 25 × 5 cm baking tin (Swiss roll tin)
9 inch pie plate	22 × 4 or 23 × 4 cm pie plate
7 or 8 inch springform pan	18 or 20 cm springform or loose bottom cake tin
9 × 5 × 3 inch loaf pan	23 × 13 × 7 cm or 2 lb narrow loaf or pâté tin
1½ quart casserole	1.5 liter casserole
2 quart casserole	2 liter casserole

Index